DANGER CLOSE

TEXAS A&M UNIVERSITY

113

MILITARY HISTORY SERIES

DANGER CLOSE

Tactical Air Controllers in Afghanistan and Iraq

STEVE CALL

Texas A&M University Press
College Station

The paper used in this book meets the minimum requirements
of the American National Standard for Permanence
of Paper for Printed Library Materials, Z39-48-1984.
Binding materials have been chosen for durability.
∞

Library of Congress Cataloging-in-Publication Data

Call, Steve, 1956–
Danger close : tactical air controllers in Afghanistan and Iraq / Steve Call. — 1st ed.
p. cm. — (Texas A&M University military history series: no. 113)
Includes index.
ISBN-13: 978-1-58544-624-7 (cloth : alk. paper)
ISBN-10: 1-58544-624-6 (cloth : alk. paper)
1. Afghan War, 2001—Aerial operations, American. 2. Iraq War, 2003—Aerial operations,
American. 3. Close air support—History—21st century. I. Title.
DS371.412.C35 2007
956.7044′348—dc22
2007013215

To those who died in the Udairi Range bombing accident
on the night of 12 March 2001

Major John McNutt, New Zealand Army
Staff Sergeant Richard Boudreau, United States Army
Staff Sergeant Troy James Westberg, United States Army
Staff Sergeant Jason M. Faley, United States Air Force
Specialist Philip Michael Freligh, United States Army
Specialist Jason Douglas Wildfong, United States Army

May the memory of your sacrifice remain as bright as
your devotion to duty.

We sleep safe in our beds because rough men stand ready in the night to visit violence on those who would do us harm.

GEORGE ORWELL

Contents

Illustrations

Maps

Preface

America had a secret weapon. Ironically, America didn't realize it had this secret weapon until the events of 11 September 2001 plunged the nation into the War on Terror. Because of the unique circumstances of the fight to oust the Taliban from Afghanistan, America's opening move sent small teams of Special Forces to link up with a loose-knit confederation of Afghan rebels. Initially this move was meant to pave the way for much larger follow-on conventional forces, but when the Afghan rebels and SOF teams started rolling up the Taliban by themselves, U.S. military leaders capitalized on their success, and the rebel-SOF combination became the main effort. When the success of this unlikely force continued, to the point of bringing down the entire Taliban regime, people looked closer at what made it work so well. What they found was a catalyst of air power experts—air force personnel who direct airstrikes against enemy ground forces—and that began the dawning awareness of this secret weapon.

This group of experts, collectively known as TACPs for the Tactical Air Control Parties in which they work, exists in a twilight world caught between two services—held at arm's length by the air force, not fully embraced by the army. In Afghanistan and Iraq, however, they played a critical role in bringing down two murderous regimes despite overwhelming odds. In fact, to a significant degree, the shocking speed with which the Taliban and Hussein regimes collapsed was due to the role played by this small group.

This is their story. It is not *the* history of the wars in Afghanistan and Iraq; in fact, technically speaking, it is not even *a* history of those wars. It is simply one piece of the bigger picture, but one that has been largely untold up to this point. It is told in their own words to give these men a chance to speak for themselves about what they did and what they were thinking. In the process, what emerges is not only a story of heroism and sacrifice but also one of incredible ingenuity and a glimpse into how and why these men have transformed modern warfare.

There is also another side to this story: The history of close air support, or CAS, is inextricably linked to the TACP story. CAS is the use of airstrikes in close proximity to friendly ground forces, usually because they are engaged with the enemy. One reason the TACP potential remained secret for so long is that in the wake of Desert Storm, when that capability really took shape, the army and the air force each developed its own unique vision of how the ideal war ought to be fought, and CAS did not figure in either vision. This is where I enter the story. I spent the last twelve years of my air force career caught up in the CAS controversy. After eight years as an air force pilot, primarily flying B-52s, I went off to graduate school, where as a budding military historian I took a keen interest in the development and evolution of air power. The United States' air power debate is full of contention, with several groups each believing it alone had the true vision, and after many decades of acrimonious debate, feelings and opinions had hardened into genuine animosity. On the one side, the air force had been dominated by bomber and fighter pilots—both of whom rejected CAS. On the other side, the army, which in theory embraced CAS, in reality had become so bitter toward airmen that nothing the air force did was right, and operationally the army retreated into a "go it alone" attitude. My interest in the air power vision debates culminated in a dissertation written on a related subject.

After completing my Ph.D., I went to work at the Pentagon in an air staff think tank that helped shape air power strategy, concepts, and doctrine. Because of my military history expertise, I ended up working primarily on projects related to integrating air and ground power. The more I immersed myself in the competing ground and air perspectives, though, the more I realized that both the army and the air force had entrenched themselves in ideas shaped as much by partisan thinking as by facts and experience. I also became acquainted with a small group of reformers who pointed to new capabilities and called for a new focus for air power—one that stressed greater coordination with ground forces and air power's ability to kill enemy ground forces. Their ideas helped shape and advance my own thinking, but in a revealing insight into the atmosphere toward military reform in the late 1990s, my ideas drew as much criticism from the air force as from the army.

After I left the Pentagon I became part of the TACP community as an air liaison officer attached to the army's 10th Mountain Division. After years of studying ground warfare and air power in books, classrooms, and joint working groups, I looked forward to this close-up practical perspective where I could test some of my ideas and theories in a more realistic setting. I also looked forward to getting to know the army better. I had come to suspect that the CAS problem was attributable to both sides of the air-ground team, and though I knew the air force quite well by that point, I felt I couldn't really understand the CAS problem until I knew better the other half of this "bad marriage." More than anything else, this assignment impressed upon me what just about any TACP could tell you without all the theory and "book learning": CAS was poorly understood by many members of *both* the army and the air force, especially at the senior levels. This is not the case with every senior officer. Maj. Gen. James Campbell, division commander of the 10th Mountain Division during my stint there as an ALO, was very receptive and open-minded about suggestions for incorporating air power into his plans. Unfortunately the exceptions prove the rule and therefore CAS potential was barely being tapped. Of course both services—again, especially at the senior levels—will tell you officially that this claim is preposterous, especially now that TACPs have shown what CAS can do, but just ask any TACP about "the bad old days."

I retired from the air force at the end of that assignment, shortly before the 11 September attacks. I felt I finally understood how air and ground power could work better together, and I left with some well-developed ideas of how the two ought to be integrated. I also kept in touch with my TACP friends. When I saw later how CAS and the TACP community were given two excellent opportunities to "show their stuff" in Afghanistan and Iraq, and when my former colleagues started telling me about the dramatic results they had achieved, I decided to capture their story on paper. This book is that attempt—not only to tell what TACPs did, but also to illustrate how it worked, why it worked, and most important, what needs to be done to ensure it goes on working.

I must hasten to add some caveats, first by stressing what this book does not claim: It does not claim that air power alone won these wars nor even that air power was *the* decisive element in victory. Some have made such claims in the past, but that is not my claim. Just the opposite in fact, because I hope I have demonstrated through the examples in this book how the TACP community and the army worked hand in hand (usually) to achieve victory, and that the formula for their success rests in the inherent properties of air power and ground forces when used wisely to complement each other. Each was essential, neither was superior. To argue otherwise would be as preposterous as claiming that the hammer is more important than the anvil or vice versa.

Second, I want to say a word on names appearing in this book. Because the War on Terror is still ongoing, and because of the nature of the

threat, some in uniform are justifiably hesitant to have their names appear in print. For this reason I have used only names of people who were
interviewed and those mentioned in the book who did not ask to have
their names withheld. The biggest area where this policy came into play
was with the many people mentioned by interviewees when describing
events. While all who were mentioned certainly deserve recognition for
their contributions, and while many of them would have been happy to
be mentioned in the book, I did not want to do so without their permission, and the difficulties I encountered trying to track individuals down
to get permission made it clear that finding everyone would have turned
into a nightmare. So if you see something like "[another TACP]," that is
the reason. Most important, don't think the individual telling the story is
trying to hog all the glory. TACPs are a lot like SOF in this regard: quick to
share credit, slow to claim it. There are some exceptions to the name policy. The actions of some people in high-profile events have already been
written about to such an extent in books, newspapers, or articles that I
felt their role was a matter of public record. Similarly, individuals in key
positions, such as commanders, are public figures and can be referred to
by name—it goes with the territory.

One great privilege reserved to authors is the opportunity to thank
the many who helped. In telling this story I have incurred a number of
debts that I am happy to repay here. Because this book is largely based
on interviews, transcribing those interviews was essential. This task fell
to four wonderful women who typed the dozens of interviews into hundreds of pages; they are Kimberly Bostwick, Jean Pickett, Janet Shaffer,
and Joan Shumin—ladies, I couldn't have done it without you.

Members of the TACP community obviously helped make this book
possible, and I thank all who stepped forward to offer their stories and
insights. I also thank those who gave leads for other contacts. In many
cases this gave me some of my best sources. Others, for various reasons,
didn't pan out; some couldn't be found, others weren't interested, and
some I just couldn't get to for one reason or another. I apologize to those
whom I interviewed but didn't include in the book—I ended up with an
embarrassment of riches when it came to good material, so I had to cut
somewhere. I chose to limit what I included to information that either
was most central to key events or presented a cross section of skills or
contributions. This in no way means other contributions weren't important or interesting.

Five TACPs deserve my deepest thanks, for they played a central role
in this project from start to finish. Colonel George "Shack" Bochain was

instrumental in sparking the whole idea in the first place. Our many discussions about how CAS ought to be used when we were serving together back at Fort Drum led directly to his telling me how well it worked when he returned from Afghanistan in 2002. Since then he has not only shared his experiences and insights but also shared his home and his scotch—well, sometimes it was my scotch. Another one who played an essential role was M.Sgt. Charlie Heidal. Charlie is something like a central point of contact for the entire ROMAD community, that is, enlisted TACPs, and when I turned to him early in my quest for people to interview he became an enthusiastic supporter and has been an indispensable help. Another who has been central to helping me understand not just the part he played (which was a big one) but also many of the finer points or more critical issues was S.Sgt. Ed Shulman. Another who played a big part in helping me "get it right," especially with the editing, was M.Sgt. (Ret.) Joel "Hotmike" Hokkanen—I couldn't have asked for a better copy editor. Finally, an old friend, Col. Byron Risner got me pointed in the right direction on TACP support for the invasion of Iraq. All five of these guys also suffered through the rough drafts not only helping to ensure accuracy but also trying to make it read a little smoother. Of course any errors or flaws remain mine alone.

Air Force Ranks and Abbreviations

Officer Rank	Abbreviation
O-10: General	Gen.
O-9: Lieutenant general	Lt. Gen.
O-8: Major general	Maj. Gen. or M. Gen.
O-7: Brigadier general	Brig. Gen. or B. Gen.
O-6: Colonel	Col.
O-5: Lieutenant colonel	Lt. Col.
O-4: Major	Maj.
O-3: Captain	Capt.
O-2: First lieutenant	1st Lt. or 1Lt.
O-1: Second lieutenant	2nd Lt. or 2Lt.

Enlisted Rank	Abbreviation
E-9: Chief master sergeant	C.M.Sgt. or Chief
E-8: Senior master sergeant	S.M.Sgt.
E-7: Master sergeant	M.Sgt.
E-6: Technical sergeant	T.Sgt. or Tech. Sgt.
E-5: Staff sergeant	S.Sgt.
E-4: Senior airman	Sr.A.
E-3: Airman first class	A1C
E-2: Airman	Amn.
E-1: Airman basic	AB

DANGER CLOSE

Prologue

Two Clear Days

On 12 March 2001 the dawn brought a beautiful clear sky to Kuwait. The weather report called for good visibility and comfortable temperatures, both of which were important because there was a major daylong exercise scheduled for air and ground units from around the theater. Known as CASEX, for close air support exercise, the event brought together aircraft from several nations and services to work with ground personnel in various locations around northern Kuwait to practice close air support— the use of airstrikes against enemy forces in close proximity to friendly ground forces. Most of the ground portion of the exercise involved air force tactical air controllers, who are responsible for controlling air attacks by identifying ground targets to be attacked, helping pilots locate those targets, and then clearing pilots to attack when conditions look reasonably safe. Most of this day's training would be "dry"; that is, the aircraft would have no weapons and all training would involve merely practicing procedures and techniques. The highlight of the exercise, though, would take place on Kuwait's Udairi Range, a large complex used by several nations for live-fire training of all sorts. At Udairi a group had set up to work with aircraft carrying live ordnance, both bombs and guns, and many people were looking forward to a day of very realistic, and therefore very effective, CAS training.

In the closing hours of the exercise, disaster struck: a navy F/A-18 dropped its bombs directly on the group controlling the strike, killing six and wounding five others. Among the dead was a New Zealand army officer, and this, along with the fact that the accident had taken place in a foreign country, made this a high-profile international affair. The news was flashing around the world on CNN before rescue operations were even complete, and the aftermath brought the small but tight-knit community of air force CAS controllers to one of its lowest points.

U.S. military leaders moved swiftly to investigate—a board was appointed the very next day—but that didn't stop public speculation and finger-pointing. Consternation within the TACP community began almost immediately when CNN reported within hours that a navy spokesperson claimed the air force TACP, a staff sergeant, had cleared the navy pilot to release his bombs. This not only focused blame on the air force ground controller but also brought several other issues—sensitive issues involving differing service cultures and long-standing service animosities—into the picture. As a result, the TACP community found itself in the crosshairs of an international crisis, and some even felt their profession was suddenly on the chopping block.

One reason for concern involved the air force's approach to controlling close air support. For decades the air force, like the marines, had relied strictly on pilots on the ground to control air attacks. From at least the Vietnam War, however, enlisted members working alongside these pilots assumed greater and greater responsibility. By the eve of Desert Storm they were authorized to independently control airstrikes. Collectively known as ROMADs (an acronym dating to the Vietnam War that supposedly stood for radio operator, maintainer, and driver), today they control most CAS missions, but as late as the Udairi accident this was still quite controversial. One marine officer, in a message posted to an online ROMAD bulletin board, spoke to this controversy directly: the fault lay clearly with the air force for allowing enlisted men to control CAS; had the air force stuck with pilots as the marines had, this would never have happened. ROMADs knew this sentiment was widespread within the army as well as the Marine Corps.

Another area of great interservice sensitivity stemmed from the fact that in many ways the air force had never fully embraced the role of close air support. This is a lightning rod issue among the services. Air force leaders and spokespeople will strenuously deny the charge and point to the great progress made in improving CAS capability after Vietnam, particularly in hardware and doctrine, and these were true advances that set the stage for current capabilities. But just about anyone in the other services, as well as most military historians, will point out that much of the air force's CAS improvements came at army insistence and that low budget priorities and the constant refrain that CAS was the least efficient use of air power prove that CAS was not where the air force's heart was. In fact, many who disagreed with the air force using enlisted personnel to control airstrikes saw it as just another example of the air force's casual attitude toward CAS, a sentiment that would surely come into play in early charges that the air force controller had been to blame for this accident.

TACPs collectively felt the weight of both these sensitivities squarely on their shoulders, but many also felt a great deal of bitterness. They had been complaining about problems with CAS procedures in the air and on the ground for years and felt they had gained little to show for their efforts. Some even thought the accident's circumstances highlighted the indifference in official air force and navy circles, and wondered how many more would have to die before officials would start listening.

Another circumstance increased the ROMADs' anxiety: The pilot was a moderately high ranking officer and a squadron commander, while the air force controller was only a staff sergeant. Many ROMADs feared the enlisted man would be sacrificed to save the officer. The navy's early release of the claim that the enlisted controller had cleared their pilot to release bombs only added to fears that one of their own was going to be made the fall guy.

All in all, this was a pretty bleak time for ROMADs. Even after the accident investigation showed that the pilot had been at fault, getting back to normal did not make things much better. Shrinking defense budgets hit their units and training opportunities hard, and the conventional wisdom for some time, especially after Operation Allied Force, the 1999 NATO intervention in Kosovo, held that major ground conflict such as they specialized in was outdated.

Almost exactly six months after the Udairi accident, on another clear and beautiful day, hijacked airliners plowed into the World Trade Center, the Pentagon, and a Pennsylvania farm field, plunging the United States into two wars that would call on the special skills and dedication of the TACP community—they were about to become America's newest secret weapon.

What Is a TACP?

Few people outside the military know that the air force assigns personnel to army units to provide a broad array of services that come under the category of air support. The air force still uses pilots to control CAS missions, though now they have been joined by other flying officers, such as navigators and weapons systems officers. Once known as forward air controllers, or FACs (a term marines still use), they are now called air liaison officers, or ALOs. Enlisted personnel have always assisted officers in critical ways, and those positions have evolved into the modern ROMAD. In fact, the traditional origin of the term ROMAD alludes to those enlisted men who assisted FACs by maintaining and operating the radios, and of course by driving the officer wherever he needed to go. In today's air force ROMADs do most of the CAS controlling, and therefore they make up the largest part of the TACP community. ALOs now act primarily as liaison and advisers to ground commanders at all echelons, and they serve as the command elements of air support units and the air support system. Together ALOs and ROMADs are assigned to ground units to meet their air support needs. Besides rank, the biggest difference between these two groups is that ROMADs work in this field their entire careers while most ALOs serve one or two tours—each tour usually lasting only two years— as an adjunct to their flying career.

This difference in tenure makes for significant strengths and weaknesses. Early reliance on pilots to control CAS rested on the logic that a pilot understands air power better than anyone, that he knows best what an aircraft can do and how best to employ air weapons. In short, the pilot's "air sense" was considered the most important factor when controlling airstrikes from the ground. As ROMADs began shouldering more and more responsibility, however, a new set of considerations emerged. By living in this world of ground combat year after year, ROMADs came to understand ground warfare better than most pilots could ever hope to in only two years; they learned how to move and survive on the ground; they better understood the army and developed an empathy for the soldier's challenges and concerns; and perhaps most important, they learned how to best influence with air power that fluid and seemingly chaotic world of ground combat. By working as a team they maximize their strengths and compensate for their weaknesses.

In the field, ROMADs and ALOs work in teams known as tactical air control parties to control air attacks. Numbering at least two people, a TACP consists of a senior member who has been trained and certified to control CAS missions and a junior member who assists and learns the ropes in the process. Those certified to control airstrikes are often called tactical air controllers, and ROMADs with this certification are known as enlisted tactical air controllers. The junior member of the TACP is variously known as a ROMAD, 1C4 (the air force's service code for all ROMADs), Charlie, Chuck, or other names best left unprinted. TACP is also a generic term for any air force person in the CAS control business.

What are the people who inhabit this unique world really like? ALOs face daunting challenges and render heroic and often unappreciated service, but to really understand the CAS control community you have to understand the ROMAD. To call ROMADs a unique breed is an understatement. Few other individuals bring so much real influence to the battlefield, and those people have much higher rank or position. But as recent wars have demonstrated, one ROMAD with a radio can have a devastating effect on the enemy's morale and fighting ability. Two other aspects, though, make the ROMAD unique: rank and organizational issues.

The military is and always has been extremely rank conscious; rank factors not only in command and giving orders, but in other often subtle but influential ways. ROMADs control more firepower than most officers, but their rank does not always reflect that control in command posts or in planning rooms where key decisions are made. Many army field grade officers, for example, have trouble taking advice from an air force sergeant. Rank is an issue within the air force as well. For one thing, there is no TACP career field for officers in the air force, so the only dedicated, full-time constituency for CAS control issues is made up entirely of enlisted personnel. The lack of high rank translates into lack of influence within the corporate air force and severely limits the ROMAD community's ability to impact decision-making in such critical areas as budgeting, acquisition, doctrine formulation, and training standards. The highest-ranking ROMADs are chief master sergeants, and while they carry a great deal of influence and command tremendous respect, they cannot go "beak-to-beak" with generals when hard decisions are hammered out.

The rank problem also has a cultural dimension. The air force's combat culture has always centered on aircraft and those who fly them. This culture was historically dominated by bomber pilots; for the last twenty years fighter pilots have held sway. Both groups have long had difficulty accepting as equals those who do not fit their cultural image of "war fighters." Part of their image is that in the air force the real fighting is done by officers, a prejudice that leaves enlisted combat troops frozen out in many ways. For example, the internationally famous U.S. Air Force Weapons School currently excludes ROMADs because they are not officers. Is this based on practical considerations of who can influence the battle, or is it simply a problem of key decision-makers clinging to cherished but possibly outmoded ideals? This exclusion denies a critical combat community valuable knowledge that could be gained by sending its members to one of the world's best advanced tactical schools. It also denies this community an important measure of respect and influence within air force culture. In air force circles, Weapons School graduates are held in such high esteem and wield so much influence they are known simply as Patch-Wearers because they get to wear the coveted Weapons School graduate patch.

TACPs also live and work in an organizational structure that creates challenges in peacetime and in war. For one thing, ALOs make up the entire command structure of every unit in the air force's tactical air control system. These officers are dedicated professionals who bring great strengths to their positions, but they serve temporary assignments outside their regular career fields, so their expertise is different from the ROMADs they command. This difference in perspective regularly creates differences of opinion when day-to-day issues or long-term policy decisions arise.

Further, many of these ALOs (but certainly not all) are not volunteers to their assignment—often they are there against their will and look on the assignment as a hardship. Not only would these officers prefer to be back in the cockpit, they often see the ALO assignment as a detour that detracts from their "real" career—a detour that will bring little respect from their peers and few rewards when it comes to future promotions or desirable assignments. At the very least, these officers do not have their head "in the game." At worst their attitude becomes a source of daily frustration that ROMADs must contend with throughout their career. One doesn't have to be around the CAS control business long to see this first-hand and sense the significant scope and scale of the problem. The problem is infinitely worse if the officer with the "attitude problem" is a commander.

Perhaps the most revealing insight into the character of the TACP community, though, is that it exists in a netherworld between two services, neither of which fully understands or appreciates what it does. TACPs are air force; they train in air force schools, are commanded by air force officers, and in many ways great and small are shaped by air force culture. But they also live, work, fight, and die with the army. To the air force they are an oddity: ground combat forces in a service that mostly focuses on fighting in the air, they also perform a mission the air force has always kept at arm's length. Add to this that by living and working on army bases there is a real "out of sight, out of mind" attitude within the corporate air force. No wonder TACPs feel like they don't really fit in with their parent service. This is especially true of ROMADs, who may spend their entire career without ever being stationed on an air force base.

But TACPs don't feel much more welcome in the army. A lot of animosity toward the air force has built up within the army, much of it because of past history and the evolution of dramatically differing service cultures. The most important historical legacy in understanding the army's attitude toward the air force is the air force's lack of enthusiasm for

CAS. This has hit the army hard for a long time and left deep and abiding scars. Some of the venom is based more on the air force's persistent attitude than on objective assessment of past episodes, and one might expect that the army would embrace wholeheartedly a dedicated group within the air force that has committed itself to fighting and dying alongside them, but the sad fact is that too often TACPs are made "whipping boys" for all past air force sins, real or imagined.

Most of the friction between the army and TACPs, though, stems from profound differences in service culture. Reflecting ageless realities of ground warfare, the army operates at a fundamental level on control through direct command. Commanders at all levels want and expect to control, not just command, all their combat assets. They may understand at a cognitive level that total control is impossible and that they must cope with the uncontrollable, but at a visceral level they yearn for control. The air force, though, retains direct control of its TACP forces and "details" them to support the army. Army commanders feel considerable frustration, therefore, that TACPs are not under their direct command, but the heart of the problem runs even deeper. The air force operates in a much more fluid environment; air operations are subject to myriad forces of nature to a greater extent than any other mode of combat, and modern air power has become so diverse, widespread, and complex, and serves so many divergent interests that the air force has evolved a highly decentralized mode of operation. It often seems chaotic and unresponsive, but actually it might be better described as "self-synchronizing." At times it seems no one is in charge and nothing can be done to influence the system, but in reality, thousands of people are in charge of critical pieces of nonstop operations, and therefore the air force has pushed a great deal of authority down to very low levels. All of this allows it to meet many conflicting demands, and at a very basic level there is a great deal of insight in the air force cliché "flexibility is the key to air power."

Some consequences of this mode of operation, though, can result in inflexibility and lead to great frustration for the army. A brigade commander, for example, may decide to push up an offensive by thirty minutes. When his TACP tells him the four sorties scheduled to support that operation cannot be rolled to the earlier time, the colonel cannot understand how all the other components of his plan—artillery, engineers, logistics—can turn on a dime but four airplanes cannot. What seems so easy, however, is actually quite complex; the aircraft in question had quite likely flown earlier sorties supporting other operations, and the big "air plan" for the entire war effort had allocated just enough time for hundreds of people in dozens of disparate operations to get those aircraft ready to fly by the originally scheduled time. To change that plan would mean not only contacting all those people but also disrupting hundreds of other carefully synchronized "just in time" operations getting other aircraft in the air to support other operations all across the theater. But this is little comfort to the brigade commander; he had been told those sorties were his and he looks at them as "his sorties"; he had planned on them, and now he is told he has no control over them. It all seems so illogical he can only conclude that if the air force really wanted to it could make this happen, and that if he had direct control of those air force assets, by God, it certainly would happen! Such impasses seem to offer further proof that the air force doesn't really want to support the army. The TACP gets blamed for this. And even if he works up a satisfactory alternate plan, the commander may be mollified but will still feel the air force system is chaotic and inflexible.

Caught between the army and the air force, TACPs marshal on, largely by knowing when to advise, when to stand their ground, when to roll with the tide, and when to grouse. Most important, though, TACPs have had to learn to thrive in an environment where technical expertise, danger and hardship, great responsibility, uncertain support, imaginative tactical skill, and standing on one's own are all part of any day on the job. It is a highly adverse environment, but fortunately it has created the conditions that have made the TACP community the very kind of agile thinking, technically adaptable, dedicated professional needed when America came calling.

Other Realities

Though ROMADs are in the air force, because they spend their entire careers living with the army, at heart they have more in common with soldiers and marines. They have that outlook common to those whose daily life is bounded by death, dirt, physical exertion, and hardship. Among the services, the air force has the reputation for enjoying the best benefits and demanding the greatest creature comforts; this is lost on most ROMADs, for by living on army posts they give up the "extras" found on air force bases, and by working in the field they sleep in the same tents, dig the same foxholes, share the same privations, and face the same dangers as their army compatriots. All this makes sense, but because they are air force they have to continually "prove themselves" to their army colleagues, and often, as they put it, have to "out-army the army." Much the same could be said for ALOs, but with one big difference—most ALOs face two years of this life then return to the air force lifestyle they have come to expect.

ROMADs must also achieve a challenging level of technical expertise. The need to operate some of the most sophisticated communications equipment, computers, and high-tech gadgetry is enough to constitute a demanding career field in its own right. For example, they not only routinely rely on the oldest radio technology—HF—but also have to work with the full range of mid-twentieth-century technology—VHF and UHF—and in the last few years they have turned increasingly to satellite communications. If this weren't enough, they also have to be able to perform rudimentary troubleshooting and repairs on these systems in the field—they even have to know how to make their own radio antennae out of basic materials.

On top of all this, they are also combat troops, ones who must be thoroughly familiar with two regimes of combat—war in the air and on the ground. They must thoroughly master the intricacies of friendly and enemy ground warfare—weapon systems, unit formations, doctrine, and so on—and they must be fully versed in the full range of air combat—aircraft and weapons capabilities and limitations, air defense systems, and airspace control and deconfliction, just to name a few. Most military members are expected to master only one area of expertise. ROMADs must know them all.

Perhaps the most important aspect of all TACPs—ALOs and ROMADs—is that because they control so much firepower that can be applied in so many ways, the good ones add the further dimension of shaping and influencing the battle that takes place where air and ground combat meet. Eighteenth-century generals used to speak of a highly prized genius known as coup d'oeil—literally "stroke of the eye." It refers to that unique ability to watch a battle unfold, recognize where and when a decisive blow should be struck, and then act quickly and resolutely enough to take full advantage of the opportunity. This is a good analogy for the challenge faced by the CAS control community and the distinctive contribution it makes. This is not as simple as some people seem to think. Exploiting air power is never about hitting everything, for there are always more targets than weapons; far more important is to get the best effect you can given the situation and resources at hand. Much the same could be said of the fluid world of ground combat—events unfold so quickly and so many factors impinge at once that the ability to assimilate everything without being overwhelmed and paralyzed by indecision has long been the acid test of combat leaders. TACPs must remain on top of both these chaotic environments if they stand any chance of being effective. And yet this is where they routinely shine the brightest. A constant theme in this narrative is how these men, some young and untested, some old and experienced, consistently faced incredible odds, unimagined circumstances, or impending disaster and still came up with solutions that not only "saved the day" but also amazed everyone around them. The fact that they have gone so long unnoticed, and to a great extent unheralded and unappreciated, only makes their performance that much more amazing.

This is their story.

Part
ONE

Afghanistan

In October, who thought we'd be in Kandahar in January?

UNNAMED U.S. GENERAL, JANUARY 2002

1. The Challenge Is Clear— and Daunting

The dust of the World Trade Towers had hardly settled before it became clear—Osama bin Laden and his terrorist organization, al Qaeda, were responsible. One other fact followed in the wake of this reality—the Taliban regime in Afghanistan, by harboring bin Laden and supporting al Qaeda training camps, was complicit in this heinous crime. When the Taliban refused to hand over bin Laden and dismantle the camps, a war to deal with both the Taliban and al Qaeda became certain. What was far less certain was how such a war could accomplish anything effective yet acceptable to world and U.S. public opinion. Decision-makers and opinion shapers were debating the options publicly and passionately. Some advocated a massive bombing campaign—"Bomb 'em back to the Stone Age!"—but few thought this would serve any purpose other than naked vengeance. With little real infrastructure and a regime that rejected modernity and wanted in many respects to see Afghan society stripped of its Western trappings, there was little bombing could do to cause the Taliban real pain.

More troubling, some advocated a major ground invasion. Sending a massive U.S. ground force to bring down the Taliban, root out al Qaeda, and hunt for bin Laden seemed the only sure way to end that threat, and according to a CBS/*New York Times* poll, 55 percent of those asked said they would accept thousands of American deaths in a military campaign against Afghanistan (*N.Y. Times,* 25 September 2001, A1). Surely this level of support opened the door for a major ground offensive. But the Bush administration seemed less sanguine, probably because the history of foreign armies in the region was ominous. Afghanistan, with its rugged terrain and long history of tribal and clannish independence, was infamous as the graveyard of European armies. Alexander the Great conquered it, but his generals did not hold it long after his death. Britain and Russia both tried to absorb it into their respective empires in the nineteenth century, battling each other in what became known as "the Great Game," but the recalcitrant Afghanis thwarted both their efforts. Uppermost in people's memories, however, was how the Soviets had met their "Vietnam" in Afghanistan, and in the view of some, this national disaster was what really started the Soviet slide into collapse. Few advocates won any real support for this option.

Adding to concerns about taking on the Taliban and al Qaeda in a conventional ground war was the fact that for years a loose coalition of Afghanis known as the Northern Alliance, as well as other groups, had waged a tenacious but seemingly futile rebellion. If these Afghanis couldn't beat the Taliban on their own turf, what chance did Americans have in this mountainous landlocked country half a world away? While this added to the pessimism of dealing decisively with the Taliban, it did offer a glimmer of hope: why not link up with the Taliban's enemies, help them bring down the regime, and then be in a better position to deal with a new, hopefully more cooperative, Afghani government?

On 7 October, the U.S. military began launching air attacks against Afghanistan targets. Not surprisingly, the Bush administration did not announce its strategy at the outset, so speculation on this point was rife in the media. Airstrikes appeared calculated to degrade the collective military capabilities of the Taliban regime and their al Qaeda allies, but by all accounts it looked like a classic strategic bombing campaign. Fighters, bombers, and cruise missiles from the United States and its coalition partners struck key buildings, airfields, radar installations, and other fixed targets generally considered part of a nation's infrastructure and vital to its defenses. The terrorist training camps were being bombed as well, which had obvious utility to the War on Terror, but many asked how an impoverished nation that had seen decades of uninterrupted warfare and that was notoriously bereft of infrastructure could be seriously weakened by these air attacks. Many speculated the attacks were meant to aid the Northern Alliance somehow, though Northern Alliance leaders were unimpressed and unsure how their cause was being advanced. Officials remained tight-lipped about the overall strategy, though some pointed out that any modern U.S. military operation would begin with just such an "air phase" to ensure air superiority, disrupt enemy air defenses, and degrade enemy political and military command and control facilities, all of which would aid whatever happened in "phase two."

After several weeks, however, it looked to outside observers like the air campaign *was* the strategy. Reports had surfaced of Special Forces teams moving into theater, but no major combat unit movements seemed to be under way that might indicate an imminent "ground phase" to follow up and exploit the "air phase." Moreover, it didn't seem like the air campaign was meant to directly help the Northern Alliance, since its officials were still complaining that few airstrikes were aimed at Taliban troop positions. This charge seemed plausible since a Northern Alliance offensive on Mazar-e Sharif had been halted and the widely touted drive on Kabul postponed. If the air campaign wasn't paving the way for either an imminent U.S. invasion or a Northern Alliance ground offensive, what was it trying to achieve?

Since most targets thus far had been of the type struck in what air doctrine calls a strategic attack campaign, many observers assumed Bush and Rumsfeld were trying to win the war with air power alone. This assumption awakened the old strategic bombing debate and brought back images of Bill Clinton's handling of the Kosovo campaign. Critics ranging from politicians like John McCain to academics like air power theorist Robert A. Pape and media pundits like Charles Krauthammer lined up to denounce any strategy based on "paralysis through bombing" and to call for conventional invasion as the only way to victory. The chorus of criticism only grew louder with a string of high-visibility mistakes as U.S. planes bombed the wrong targets. Inexplicably, Americans targeted a Red Cross relief warehouse, not once, but twice. "Collateral damage" and large numbers of civilian casualties were being widely reported, and not just by the Taliban. By late October America's war on terror in Afghanistan appeared, publicly anyway, to be like a ship without a rudder, and the critics were becoming more insistent.

But events in Afghanistan were poised for a dramatic turnaround. In the weeks between late October and early November a significant number of new Special Forces teams infiltrated into Afghanistan and linked up with various Northern Alliance elements, as well as U.S. and Coalition units already in theater. One key component of these new teams was air force ROMADs known as SOF TACPs. These individuals were part of a program that had started in 1994 to select highly experienced ROMADs who were then given Special Forces training and sent to work with SF units around the world. Though they were regular air force, they were Special Forces in everything but name. Originally the SOF TACP program had been intended to train SOF forces in how to conduct "emergency CAS," but the mission expanded and they gained a permanent position on many SOF teams as something like "super TACPs." The job of these SOF TACPs in Afghanistan was to link up with friendly forces, get as close to enemy positions as possible, and then call in airstrikes.

Bringing in CAS experts brought several immediate advantages. First, by getting in close enough to see what was being hit and having the train-

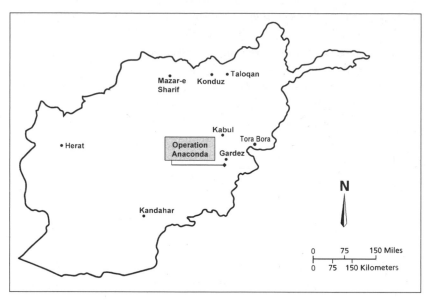

Afghanistan

ing to ensure the greatest possible accuracy in aiming, these controllers could greatly reduce the problem of errant bombs. Second, one of the reasons airstrikes on enemy positions in front of Northern Alliance forces had been so few was that without some form of control on the ground to guide the airstrikes, the possibility of bombs falling on Northern Alliance forces was significant and would have had a disastrous impact on the tenuous relationship U.S. leaders were trying to build with the notoriously fickle rebel leaders. Third, these new teams could begin probing for enemy units in other areas of suspected strength.

These second and third advantages offered obvious utility, but there was a less obvious benefit—a new capability had been taking shape for several years that few had fully appreciated. The stunning success that followed not only demonstrated the new capability in dramatic fashion but also took a lot of military experts by surprise.

The Fall of Mazar-e Sharif

The first major city to fall to the rebels was Mazar-e Sharif, and the collapse of Taliban forces holding the city was so sudden and so surprising that on the same day that newspapers reported the city's fall, they published articles criticizing theater commander Gen. Tommy Franks's overall strategy. One of the catalysts for this success was S.Sgt. Stephen Tomat. A SOF TACP stationed at Fort Bragg, North Carolina, Tomat is with the 22nd Air Support Operations Flight, which supports 5th Special Forces Group. In early November, Tomat's SOF team linked up with one of the Northern Alliance's strongest, and most notorious leaders, Gen. Abdul Rashid Dostum. Dostum's forces were south of Mazar-e Sharif and had been trying to move northward to take the city since before the September eleventh attacks. SOF and other U.S. government agencies had linked up with Northern Alliance units prior to Tomat's arrival, and they had been calling in airstrikes on suspected enemy positions, but as Tomat says, "these teams were of the mind-set . . . that they [could control CAS] from twelve kilometers away or more." The problem with this approach is twofold. In Tomat's words: "One, it's not effective—you obviously can't get 'eyes on' the target . . . and two, you're more than likely incurring a great deal of collateral damage, not to mention civilian deaths." Tomat made critical changes right away, and those changes made quite a difference.

> After about a week of bombing, the command staff . . . determined that it was vital that they get a TAC-qualified individual on the ground. I was then told to get my stuff ready; had about three hours to get on the bird . . . and then we finally [made it] into our link up point [and] infilled down into Dahee. . . . The main mission of the team was to secure the two northernmost airfields in northern Afghanistan for resupply and for reinforcements for future operations. [One airfield is] located just south of Mazar-e Sharif and there's another one off to the east. The second mission was to open up the land bridge . . . into Uzbekistan to provide a land route for reinforcements. . . .
>
> You can see just how the people lived out in that area. We were lucky to have some place to sleep. Later on we moved up into the mountain regions and found a number of caves and areas to sleep in [and] to conduct CAS from a little bit later on. Once we infilled, it took about a day for General Dostum to come down to our area. It was there that I assessed the situation; the team captain informed me of what was going on. [Dostum's people] were thinking to call CAS onto these towns from [twelve kilometers away]. . . . It was at that point I told . . . General Dostum that we need to get eyes onto the targets to be effective. I would prefer [to be] within a kilometer of the enemy positions, so I could determine what I was striking. My main focus was to strike the [command and control] nodes initially, where I know the command elements were going to be located. I know that once the command structure falls, the grunts aren't going to have the leadership to carry out orders. . . .

We then moved from just south of Dahee . . . up the riverbed in order to avoid mines to an area south of Chopchau. The Taliban had taken all the mines from the Russian war and placed [them] in what they thought were avenues of approach. Just to the south was a village that had been razed, destroyed, literally leveled by the Taliban. There's nothing left of it. [From] that point, we were going to conduct our operations to push the bad guys out of this area so we could move north up into Mazar-e Sharif. . . .

Now keep in mind, we moved this distance by horseback and foot. There's one point where we walked because our horses were just dead dog tired, I mean literally. These are not horses like Western horses, they are like large dogs. And the saddles we're sitting on were literally two-by-fours covered with a piece of carpet. And because the Afghans were not very big guys their stirrups were extremely short. So we were sitting on [these horses], our asses were sore, our knees were literally up to our chests. But that was pretty taxing on the body and on the horses, so there was a good sixty to a hundred kilometers we actually walked on foot to give the horses a rest. Eventually we got some four-wheelers brought in to us just south of Mazar-e Sharif. . . .

The Taliban and al Qaeda had blocking positions to prevent us from moving north. For years the [rebels] had been fighting the Taliban; the Taliban had just virtually overwhelmed them and set up bunker systems and taken over towns and villages. This whole area, because it's a river system, is heavily populated, relatively speaking.

Once I got into the area of Omulton . . . it took me about three days to recon the area and find the command and control bunker system. They had ZSU 57-2 [like many antiaircraft systems, it can be used in a horizontal mode as a direct fire weapon], a tank, and a bunker system, and these bunkers, which are almost in a line, is where the command and control center was. We found out that night that Mullah Fazil and Mullah Rezat were at this position. Mullah Rezat was deputy minister of defense. He was the number eleven guy that we were to capture or take out. Mullah Fazil was the army chief of staff—the number four guy that we needed to either apprehend or take out.

Because they operate deep in enemy territory, SOF teams depend on stealth and face the constant threat of discovery. With their small numbers, this could be disastrous, and quite often air power is the only heavy firepower available. About the time Tomat completed his reconnaissance, part of his team was compromised and the enemy launched an attack.

Mullah Fazil pushed northeast with his convoy in order to flank [their position]. . . . I called in an F/A-18 [for] a gun run . . . but he'd have to "break the deck" [descend below the minimum altitude restriction]. So I asked him to get permission from our command sources. He did so; he broke the deck; and I talked him in onto the target. No sooner had he struck the target, we heard over the radio . . . that Mullah Fazil was on the run. We could watch them—they looked like ants—they just scattered. That initially broke that contact with the enemy. Then a B-52 was called in on the remainder of the targets. He dropped like twelve Mk-82s onto bad-guy positions and our guys pulled back at that point.

Next Tomat turned his attention to the command and control complex. For this he called on a new weapon in the CAS arsenal, the JDAM, a conventional bomb fitted with a GPS guidance system. It was designed in the wake of Desert Storm for use against fixed targets in a strategic attack role. Here we encounter a theme running throughout this narrative—the ingenuity TACPs showed in finding creative ways to deal with unanticipated and often unimaginable situations. Such ingenuity has long been a hallmark of the American soldier, from Bunker Hill to Normandy, so seeing it alive and well in modern-day airmen shouldn't be surprising, but it is inspiring, and on several occasions it was lifesaving. In this case, JDAMs were pressed on short notice into the CAS fight—a role for which they were never intended. One reflection that this was unanticipated is that there were no established tactics, techniques, or procedures for their use in the CAS role, but TACPs adjusted on the fly, not just in adapting current procedures but, most importantly, by incorporating the weapon's unique capabilities into their way of thinking and doing business. The uniqueness of the situation was not lost on Tomat, but he also realized that innovation on the fly was a two-edged sword. As he explains, to leap into the battlefield of the future you need to have a solid grounding in the basics, and you must have the conviction to stick to the rules no matter what. Tomat's conviction would be put to the test when he got into the middle of Mazar-e Sharif itself.

I then went [after] the command bunkers . . . with a B-52 with six JDAMs. . . . The fact that I'm utilizing a Vietnam-era airframe in [an unconventional warfare] scenario with a twenty-first-century weapon was absolutely awe inspiring. I had goose bumps. When I called in that strike, every single one hit direct on. No problems whatsoever. I know the media said, "Well, they're not accurate"; bullshit. If you utilize the tools you have in hand . . . they will strike your target where you want them to. . . . I knew prior to coming into [this] country what I could do with the JDAMs. . . . I went back to old school utilizing the map and the compass and stuff like that—you can't go wrong with that. . . .

[Striking that bunker system killed] Mullah Rezat, the secretary of defense, and 150 of his men. . . . As soon as I struck it General Dostum's forces on horseback took that area over. . . . We captured the aide to Mullah Rezat, brought him back to our OP. . . . He was slightly wounded in the arm, very flush and visibly nervous. It was then that General Dostum told him to get on the radio and tell his troops, the Taliban, that the Americans are here, to give up, and to go home. Not more than an hour or two hours after, we took the town of Boybache as a consequence of destroying these bunker systems. We moved into Keshendeb-ye and we continued to the west and then up to the mountain of Homoltek. . . . As a consequence of destroying the command structure here, these villages fell without another CAS strike or another U.S. forces action on [them] against the Taliban or al Qaeda. . . . Within literally seven days we were up just south of Mazar-e Sharif. [Task Force Dagger] couldn't believe it.

Taliban and al Qaeda forces fled in two directions. One group moved northeast toward Konduz, the other north toward Mazar-e Sharif. Dostum pursued the latter remnant, which rallied as it approached Mazar-e Sharif. Tomat relates the next phase of the running battle:

Before we got into Mazar-e Sharif there is a mountainous pass. That's an ideal spot for bad guys to keep me from moving and to make your day go bad. So we split up [into] three CAS teams. We moved one CAS team up to the eastern ridge, the other CAS team . . . went off to the west, and then myself with General Dostum, the team captain, and [another member of the SOF team]. Our mission was to be the main push through the pass. Prior to that push—I mean immediately, within minutes of that push—there was a BMP-21 and a ZSU 57-2 that laid down fire all along this ridgeline, the valley, and back up the other ridgeline. In effect it pinned down the [eastern] CAS team. So I clambered up the hillside and found me a good hiding spot and called in the strike on the bunkers immediately on the northern side of the pass, the ZSU, and the BMP . . . [using] F-18s and JDAMs.

From his position on the hillside, Tomat could also see a column of trucks and infantry moving along the road to attack. For this Tomat again came up with a creative solution. He had a B-52 on station loaded with twenty-seven Mk-82s, five-hundred-pound general purpose bombs—so-called dumb bombs. "What I had done was establish a bomber box," he said, referring to an imaginary area within which he wanted those bombs to fall. Tomat created this box to maximize the effect of the bombs to be dropped, positioning it so it would take out as many enemy troops and equipment as possible. He then passed the coordinates to the bomber, which dropped on his clearance to place those bombs within the box. Those bombs took out five trucks, as well as many enemy soldiers.

This engagement paved the way for Dostum's forces to resume their march northward, and by morning the way was clear into Mazar-e Sharif. As they moved through the villages newly liberated from the Taliban, Tomat was struck by the reception they received from the villagers and what it said about what these people had suffered under the Taliban regime. "That was almost surreal to have these individuals cheer us on. I knew what the Taliban had done to these people over the past four years, but [not] until the subsequent month [spent] in Mazar-e Sharif did I get the full scope of the torture they put these people through. It was actually horrendous. All in the name of religion; it's sad."

That day's march brought them to Qala Jangi, a village on the outskirts of Mazar-e Sharif and the site of a notorious prison uprising a few weeks later. The SOF team didn't get to spend much time there, however, for as Tomat relates, they soon received information that led to the collapse of Taliban authority in Mazar-e Sharif.

> We weren't there for more than three or four hours when [intelligence] gave us word that we had Taliban and al Qaeda holed up in Mazar-e Sharif, the city itself. This time it was about nine hundred of them in the center of the city. They were holed up in a large building, formerly a school [a madrasa, a school for religious training.] They said they were not going to surrender to General Dostum or to the Americans— that they were going to fight to the death, and they proved that when they killed the peace envoy we sent to them to ask them to lay down their arms.
>
> It was then that the team captain asked [me and some of the SOF team] to move into the city and take that target out. We then moved into the city with Commander Fakir [one of Dostum's lieutenants]. Commander Fakir was actually from the city and he had a house there. So he was intimately familiar with where this building was.
>
> Keep in mind, I'm sure you've seen *Black Hawk Down;* that's the scenario. . . . I asked Commander Fakir specifically for a building near the target area but high enough that I could see at least a good majority of the city. It was almost surreal because we came into the city in the back of a pickup truck, there's five of us, Commander Fakir with a couple of his guards in the cab, the rest of us were in the back of the truck, guns up, we're looking around, checking for bad guys, on the

rooftops, in the windows, on the streets, the streets were packed full of people, we're winding and making turns, and going through each of the small back roads, and finally made it up into this building, a big old five-story building.

We go up to the rooftop—perfect view of the target area. I have buildings on my left and my right that I have to be concerned with. I did not expect the target area—the building—to be so close to the other shops. But that was something I had to deal with at that time. There was a compound on the other side to the east of the building, and the building was oriented basically north/south.

As I set up my [binoculars] and my SOFLAM I could see individuals walking in and out of the rooms with their weapons and moving crates and stuff from room to room, going in and out of the courtyard. A lot of individuals, nine hundred of these guys, were holed up in this building. I set up the SOFLAM and we called in for [a highly qualified pilot] because this was a high payoff target and it was in way close proximity to civilians and friendlies. . . . I plotted the target—oh, by the way, the map I was using cannot [be used to] call in a strike—not in an urban setting. So I asked [others in our group] if they had any maps of the city. [One guy] pulls out this old Russian map—it was at least ten years old.

Tomat's map problem left him with a unique technical dilemma, one with overtones that would test both his ingenuity and his integrity. Because of the close proximity of other buildings, the two most precise options in this situation would be either a GPS-guided weapon such as a JDAM or a laser-guided bomb. Tomat's map problem, though, precluded his using JDAM because he could not manually double-check his GPS coordinates. His regular map gave him accurate terrain information out in the countryside that he could use to triangulate his position with his compass to crosscheck his GPS, but it had no real reference points inside the city; the Russian map gave detailed information but was unreliable. Others in his position might have been tempted to just trust the GPS, but Tomat knew many vagaries in the technology meant a considerable error could enter the equation and he would have no way to catch the error. He still had the laser option, but the aircraft that showed up to support him was about to make this option impossible as well.

So, a couple navy aircraft check in, I give them the nine-line; he first says, "I've got JDAMs on board—how about we use those?" I said, "Sorry, we can't use those because I can't confirm the actual coordinates utilizing the map with the GPS and the SOFLAM. What I prefer is utilizing the laser." He comes in on the laser run-in and asks me to "lase on"; he pulls off; "no spot"—he didn't see it. He does this twice; he's not picking up the spot [the laser energy]. I know my laser's working fine 'cause I'd used it prior. So I don't know if being in the city impeded picking up the laser spot or if there was something wrong with his laser spot tracker.

With GPS and laser-guided weapons out of the picture, Tomat's only remaining option was to do a "talk-on"—to verbally guide the pilot's eyes onto the target so the pilot can designate the target with his onboard targeting system. Many consider "dumb bombs" as hopelessly inaccurate in an era of "precision weapons," but a new generation of cockpit targeting systems incorporating computers and high-tech optical devices are so accurate that some observers have coined the phrase "dumb bomb, brilliant aircraft" to describe the new capability. The only problem was that the pilot was going to have to "break the deck" to be able to see what Tomat was talking about, and this brought a danger for Tomat and his team.

So I said, "That's fine, I'll do a talk-on." [It] took me about fifteen minutes to talk him onto the target, for me to know for sure that he saw the exact target I was telling him [to strike]. By then these guys are getting restless in the building because [they] know "we got birds in the area," so they know birds means bombs, bombs means . . . some guys were around there directing the aircraft.

I finally talked the lead aircraft onto the target, he says, "I got it," he comes in, first bomb right off the rack shacks right through the center of the building—exactly in the center of the building. This is like a hornet's nest—maybe killed a hundred, 150 of the guys, if we're lucky, on that first bomb. Number two [second aircraft in the formation] comes in—goes to pickle—bomb hung [would not release]. He says, "I'm going to have to RTB [return to base], I got bombs hung." And I say "Well brother, we just stirred up a hornet's nest, we're 340 meters away and we're getting shot at right now 'cause they know we're here. I need you to come in and figure out some way to get those bombs off the rack."

Number one came back in. He had three more remaining and he said, "No problem." He comes back in, below the deck and all three at the same time. Just levels the place, absolutely levels it. We found later about eighty of the bad guys survived. Of that eighty, only thirty lived because after we released the remainder of the ordnance, these guys just scattered out of the rubble and as they were scattering they moved into the surrounding buildings. It was there that the citizens of the city took over and just started shwacking on them in the streets.

From that time on, we liberated Mazar-e Sharif and the surrounding areas. We went on to conduct other operations—search and destroy [missions]—but we didn't actually conduct CAS nor any destroy missions, just search out and see if we could find any high value targets [important enemy leaders].

2. Integrating the Special Forces—Close Air Support Team

The fall of Mazar-e Sharif, especially the speed and totality of the Taliban's collapse there, came as a major shock to many people around the world. It was a badly needed morale boost for anyone yearning to see justice meted out to the Taliban and al Qaeda. It also silenced those critics claiming the Rumsfeld-Franks strategy was doomed to failure. More important, though, it showed the world there was something significant in marrying Special Forces and air power with a seemingly insignificant force like the Northern Alliance. After years of losses, the Northern Alliance seemed unlikely to pull off such a stunning victory on their own, so obviously SOF teams and air power must be key parts of that victory.

Military leaders realized that somehow air power, particularly in the form of CAS, was the great catalyst in this equation, but exactly why was not clear. Many observers ascribed the success to technology and weapons that had emerged in the previous twenty years. Precision guided munitions, which made their public debut in Desert Storm, got a lot of press, and the U.S. military had integrated them into routine CAS operations, but the wider public wasn't aware of this prior to Afghanistan. In fact, so much had been done in this area that some observers believed the big revolution in Afghanistan was simply guys on the ground with laser pointers designating targets for precision weapons.

New weapons weren't the only part of the revised CAS picture, though. Even the so-called dumb bombs gained new importance because they were now being dropped by highly accurate aiming systems that could be relied on even in close quarters. Extraordinary new advances in reconnaissance had also done a great deal to transform the air-ground team. Satellites and unmanned aerial vehicles significantly increased what soldiers and airmen could see and how quickly the images could be sent to them. Various means of monitoring energy emissions across the electronic spectrum helped troops know what sorts of units or weapons systems were out there and where they were located, and cosmic radar sets could detect and help identify units and weapons moving on the ground. But for all their glitz and sex appeal, new technology and gee-whiz weaponry were not the real secret to what was happening on the ground in Afghanistan.

Some perceptive observers realized that what was really different about recent events in the war was a new operational concept. So the question of the day was how to identify that concept, how to harness it, and how to make it work on a routine basis. The natural tendency is to ascribe great capability to technology or weapons, but in reality the most important factor is how you *use* that technology or weaponry. A critical level exists in warfare between the tactical level—"the grunt's eye view"—and the strategic level. Known as the operational level of warfare, it might best be thought of as how military organizations conduct business—their mode of fighting, how they integrate various combat arms throughout the theater, their organization and logistics, in short, how they translate tactical level capability on a day-to-day basis into strategic level success. It is the operational level that often spells the difference between success and failure. What most people think of as doctrine is really the codification of concepts or modes of operating at the operational level of warfare. At the operational level in Afghanistan, what the Coalition was doing had never been done before; moreover, it hadn't even been anticipated, and so the secret to recreating what had happened at Mazar-e Sharif was to figure out what had worked there and weld it into an operational concept that could be applied across the theater.

One problem with knitting normal SOF operations into a theater-wide operational concept was the challenge of applying air power to routine SOF techniques on a massive scale. Essentially, because Special Forces travel very light, their primary heavy weapon across this theater was going to be CAS, and that meant substantial air power. The difficulty was not that SOF personnel were unfamiliar with controlling CAS. SOF teams often called in airstrikes on specific targets, and CAS is always available as a last-ditch defense, so all SOF fields receive some level of CAS control training, and some fields, particularly combat control teams, receive more than others. The problem was that across the SOF community no single area specialized in CAS control as its primary mission. For example, combat control teams are primarily responsible for going into hostile territory with other Special Forces to establish landing zones or seize airfields and then controlling aircraft traffic into and out of those landing zones or airfields. Thus SOF levels of expertise weren't as high as those who specialized in controlling CAS—air force TACPs.

This lack of CAS control expertise had not been a problem before because CAS normally was not used a great deal. SOF specialties reflected skills that had been most needed in SOF operations up to that point, and their limited need for air support had kept their lower level of CAS training from being a problem. But now they were being called on to use CAS at unprecedented levels and in myriad situations and circumstances. Added to this was the extremely delicate political environment, both in Afghanistan and around the world. Taken together, the potential for a single mistake leading to incalculable harm to the war effort was high, and the opportunities to commit such mistakes were even higher.

There was a solution at hand, but it wasn't part of standard operations. The SOF TACP program had existed for about seven years, but originally SOF TACPs were intended to be instructors to the SOF community—to give them more CAS training. This program was not originally meant to bring TACPs into the SOF mission, but by the eve of Operation Enduring Freedom, as the Afghanistan war was officially known, SOF TACPs had become deeply integrated into special operations around the world, and in the process had received a great deal of SOF training. Still, they were not fully integrated and were not officially classified as Special Forces. Though they were assigned to specially designated units set up to support SOF missions, those units and the SOF TACPs themselves were still officially assigned to the conventional side of the air force under Air Combat Command rather than the Special Forces side under Special Operations Command.

Turning to SOF TACPs as a solution in Afghanistan was primarily a matter of informing leaders that a better option existed. A key person in this was Col. Mike Longoria. A career special operations air force officer, Longoria was commander of the 18th Air Support Operations Group, the unit responsible for supporting U.S. Central Command, the regional command tasked with running this war. Longoria's presence in this post at this time was an example all too rare in military history of the right person being in the right place at the right time. With his extensive SOF background, but in command of the TACP community charged with providing CAS controllers for this theater, Longoria was in a perfect position to bridge the two worlds that needed to come together to forge a new operational concept in the heat of battle. According to Longoria, he first met with resistance when he proposed using SOF TACPs:

> Nobody wanted us. We kind of forced ourselves on people and then within a day or day and a half they couldn't live without us. Literally couldn't live without us. . . . I'm talking about the leadership . . . those

are the people we kind of forced ourselves on. Did I think Special Tactics guys [air force SOF] could perform . . . a predominantly SOF mission? You bet; I have every confidence in the world. But I also know that
because it was heavy kinetic air [conventional bombing], not just SOF
air, we needed what we normally integrate into this piece, and that
was the ALO and the ETAC—guys who fly and drop bombs for a living.
Even though I'm a Special Tactics guy I have a great appreciation for
our [TACP community]. I don't want to participate in an activity where
we don't use their expertise and tap into that vast weapons system
experience. We need to use that; we'd be stupid not to. I don't need
them to be SOF experts—they're air power experts—and we need to
integrate them into this fight.

Longoria also stressed that putting TACPs with SOF teams would work
smoothly and actually complement SOF capability.

SF guys are better at cultural integration than anybody in the world.
They are the best. . . . Air force guys . . . are capable of the employment:
they can jump out of airplanes with the SF guys; they can assault with
the helicopters and do all these kind of things; they can hump a ruck
just like the SF guys do. But what the SF guys bring is a cultural sensitivity and a sense of how to integrate with other land forces in an appropriate way. And they're good at it. Our guys are more technically
oriented . . . so if the mission required cultural sensitivity, SF hands
down. But if the mission required just simply directing air power, there
is nobody better in the world than ETACs or Special Tactics guys. Nobody better in the world.

Winning over leadership wasn't hard—as Longoria said, they quickly
learned they couldn't live without the conventional CAS expertise—but
tapping the full spectrum of that expertise wasn't just a matter of getting
TACPs into the field. Some very critical components and expertise were
missing at the headquarters level as well. In a theater of war, the normal SOF mode of operations is to work in the margins. They use the big
fight—the tank battles, the air campaign, the diplomatic negotiations—
as cover to slip unseen into where they need to go, and often make their
essential contribution unnoticed and unheralded. So their organization
and operational modes are geared toward being a small part of a much
bigger military establishment running the war. In Afghanistan, however,
the SOF campaign *was* the main theater-wide effort. This meant that the
SOF community and its command and control infrastructure suddenly
found itself having to carry much of the weight of running a theater-wide
war and achieving theater-wide operational level goals.

One area where this unfamiliar role created problems was with the normal means for integrating close air support into the ground campaign. After decades of wrangling over CAS, the army and the air force had evolved a very effective system covering nearly every aspect of CAS from planning to execution—how to request it, plan for it, control it, who makes key decisions about levels of CAS support, and perhaps most critically, how the sorties actually available for CAS get divided among the various units in the fight. This system is made up of two parts: the air force's theater air control system and the army air-ground system. Together it is known as the TACS/AAGS system, and it is the doctrinal basis for integrating CAS into ground combat across an entire theater. There was only one problem when it came to Afghanistan: the mechanisms for making the TACS/AAGS system work assume that any ground campaign is going to involve a conventional army presence, so those mechanisms are folded into conventional army units and conventional army operations. As the conventional army structure sets up in theater, these elements roll with the mobilization plan. Since the full conventional army structure had not been set up in Afghanistan, the full TACS/AAGS system was not set up either, and as the SOF campaign emerged and the CAS portion of that campaign unfolded, some of the most critical portions of the TACS/AAGS system were missing. At first, true to their can-do ethos, the initial SOF personnel did superhuman work trying to fill the gaps, but they didn't have the training, experience, or manpower to perform the many critical functions needed to make a theater-wide CAS program run smoothly.

Colonel Longoria identified this need right away and took steps to fill the gaps. The main SOF effort was organized into a command dubbed Task Force Dagger, headquartered at a classified location in theater and commanded by Col. John Mulholland, an Army Special Forces officer. In a visit to TF Dagger, Longoria noticed that a handful of Special Forces troops in that one headquarters were trying to do the jobs normally done by several echelons of TACP personnel assigned to do nothing but keep their portion of the TACS/AAGS system running smoothly. Normally CAS requests go to TACP cells at army tactical operations centers located at battalion, brigade, and division levels, and are then handed up to the critical nerve center, the air support operations center, which coordinates all CAS efforts for at least an entire corps, and often for an entire theater. All these cells normally comprise more than a hundred personnel highly trained in both CAS procedures and the inner workings of the TACS/AAGS system. In Afghanistan, however, all echelons were collapsed into one headquarters at TF Dagger. There were no battalions, brigades, divisions, or corps, just this one headquarters, and the entire process rested in the hands of a few Army Special Forces troops with familiarity in the TACS/AAGS system. Longoria offered to send a team of ALOs and ETACs to take over this critical function, and they not only did a great deal to smooth out the flow of CAS requests and coordination of CAS related issues but also linked into other parts of the military establishment that could help influence CAS issues.

A key part of this team was Lt. Col. George Bochain, at the time commander of the 20th Air Support Operations Squadron, attached to the 10th Mountain Division at Fort Drum, New York. An F-16 pilot by trade, Bochain joined TF Dagger just as the battle for Mazar-e Sharif was beginning. Bochain describes what he found:

> [Colonel Mulholland] did not have a centralized planner in his staff that would be able to tie that all together, and he was spending a lot of his time focusing on [this problem]. . . . He needed somebody to dedicate his entire time to managing that piece for him 'cause he had a lot of other things going on. He and his command structure at that time were doing what they could with what they had, but they really had not done this before. It's not anything you would expect them to do; it is what guys like me do for a living.
>
> There was a targeting cell that had been set up, and there was a fire support cell, and the folks had done a really great job of establishing a process, however there were many things that needed to be fixed. The folks running the targeting cell—again, hardworking, incredibly dedicated, smart people that had no targeting experience. Fire support was being run by four Special Operations tactical air controllers with the highest rank being a tech sergeant, and again, they did a remarkable job of just setting this up and having a process in place to do the first phase of this thing at Mazar-e Sharif. The difficulty was that a tech sergeant does not have the instant access to the commander that is required when you have to make a decision or provide advice on what air power can do. Even though these guys are as good as they come, there is a level of experience in there and access to the commander that wasn't present. [Additionally,] we had to coordinate with all national agencies, and that required a different type of expertise, and a certain amount of horsepower too, in order to have credibility with these agencies scattered all over the world.

But just getting CAS experts into the TF Dagger headquarters didn't make this a smooth or easy job, largely because the ground campaign was almost entirely SOF, an approach that had not been anticipated. As

Lt. Col. George Bochain stands outside a base in western Iraq. Bochain, a principal architect in forging the SOF-CAS operational approach early in the Afghanistan war, helped lead operations in western Iraq.

Bochain pointed out, "We were battalion, brigade, division, and corps all wrapped up into the same six-man element. We did all the way from minutia tactical to the overarching strategic planning for this task force, all with six guys at a table."

Getting an ASOC up and running at TF Dagger wasn't the only challenge Bochain faced with this new SOF operational mode; the SOF forces out in the field were going to have to make some adjustments as well. One other role of an ASOC is to parcel out CAS according to the ground commander's allocation decisions and priorities. Since there can never be enough air for all the things you would like to do, someone is going to have to make some hard decisions. That starts with the overall theater commander who decides how much air to devote to such tasks as air superiority, strategic attack, and CAS. Once he decides how much will go to CAS, the ground force commander, who is supported by that CAS, decides how he wants to divide it among his units. This sounds logical in theory, but in practice it can lead to problems because bad things never occur in sequence, they invariably come all at once. So what often happens in warfare is several units call for air support at the same time and the ground commander must decide who gets priority. He can base this on many factors—he may think one threat is most severe; he may want to focus the air to help his main effort; or he many want to use the air to help his secondary effort hang on. Whatever his reasoning, and even though the ground commander makes the decision, it is the ASOC that has to deliver the bad news—who does and who does not get CAS—and this is the basis for many bad feelings among army guys toward the air force: the ground commander may have made the decision, but to the guy pinned down in a foxhole it seems like it was the air force that wasn't there to help him when he needed it.

The conventional army has had to live with this dilemma and has learned to deal with it, but Special Forces had generally been exempt. Because the weight of their efforts had always been so small in comparison to the conventional war going on around them, and because their unplanned CAS needs only came with real emergencies—such as when a team deep behind enemy lines had been discovered and was under attack—their procedures had called for them to go straight to the combined air operations center. The CAOC, also sometimes called simply the AOC, is the control center coordinating all air activity—everything from air refueling and air transport to reconnaissance and air superiority—for the entire theater. The CAOC would pull whatever was available from whatever mission it was on because SOF emergencies trumped just about anything else going on in the conventional war. Now with SOF teams being the main effort and using CAS as their main weapon, the chances of situations arising where there wasn't enough CAS to go around was a very real possibility, so Bochain fell back on the standard theater CAS allocation procedures: he directed SOF teams to request CAS through the ASOC instead of going directly to the CAOC. According to Bochain, this did not go over well at first.

> Early on the [orders] were written that the teams would go out and contact the CAOC directly and get air directed to them. That was the big thing that we changed immediately because the CAOC is the wrong level to be making battlefield decisions on priority of air. Once the CAS has been allocated down to the ground commander, it's up to the ground commander to decide where it goes. . . .
>
> So we told [the SOF teams], "You need to put all your requests through us," and they're looking at us like, "Hey, when I was in fight X, country Y, I could go straight to the [CAOC] and they would send it directly to me." So you had to educate them that this was a different game. "We're running multiple airstrikes at the same time. We have

to prioritize at the ground commander level—who gets what, when, where, why—and if you're out there [operating] on your own, you don't know the rest of the picture, the other teams out there that are not part of your playbook." . . . So they were concerned about that. I'd be concerned too, because it was a perfect world for them with the original setup. We had to be the guys that said no. . . . It was a little bit of training and salesmanship, "There's a reason for this guys, trust me."

The breakdown in the normal TACS/AAGS system was not just confined to TF Dagger. Another critical part of the system is the battlefield coordination detachment located in the CAOC. The BCD is staffed by army personnel, and it serves as a link between the ASOC and the CAOC to help integrate CAS into the rest of the air war and to advise CAOC personnel on army needs. As with the ASOC, though, this detachment normally works with the "big army" and does not have a routine role in SOF efforts. Moreover, there is a significant firewall keeping them from establishing such a role—security clearances. Because of the nature of SOF operations, anyone working with them needs not only a top secret clearance but also the further classification that grants access to sensitive compartmented information. Taken together, the ASOC and BCD problems meant that two of most critical parts of the TACS/AAGS system ensuring smooth CAS coordination at the operational level were absent at the outset in Afghanistan, the very period when CAS was emerging as the secret weapon in this new style war.

There was a group at the CAOC intended to coordinate SOF needs—the special operations liaison element. Normally a small team—usually only two on duty at a time—they coordinate the limited air needs of SOF teams scattered amid the much bigger conventional war. Faced with coordinating all CAS needs across the vast Afghanistan theater, the SOLE was initially as overwhelmed as its counterparts at TF Dagger. Colonel Longoria realized this problem was as acute as that at TF Dagger and sent what he had closest at hand. The first to arrive in the early days of the war was S.Sgt. Ed Shulman. A SOF TACP assigned to the 19th ASOS at Fort Campbell, Kentucky, and aligned with 5th Special Forces Group, Shulman had just deployed to Kuwait in support of routine operations there when the Afghan war started. Shulman describes how he ended up in Afghanistan and what he found:

[Colonel Longoria] went out to Kuwait to try and get a . . . better feel for what was going on. He linked up with me in Kuwait and we started talking to some of the flying squadrons that were flying out of Kuwait in support of [Afghanistan], particularly some of the F-16 units. . . . They started talking about a lot of the problems [CAS controllers] were having: unfamiliarity with the techniques, the methods of employment, your standard CAS [tactics, techniques, and procedures]. The pilots were having to take a lot of time to explain the equipment they were using; they weren't really getting the feedback from the guy on the ground they needed. That of course made us go, "Hey is that our guys?" . . . We started looking into who the call signs were and trying to find out what the deal was, and that took us to the CAOC in Saudi.

At that point [Longoria] grabbed me, being the only [SOF TACP] within arms reach . . . and we went down to the CAOC on a three-day fact-finding mission. We got in there and started briefing with the guys in the SOLE and immediately started to see what the problem was. The big problem was there was no system in place to link the air war to the ground picture; it was all being done at echelons above reality and then pushed down to a tactical level. But there was no translator for that. What I mean is that basically the SF teams were pushing [CAS requests] up to the [TF Dagger], from [there] it was going to the SOLE, and then the guys from the SOLE—two Special Forces NCOs and one warrant officer who were all really sharp guys but they were basically being tasked as an ASOC—they had no operational experience doing that.

These guys are basically running what I called the "sticky note ASOC," where you've got people running around a building with little yellow sticky notes going, "Hey, Tiger XX needs CAS," "Hey, Cobra XX needs aircraft," "These guys are troops in contact," and it was completely disorganized. It was a mess. You'd see notes stuck up on computer screens, "Cobra whatever needs CAS now!" I'm going, "Hey is that something that needs to be worked? Do you guys not have time to talk?" And they're like, "Oh, that's from yesterday." So you can see . . . how stuff like that can break down really quickly.

So Colonel Longoria identified that; I identified it. I started from the day I got there asking some questions and then I wound up getting locked into the operations floor. And I basically just kind of made a home for myself, and those guys right away were like, "Hey, yeah, you know how to do this stuff?" The focal point for all that [was] the commander of the SOLE . . . a combat control officer, a prior service marine; again good smart guy . . . he was the one that was kind of like, "Hey, yeah, come here, sit right here, help us out with this."

I deployed on three-day orders and stayed two and a half months. When I initially got there I established the systems. We got right up on mIRC Chat—it's like [an] instant messenger–type online chat protocol, but we were using it over SIPRNET. We didn't have any direct radio contact with [TF Dagger] . . . so I opened a dialogue with them and as soon as I typed in "hey, . . . it's Ed," all of a sudden I got this long, "Hey,

*S.Sgt. Ed Shulman mans a .50-caliber machine gun on his team's
gun truck in western Iraq. Shulman played a key role in helping the CAOC
adapt its operations.*

oh God, we're so glad you're there, nobody's been there before, this is
going to make stuff easier." . . . They were tracking things effectively,
but they had no way to communicate what they were doing to the
guys at the CAOC. . . .

[Another thing] having an ETAC in the CAOC created was a facilita-
tor. . . . Not a soul in the CAOC [understood CAS]—there was one major
that was a prior ALO that I started talking to that became a pretty good
ally—but I was dealing with navy [captains] that, with all respect, didn't
have a clue about how to fight an air war. They didn't understand CAS;
they didn't understand how it worked; they didn't understand why
[SOF] teams on the ground that were under fire couldn't tell [the CAOC]
twelve hours in advance that they were going to be under fire. They
just didn't understand why the situation was so dynamic. I can't stress
this enough: everybody really knew what they were doing [in their own
area of expertise]—I couldn't have done what I did without them being
smart [about that]—but nobody knew how to tie it together.

Another consequence of the unanticipated role for SOF and CAS in this
new style war was that not all SOF TACPs were equipped with all the new

high-tech weaponry. The same kind of flexibility and ingenuity shown by Staff Sergeant Tomat was needed at the CAOC and ASOC because they needed to match air assets to small isolated teams spread throughout the theater. Once again, Shulman offers an insider's perspective.

> When it came down to [SOF] teams on the ground with different types of equipment there was nobody in the CAOC at the time that could look at the ATO and identify [which teams needed which aircraft]— they were just sending aircraft. So you'd get one team that was all set up to use JDAMs . . . [who] would get a plane that showed up with all LGBs when they didn't have a laser. And then the guys that didn't have any way to derive coordinates effective enough for JDAMs would get a bomber full of JDAMs. Those were the kinds of problems that were going on. I was able to look and say, "Okay, this is what all the teams have, this is what their capabilities are."

Fixing the staff problems at the headquarters level wasn't the only element needed to develop an operational concept for this new style of warfare—the other essential missing ingredient was a vision of what air power could do in the unique circumstances of this particular war. Furthermore, what was needed was not just a vision of what CAS could contribute to the conventional fight in a general sense, but what SOF and air power could achieve when fused in the midst of this unique war. SOF forces faced this same challenge, and Colonel Mulholland deserves special recognition for his genius and trailblazing efforts. The other critical part of the equation—the man who provided the vision of what air power could contribute through CAS in Afghanistan—was Lieutenant Colonel Bochain. Together, these two men crafted the fusion of SOF and CAS.

Bochain first had to start with his commander's intent. That centered on finding which members of the anti-Taliban rebellion could be depended upon (a very subjective proposition, to say the least), getting SOF teams to those elements, and then helping them expand their control of portions of Afghanistan to the point where the Taliban lost its grip on the nation.

This was not going to be a linear war. As befitted the SOF heritage, it was going to be quite unconventional. "I don't say there was any template that was built that said, 'Okay, we're going to send in twenty-seven teams and they're going to contact these twenty-seven different tribes; that is all going to be coordinated together and we're going to push forward on a conventional front and then we'll march into Kabul and declare victory,'" Bochain observed. The commander's intent also called for a highly decentralized war effort across the theater. The different factions in the anti-Taliban rebellion had various motives for assisting the United States and had often competed with and even fought each other. No SOF team working with a rebel faction could conduct its piece of the war the same as any other piece, and each team had to operate with an eye on the other factions.

Mulholland also knew how he wanted Bochain to fit air power into this goal. According to Bochain, he was told to "somehow mold extremely violent air power into a way of destroying the enemy without using excessive power or having any kind of unnecessary collateral damage and loss of civilian life, at the same time protecting our troops." Bochain had a lot of latitude in finding the best way to accomplish that mission. The real challenge would be juggling the competing imperatives on a day-to-day basis. There would be no constants in the air support campaign, except the constancy of change—each day would bring a different theater-wide picture, a different array of assets, and different constraints. Through it all Bochain had to use air power to keep up the operational momentum.

Bochain described three main pieces of the operational concept. In one piece, SOF teams would continue to scour the countryside looking for significant targets that could be added to the list for the strategic attack campaign. This campaign focused on such things as communications facilities, command and control infrastructure, logistics centers, and military bases. As the main focus of theater operations, TF Dagger had significant input into what went on this list. But Bochain wanted to ensure that the bombing campaign served the new operational concept rather than devolving into bombing for bombing's sake. "We could bomb those targets indefinitely," Bochain said, "and just make more rubble out of rubble. Not a lot of people understood that. This was going to be a different type of war."

The second main piece focused on linking SOF teams with reliable factions of the Northern Alliance to help them succeed against the enemy. As Colonel Longoria had thought, by linking SOF TACPs and SOF teams the strengths of air and ground complemented each other. The SOF team, strong in the cultural integration skills needed to win the acceptance and sustain the sometimes shaky support of the rebel warlords, put the CAS expert in a position to provide the firepower advantage that tipped the balance in favor of the Northern Alliance.

Why did CAS provide such a powerful boost to these rebel forces? True, the Northern Alliance had been fighting the Taliban and al Qaeda for several years and something like a stalemate had emerged, so any boost to the firepower of one side or the other was bound to have a telling effect. But something more was going on. Improved air power capability in the ground attack role was creating a new dynamic that had gone largely unseen in America's most recent military campaigns. With U.S. air power so effective against ground forces, particularly massed or maneuvering ground forces, the best defense would be to disperse and hunker down. But if there is a friendly ground force nearby, this dispersed and immobilized enemy is now vulnerable to defeat in detail unless it can mass and maneuver against that ground force, which once again makes the enemy army vulnerable to U.S. air power. So when TACPs were coupled with Northern Alliance armies, the Taliban and al Qaeda were faced with this air-ground dilemma. As long as the Northern Alliance force remained in a position to threaten Taliban forces, the enemy couldn't disperse without surrendering control of Afghanistan, so they stood in place and remained lucrative targets for American air power. As the success in Afghanistan shows, it doesn't take a massive modern army to be an effective foil in this air-ground dilemma.

The third piece of the new SOF-CAS operational concept involved SOF teams going out to check areas of known or suspected enemy strength and, as Bochain described it, "kicking the anthill." Because of the rules of engagement, and because both enemy and friendly factions were interspersed in the general population, Coalition forces could not assume that what looked like a Taliban or al Qaeda concentration was indeed hostile. Once that force proved its hostile intent, though, Coalition forces could engage them with all the force necessary and justifiable. As Bochain points out, this approach very quickly came to predominate:

> The most valuable thing we had was to make contact with the enemy in a purely CAS/troops-in-contact role with a very few number of [SOF] guys operating pretty much autonomously. We said they were with the Northern Alliance, and the Northern Alliance was responsible for protecting, feeding them, that sort of thing. But when we came down to the actual execution of the mission, most of the time it was just a few of our guys going forward with the Northern Alliance hanging considerably back, and they would get up into a position where they could observe and then call in airstrikes. Initially the Northern Alliance didn't think any of this was going to work. After a couple of successes, that's all they wanted to do. They did not want to engage the enemy until they'd been bombed, bombed, bombed, and bombed again and they would drive in with their guidon and declare victory. So they saw early on that, "we don't have to kill thousands of our own guys"—this air power thing is a whole new role to them and they liked it.

> Our guys were then in a position of sometimes taking increasing risks, because time and again we were able to get them whatever they needed to bomb their way out of a difficult situation. . . . There's as many different techniques as there are people, but I would say the general characterization is we got more aggressive once we figured out the system, responsiveness time, the effectiveness of the weapons, [and then] refined the process. The guys would get up there pretty darn close and engage. If they didn't have that almost instant responsiveness of air, if they didn't have that "warm-fuzzy" that they could get [air], there was no way they would press up that close. They needed time to react and that time to react shrank the more responsive the air got.

This "baiting the hook" approach involved great risk, and again the linkup between SOF and SOF TACP proved to be just the sort of complementary capability needed to meet this risk. First, besides being experts at cultural integration, Special Forces make up about the most lethal small combat teams on earth. So if in seeking out enemy forces these SOF teams encountered a force that was "proving its hostile intent," up to a certain point the team could deal with that force with its own weapons and capabilities. These capabilities include disengagement and evasion, another SOF strength. If the threat proved to be more than the team could handle on its own and disengagement was impossible, or if the intent was to engage with maximum effect, the SOF TACP could bring tremendous firepower to help. In really desperate circumstances, though, where even with the employment of CAS the situation might still be in doubt, having one of the most experienced CAS controllers in the world can be the only thing that stands between life and death for the team, and even in those situations, the SOF TACP may have to call on all his ingenuity and every trick in his kit bag. That risk, though, could also bring huge dividends, as Bochain relates.

> The most [extreme] scenario of that was north of Konduz. There was a village up there called Barouc, and we knew the Taliban were massing in this town; estimates were in the low thousands. A lot of these forces had come out of Konduz because we were hitting targets near Konduz; they were looking for a safer place to get to and they essentially took over this hamlet. Reportedly they did a lot of nasty things in there to the local population. . . . So we sent in one of our SOF teams to get into a position to get a better sense of who was in there, maybe call in some airstrikes on some of the perimeter elements that were isolated from this town to minimize the collateral damage, and also just to probe to see what was going on in there, to see if we could draw them out.

So we had essentially four or five guys—a couple of Americans and a few Northern Alliance guys—driving up in close proximity a few kilometers away from what we thought was a couple thousand Taliban. Not very good odds, but they had a decent escape route and thought it was relatively clear. So they go in, isolate a couple of areas that are confirmed Taliban, call in a couple of airstrikes, all hell breaks loose. . . . [The enemy] pretty much determined where the airstrikes were being called in from and decided to attack.

This team [had been working] a couple of fighters as they were probing these targets and essentially the next radio call is "Oh geez, here they come!" "How many?" "There's a thousand to fifteen hundred, all of them coming at me!" "How far away are they?" "Three kilometers." "What's their speed?" They're passing this information back and forth. "Okay, Solar [the ASOC's call sign], what have you got for me? I need something right now!" "We got another formation of fighters." "That's not going to cover it; I need something to take out essentially a grid." And the formation of this valley as they were coming up to his [observation post] nicely funneled the concentration of all these guys coming at [him]. He saw this as hitting a home run and said, "I'm going to stay here and set this trap, draw them up to me." We told him we had B-52s available but it was going to take twenty to thirty minutes for them to get there. He said "Great, what do you got in the meantime?" We got a couple more fighters and he did some harassment bombing. . . .

He built a bomber box set up like a grid pattern to match this area in this valley. He did a very nice job of forming it. We put him in contact with the B-52s and they did their coordination, but as they're getting closer, the tempo and the excitement in his voice, you could tell things were getting dicey. He said, "Okay, I can only stay here for ten more minutes." "Oh, I'm taking shots from some guys coming in from the side!" "I can only stay five more minutes to control this air." Then the last transmission was essentially, "I don't know if I can get out of here, I think my escape route may have been cut." So his last request was, "If you do not hear from me, bomb the bomber box that I gave you." The implication was, "They got me and you might as well bomb it anyway because it's the end of the game for me."

So at this point we get the commander, explain to him the situation and tell him that his guy had requested to execute this mission even without his final control because the mere fact that we had not talked to him tells us he has probably been captured or killed. . . . This is a very tough decision for the commander and it's his alone to make. . . . So a pretty tough three or four minutes—seemed like an eternity—as the airplane is checking in with no contact with the ground FAC and the last thing you hear is kind of like ricocheting and bad stuff going on. So we're all sitting there, your stomach is getting tied up in knots, the whole tent is silent and all eyes on three or four folks staring at this radio with the commander making this decision. Finally he said, "All right, do it!"

[We] relayed to the B-52s, "mission's a go, clearance given on our order. No final control required." So the mission goes, we still don't hear anything from the SOF team. The aircraft check out. . . . Every minute that goes by we think we probably just killed our own guys. Probably ten minutes later we get a radio call, "Solar, Solar, team XX, thank you, thank you, thank you!." . . . "Is everybody okay?" "We're all fine!" And that was as close as I ever want to see it again.

As it turned out they pretty much were getting overrun, had to grab all their stuff, had to run. . . . They get into the car and the car doesn't start. Took them a bit to get the car started as the enemy is closing in behind them at exactly the moment the B-52 strike comes in and perfectly hits this box that this guy had developed on his esti-mation—"this is about where they'll be in ten to fifteen minutes from now"—and he said it was a glorious thing, this B-52 carpet bombing hit perfectly in the box. . . . He said, "I think you got 'em all, but I'm not sticking around to count."

The operational concept hammered out in Afghanistan "on the fly" be-came the basic blueprint guiding SOF-CAS operations throughout the phase of the war that ended Taliban control. It was a melding together of two areas of American advantage—what Washington insiders would call "asymmetric strength"—and it drew on the inherent strengths of each while mutually masking disadvantages. Significantly, it was hammered out by practitioners in each field who were not only experts but also cre-ative thinkers and who remained solely focused on drawing out the best capability to accomplish the mission. There was no hint of partisanship— "my service must take the lead" or "my branch must predominate"—but then this too is characteristic of Special Forces. Most important, though, they developed this operational mode of warfare to fight a war that was not only unprecedented but unanticipated. They went out to run a war on a high wire without a net and without a rehearsal. One anecdote cap-tures their lack of guidance from past practices: according to Bochain, the troops at TF Dagger put a sign over their shredder that said, "Put doc-trine here." They were not held back by practices of the past, instead, they were guided by their vision of what could be done.

3. The Fall of the Taliban Regime

After the fall of Mazar-e Sharif, the surviving Taliban and al Qaeda forces from that area retreated northeast to the city of Konduz. Konduz had been a Taliban stronghold and now it was reinforced. With the Northern Alliance advancing rapidly throughout Afghanistan, Konduz was the Taliban's last northern power base. Pressuring the enemy in and around Konduz was General Muhammad Daud, a rebel commander who was part of the Northern Alliance. On 8 November, about the time Staff Sergeant Tomat was helping close the noose around the Taliban in Mazar-e Sharif, another SOF team, including M.Sgt. Tim Stamey, infiltrated into Afghanistan and linked up with Daud and his forces. Stamey, a SOF TACP with 5th Special Forces Group and stationed at Fort Bragg, North Carolina, was one of the most experienced TACPs in the business. Lieutenant Colonel Bochain, Stamey's commander in Afghanistan, describes him as, "the poster child of what a TACP ought to be: calm, southern drawl, real easy, doesn't want to take credit for anything he did himself."

Just getting linked up with Daud presented a series of challenges. Stamey and his team were flown to their rendezvous point in an old Russian "Hip" helicopter they dubbed "SGLI Air;" SGLI stood for Serviceman's Group Life Insurance, the life insurance provided to every military member. The outward appearance alone was enough to make Stamey uneasy: "It was leaking—I mean, not dripping but literally a stream of fuel coming out the bottom of it." Stamey later learned that two weeks after he flew on this helicopter it crashed, killing some high-ranking members of the Northern Alliance.

The team found Daud's forces just east of Farkhar, southeast of Konduz. According to Stamey, Daud's initial reception caused some consternation. But that attitude changed, bearing out what Bochain had said about Northern Alliance regard for what Americans brought to the fight.

M.Sgt. Tim Stamey outside Konduz. The capture of Konduz effectively ended Taliban control in northern Afghanistan.

[Daud's team] moved us into a safe house on the east side of Farkhar right on the edge of the mountains. We bunked there for the night. The following morning General Daud showed up and met us for breakfast. He gave us the mujahaddin hats and scarves, and "Hey, glad you guys are here," this, that, and the other. We started asking about his forces and what we could do to help them, advise them, assist them on their portion of the land war. Well we were told, "Nope, don't need any help." "Well, how about the airstrikes?" "Nope, we can do it on our own"—the whole machismo thing. He did not want to accept any help from us. Okay. So he left and we're sitting there and we're like, "Now what the heck are we supposed to do?"

That afternoon one of the other commanders came up to us and said, "Hey would you guys like to go out and see the front line?" And we're like, "Oh yeah, love to!" So [the team captain], one of the commo [communications] guys, and I, we took off and went up to this area just to the southeast of Taloqan, the northwest side of Farkhar up to the front lines. We get up there and one of their tank officers is up on the hill and he's pointing out enemy positions . . . and there's tanks and stuff dug in right along through here. . . . We see a ruckus coming up this road [that] runs up the valley here; there's guys on horses, trucks, and a couple T-55s [Soviet-era tanks]. And we're like, "What the heck's going on?" "Oh, we're doing our big offensive." They didn't tell us nothing about this this morning during breakfast. They come rolling in and start getting hit from the tanks up on the ridgeline and getting hit pretty good. The tank officer says, "Get us aircraft!"

Stamey called the ASOC to request air support, but since nobody knew anything about Daud's offensive, no CAS sorties had been scheduled. In fact, it must have been a pretty quiet day across the entire theater, because there were no CAS sorties scheduled anywhere that could be diverted to help out. Stamey submitted his request at about two or three o'clock in the afternoon and was told the first sorties wouldn't be available until seven o'clock that evening. Before then, though, Daud's forces broke through and moved northwest, seizing the city of Taloqan, which lies approximately thirty-seven miles due east of Konduz.

In Taloqan the next day Daud informed the Americans he was resuming his offensive on Konduz, and once again stated he didn't need their help; in fact, he didn't even want to bring them along. Stamey countered with his own suggestion of what they could contribute, "I know you don't want us, but we need to come along here and get involved. We got aircraft going in and bombing all the time, where I don't know. . . . We got other [SOF] teams going around. They see you all moving in force like this you may end up getting bombed. If we're with you and we see the aircraft, we'll contact them [and] tell them not to bomb here." This won Daud over, and the team moved out with Daud's forces as they pressed on westward.

Shortly after leaving Taloqan, the group came under attack. The road to Konduz runs through a long mountainous pass between the two cities. As Stamey recalls:

We moved out in a convoy and we're in a little bitty Russian jeep about the size of a CJ5 or CJ7. . . . We're the fifth vehicle in the convoy. . . . We get up to this pass and . . . all of sudden we start getting shwacked with tank rounds. . . . You could see them when they hit the road, they're taking out chunks. All this shit hit and they're just losing vehicles left and right. Everyone turned around. It looked like in [the movie] *Road Warrior* when you see all the vehicles running across with all the dust and everything else. We'd been briefed [by Daud's people] to stay on the road 'cause there are mines on the side of the road, but as soon as they started losing vehicles, it was total chaos. . . . They just spread out along the valley floor.

The losses from this ambush amounted to five vehicles and an untold number of Afghan troops.

After returning to Taloqan, Daud approached Stamey and asked for airstrikes on the forces that had just attacked them:

"We want air and we want air now!" And I'm like, "Well who am I supposed to hit?" "Well, you know . . ." pulling out a map, "why don't you hit right here?" I said, "No, I can't see any of this; the rules of engagement [stipulate] I'm required to have eyes on target." "Well I know they're right here, and they're right here." "I can't do that," and he's getting really upset with me. "Why not? I'm telling you they're right here!" And I said, "Here's the problem: if there are any civilians there and I bomb them, even if you tell me to bomb them, I'm the one that goes to jail." "I've got to have air on them targets!"

With that, Stamey and the SOF team got Daud's approval to go back up to a pass close to where they had just been, from which Stamey could see the enemy forces. "We got up there where we could see inside this gap—you could see all the forces massing for a counterattack. I took F-18s and we shwacked and we shwacked them—I think I had two sets, this one and then thirty minutes later another set of F-18s. With the second set I was literally [using] spotting scopes to catch some stuff farther off 'cause with the first set the guys dispersed and started seeking cover. I found some other targets and hit them. That's all I could see . . . through that gap."

The team returned to Taloqan, and Daud moved some of his forces up to occupy a position near the site of the original ambush. Once again Daud started pointing out to Stamey locations he wanted bombed by coalition air power, and once again Stamey objected, "I'm not going to be able to see them." At this point, Daud revealed what had likely been his objection right along; according to Stamey, Daud said, "Well I'm not going to put you guys up there 'cause I was told by some other government agency that you guys are not to get hurt, I can't put you up there, it's just not going to happen." One thing weighing on many people's minds was the effect American casualties would have on public support for the war, and by extension, official U.S. resolve to prosecute the war. Whether or not "some other government agency" had really told Daud to ensure the safety of the SOF team, surely Daud was savvy enough to be concerned about what might happen if he let some gung ho SOF guys stick their necks out and one of them got killed.

At a temporary impasse with Stamey, and perhaps feeling that the previous day's airstrikes might have broken the back of Taliban resistance in the immediate area, Daud moved his forces out again the very next day. As Stamey reports, "The exact same thing happened. [We] started getting fired on [in the general vicinity of the previous day's ambush]. [Daud] got a lot smarter and his trucks were spread out; they weren't all bumper to bumper this time. They lost a couple more trucks and some more guys."

With his forces again under attack, Daud appeared more willing to let the SOF team put themselves at risk to call in airstrikes. Stamey and the SOF team then moved back to the hill from which they had controlled air the previous day and enjoyed the same results they had achieved earlier. "There the [Taliban] are massed, the same thing again, and we shwacked it, stopped the counteroffensive. So there's two days we'd done the same thing."

By the time the Afghanis and the Americans got back to Taloqan for the second time in two days, both were frustrated. What little equipment Daud had was being whittled away in exchange for very little gain. For their part, the SOF guys were frustrated because they felt their hands were tied. "He kept treating us like we were children." They pleaded with Daud, "let us just do our job. . . . Just let us move up on our own . . . and we'll shwack the shit out of them." Finally Daud agreed, and the team moved out at four the next morning to a point somewhere near the southern end of the pass between Taloqan and Konduz.

> So four of us moved out and we moved up to the side of the pass here and hid our jeep in a ravine. We humped up the hillside. [It] was really, really steep—rocks and literally climbing and scratching and pulling on all fours, climbing on the side of this mountain. We got to the top . . . cut straight across to the western side of the ridge and then moved on up until we got to a trench . . . about time it was starting to get daylight. . . . As soon as we moved up there you could see the whole valley. . . .
>
> Didn't even have time to get the radio out or anything—we started to get fire right down below us about 350, 400 meters. There were some mud huts right down the bottom of the hill and guys were shooting at us. This got the attention of the guys on the hill to the southwest. The guys up on that ridgeline just start cutting loose on us

with a DSHK; they're not very accurate—they kick up a lot of dirt when they go through—but they're ugly, let's put it that way. He's up above us, so he's got us pinned down. Our guys are returning fire on the guys right down below us, and I'm trying to get the damn [satellite] antennae set up, but you know how getting those things set up and getting the right elevation, getting it oriented the right direction, plus there's not room to do this in the trench, so I'm having to do this outside the trench.

So I get this thing set up finally, and get up on the radio and called the ASOC and say, "Hey we're pinned down, I need aircraft in here now," and they could hear what was going on over the handset. They tell me, "Contact KMART [the CAOC], it's an emergency." I called KMART and they said, "I have a B-52, he's about ten minutes out, contact him on the strike [frequency]. . . ." So as soon as they said that [the B-52 pilot] called me, "Hey, Texas 11, this is [B-52 call sign.]"

So I brief him and I brought him in on the DSHK and he obliterated the ridgeline there. If I remember correctly he did not have JDAMS, he just came in with Mk-82s. The Buffs over there were incredible. Everyone talks about JDAMs, hey, the guys were accurate as shit with their dumb bombs too.

That still left the troops firing on them from the hamlet at the base of the hill only 350 meters away, but the entire valley was filled with massed enemy forces.

Once I got through with [the B-52], I got everybody's brother there waiting on me. I love the B-52s, but 350 meters I'm not going to have him drop that close to me. Those guys [shooting from below], yeah they were shooting at us, but we were returning fire so they could not move up the ridgeline at us, so we were good.

I got bombers and I got fighters all over the place, so I stack my bombers to the north and my fighters to the south. I'd bring a bomber in and then I'd bring in two sets of fighters right behind him, and then bring the bomber back around and drop again, then two sets of fighters. I had Strike Eagles [F-15s designed for air-to-ground operations], F-14s, F-16s, F-18s, B-1s, and B-52s all at the same time. All this started at six o'clock in the morning and the valley was just littered with targets—they were just frigging all over the place. . . .

I controlled airstrikes from then until 1:30 in the afternoon and finally got a break. I contacted [the ASOC] and said, "Knock it off [stop sending aircraft]. I can't see any more targets. This whole valley is covered with smoke. I'll let you know when the smoke and dust is clear if I can." I said [to one of the SOF team members], "I need a drink of water," 'cause I hadn't had anything to drink, and I looked at my watch and it was 1:30 in the afternoon. From the time we contacted that first B-52 it seemed like an hour, but from the time he started dropping until 1:30 that afternoon it was seven and a half hours straight of bombing.

The smoke and stuff cleared later on and we're sitting there and one of Daud's commanders picks up his radio, a little Motorola, and he's talking on the thing and somebody is talking back to him. We don't understand, but [our translator] is getting all excited and we're like, "Hey, what's going on?" and he says, "It's the Taliban." "It's the what?" "The Taliban." "What about the Taliban?" "They're talking." "What do you mean they're talking? On your radio net?" "Yeah!" "Well what are they saying?" "They're saying they will give us money if we turn over the Americans." We're like, "What Americans? Us?" "Yeah, the ones that are directing the airstrikes." We say "You didn't tell them we were here did you?" He said, "No, we told them you were over on that hillside." "Shit! You shouldn't even have told them what Americans; these airplanes just showed up. You should have never told them we were there." And we're like, "Well how in the heck did they get on your freq?" and he goes, "Oh, easy, they got the same radios." "Yeah, well, how do you all program your freq set or change your crystals on your radios?" "Oh, it's easy, Taliban's channel one, we're channel three." "And how about on their radios?" "Taliban's channel one, we're channel three."

So when he got off the radio, bam—here starts coming tank rounds, and I said, "I don't know if you told them the other hillside or not, but we're getting tank rounds." [The ASOC] had already sent all my aircraft somewhere else and it took maybe an hour and a half before they got more air. Luckily the tank ran out of ammo, and I thought, "okay, we're good," and then, hell, here pulls up a truck, more ammo, he starts firing at us and then he runs out of ammo again. Finally we got some more aircraft and we shwacked that tank, and then there were a bunch more targets. Once we hit that tank they come out of places and start trying to hide, so we ended up bombing until way after dark.

Throughout this all-day battle Stamey called on some of the most advanced equipment the U.S. military had in its inventory, but this equipment was not the panacea often depicted in the media. Like Staff Sergeant Tomat, Stamey took pains to emphasize the importance of relying on the basics to back up the gee-whiz gadgets. "We were doing all of our target coordinates off the SOFLAM getting the distance, and using our compass to shoot the azimuth. We had two guys lase . . . so you got two guys giving you distances . . . you got two guys giving azimuth . . . myself taking information down, and then we would plug it into two different GPSs, we'd come up with the coordinates, 'Are my coordinates the same as your coordinates?' 'Roger that,' . . . and we would look on the map and agree, 'Okay, this is where the target is on the map,' and get the target elevation off [the map], so there was a lot of redundancy there."

The process Stamey describes took a lot of time, and in a combat environment, with threat, stress, and adrenalin levels high there would be tremendous temptation to cut corners. What kept Stamey and his other team members honest was not only the knowledge that a mistake could prove deadly but also the professionalism to master the basics and realize that the only way to do the job right was to rely on those basics. It also helped that Stamey could depend on his SOF team to help carry the load. "We all worked together as a team, and . . . this team I was with, ODA 586, was one of the best teams I ever worked with. They were outstanding. They didn't question me, including the captain. I ran the whole show. . . . They knew I was the subject matter expert for the CAS, and they did what I asked, and they did an outstanding job. I couldn't have got TACPs to work with me any better than those guys worked for me as far as locating targets, getting target coordinates, tracking stuff, switching over, lasing for LGBs that were coming in, I mean they were just all over it."

One other critical element contributed to the team's effectiveness: Stamey himself. For one thing, he brought some unusual talents to the battlefield. He was a top-notch sniper and, by all accounts, remarkably cool under pressure. According to Bochain, Stamey's commander, "He was surrounded multiple times, and in between airstrikes he's picking guys off with the sniper rifle, just to call in the next airstrike." Stamey's ingenuity in coming up with creative solutions to unanticipated problems was also a key part of this successful campaign. "He had all kinds of techniques," Bochain explains, "for how to flush the enemy out of their entrenched position, because even a two-thousand-pound bomb—if a guy is dug in, it's hard to dig him out of his trenches. So he developed his own little on-the-spot techniques to flush them out of there. . . . He could do an air burst over a fortified position to blow their eardrums out; bleeding from their eyes, nose, and ears, stunned, they'd come flying out of the trenches and he would have an airplane waiting to nail them. . . . Here is a guy sitting here thinking about how to do this in a logical, gruesome, necessary, efficient fashion."

At the end of that day's bombing, Stamey and his team headed back to Taloqan. Upon their return they found that General Daud was quite pleased with their work and had a much different attitude toward their going out and working on their own. "We're cleared hot to drive forward and do whatever we want to do from here on out. He had moved back up on that hill that had got hit the day before and got to see a lot of this and he was just ecstatic." Stamey would spend the next eight days bombing Taliban and al Qaeda forces in that same valley from various locations along the ridgeline, prompting them to fall back toward Konduz.

The next day, Stamey saw one consequence of his efforts. Three days of bombing, especially the third day, set off a steady stream of Taliban defectors, mostly Afghani, surrendering to Daud's forces and joining the rebel side. Daud's men would question them as they came over, and this steady stream helped improve Daud's intelligence on his enemy's forces and disposition. Through this intelligence, Stamey learned the location of the Taliban headquarters, and he called in an airstrike on that building on the fourth day. "When we hit that [headquarters] it was like hitting a damn hornet's nest with a stick. Guys came out all over the place, and then we had Buffs [hit them] and we just annihilated that whole area."

Unfortunately, once Daud saw what CAS could do, he ceased his aggressive offensive tactics. This sudden passivity, which would last eight days, coupled with the deadly effect of U.S. air power, prompted the enemy to dig in. This significantly reduced Stamey's bombing opportunities and correspondingly reduced the effectiveness of air power on the enemy. As Stamey saw it, "The Northern Alliance quit fighting. They just hung out, which started exasperating us at the end of that eight days. It's like, you know, you give me a company of Rangers and we can go ahead and take this place—just somebody to show some kind of force. Because they're just hiding out from the air." Both halves of the air-ground dilemma were arrayed against the enemy in that area, and by mitigating the effects of CAS the enemy was vulnerable to ground attack and defeat in piecemeal. When Daud's forces left the fighting to air power, though, the enemy was saved.

West of Konduz another rebel commander was not nearly so passive. General Dostum, fresh from his victory in Mazar-e Sharif, was driving hard to capture Konduz himself. With the southeast sector quiet thanks to Daud's defensive posture, and with a hard-charging enemy closing in from the west, the Taliban shifted much of their force to meet Dostum. Staff Sergeant Tomat continued with Dostum's forces and saw some additional action, but not much. "We were ordered to go to Konduz in the event that we needed CAS along with Tim Stamey. We'd be on the west and they would be on the east. We'd hammer and anvil them in between. Well, what we did once we got into that area, we called in for AC-130 support and took out some targets there, and then we set up a kill box for them, and took out some targets there." The reason Tomat saw so little action was that Dostum opened negotiations with the Taliban forces in and around Konduz. With the enemy trapped in what became known as the Konduz pocket, Dostum sought, as he had done with the Taliban forces inside Mazar-e Sharif, to limit casualties by offering his enemy the chance to surrender. He clearly saw a carrot and stick approach as the key to negotiations, and here too Tomat played a role by calling in coalition aircraft to do what is known as a "show of force"—an aircraft flyby that sends the message, "This aircraft could just as easily be dropping bombs on you."

Daud's immobility ended on 22 November. By that time Stamey and the SOF team had worked their way to the end of the pass between Talo-qan and Konduz, putting them about two-thirds of the way to the city. All that stood between them and the Taliban's last northern stronghold was a relatively flat plain and the battered remnants of the enemy's forces. Those forces were even further reduced by shifting men to meet Dostum to the west and by those who defected. It seemed that with a few more days of bombing the SOF team could have taken Konduz by itself.

Stamey started that day unaware of Daud's plans. He and the team moved out to their position to look for CAS opportunities. "All of a sud-den I hear [our translator] on the radio and, 'Hey, Daud's forces are mov-ing—they're finally doing their offensive.' Finally." Once Daud's forces moved out, the enemy disposition changed quickly. With the threat of a ground force offensive, the enemy had to coalesce to meet that danger. This made them more vulnerable to air attack, which Stamey was quick to exploit. "When [Daud] started doing his thing, [the enemy] came out of the woodwork. They [Daud's forces] start moving across, not a whole bunch of them, but his force is finally moving, and these guys came out of the woodwork. And BAM! it was CBU heaven then. I mean, we had a couple Buffs loaded down with CBUs that day and were hitting troops out in the open. We had our third or fourth best day on that last day."

That day's bombing also highlighted some cultural differences.

Just south of Khanabad [a town on the outskirts of Konduz], we had a bunch of guys that were holed up in some adobe buildings and they were firing mortars and stuff and we had a B-52, check in and the gal on the radio sounded like an angel. [I] had the radio turned up 'cause we had been firing back. . . . She comes in, "Hello, Texas 11, this is [B-52 call sign]" and [the interpreters] just stopped dead in their tracks. "Is that a woman?" "Yeah." "A woman pilot?" And then I said [to myself], "Okay, I know where they're going with this," ya know: it probably wasn't the pilot talking to me, probably the [navigator] or something.

I went, "Yup, yup, she's the pilot." . . ."Is she gonna bomb?" And I said, "Yeah." Now they're getting all worried. "Is she was going to hit where she's supposed to hit?" "Oh yeah," and I'll tell you what, she shacked everything. And it was awesome. I mean, every bomb she dropped was a shack and we were ecstatic. [The Northern Alliance guys] didn't even want to mention it, didn't even want to talk about it.

Stamey's air attacks had a devastating effect on the enemy's effectiveness. Once again he was reminded of hitting a hornet's nest. "They were coming out of the woodwork." Again he called on aircraft armed with CBUs, catching many enemy troops out in the open and on foot, and this broke the back of the resistance. Daud and his forces moved into Konduz so quickly that TF Dagger headquarters was momentarily caught off guard—Dostum was negotiating the Taliban's surrender west of Konduz, so they thought that was who must be in the city, and at first they couldn't believe the city had fallen to Daud.

The capture of Konduz effectively ended Taliban control in northern Afghanistan and opened up a wide swath of territory to the Northern Alliance. It also pretty much ended Stamey's CAS role in Afghanistan, and he spent the rest of that tour assisting his SOF team with the many other SOF duties—surveying airfields, getting hospitals running again, clearing caves and weapons caches, and doing humanitarian aid work. He was Special Forces in all but official designation.

As rebel forces were tightening the noose on Konduz, the Northern Alliance also drove the Taliban out of two other key cities. On 12 November Ishmael Khan captured Herat in western Afghanistan with hardly a shot, and the next day the Taliban abandoned the capital city of Kabul as rebel forces approached. With Afghanistan now largely in the hands of the rebels, the Taliban's last remaining strongholds were Konduz, in the north, and their spiritual birthplace, Kandahar, in the south. With the Northern Alliance made up mostly of Uzbek and Tajik tribes, though, tribal loyalty suddenly came to the forefront.

Tribal and clan identity had complicated Afghanistan's recent wars and was close to the heart of the current rebellion, for most Taliban belonged to the Pashtun tribe. Afghanistan's largest tribal group, Pashtuns had long dominated Afghan politics. Thus while the religious oppression brought by the Taliban was the primary motivation for rebellion, tribal allegiances certainly facilitated the willingness of non-Pashtuns to rebel. Many observers in Afghanistan and around the world speculated that Northern Alliance success might actually drive Pashtuns into a tighter bond with the Taliban. These concerns increased as the Northern Alliance pushed farther south, for southern Afghanistan was predominantly Pashtun. The closer Northern Alliance forces got to Kabul, the more U.S. and international observers urged their leaders to remain outside the capital until some sort of interim government, with representation from all Afghani tribal groups, could be hammered out. They feared that forces made up largely of a few smaller tribes marching triumphantly into the capital might look too much like a coalition of minorities imposing military domination on Pashtuns. Such a perception could keep Afghanistan roiling in civil war. When the Taliban evacuated Kabul without a fight, these concerns were overcome by events, and the Northern Alliance moved in to restore some semblance of order. Marching farther south than Kabul, though, would definitely look like an invasion of Pashtun territory, so the Taliban retreat to southern Afghanistan posed a real dilemma for anyone seeking stability in a post-Taliban regime.

Almost from the start, the United States sought to support dissident leaders within the Pashtun community who might lead a Pashtun uprising against the Taliban, especially in southern Afghanistan. The leading candidate was Hamid Karzai, the head of a major Pashtun clan who had served in various positions in the pre-Taliban Afghan government and who had strong ties to the deposed Afghan king. A vocal critic of the Taliban, Karzai had been in exile in Pakistan, but in early October he returned and began talking with Pashtun leaders. Slowly an opposition movement was formed, particularly in Uruzgan province, north of Kandahar, as Karzai gathered military forces. Another Pashtun leader, Gul Agha Sharzai, gathered his own army, and he too joined the rebellion. By the time Kabul fell, Karzai and Sharzai were gaining momentum and started pressing in on Kandahar from two directions—Karzai from the north and Sharzai from the east.

One distinct difference in this southern effort was that unlike the Northern Alliance that had been fighting the Taliban for years, Pashtun rebels were raising forces from scratch. Those forces needed to be organized, trained, and equipped before they could present a serious threat to Taliban authority. On top of that, the fight to oust the Taliban from Kandahar was expected to be fiercest, not only because they were battle-hardened and experienced but also because most observers expected them to fight to the last to keep their own hometown, as well as their last toehold on power in Afghanistan.

With Karzai's force was SOF TACP T.Sgt. Sean Minyon. Minyon, who is originally from Colorado Springs, Colorado, is stationed at Fort Carson, and though he normally supports 10th Special Forces Group, also located at Carson, he volunteered to augment the 5th Special Forces Group to help with the massive scope of this war. He arrived in theater in mid-October. When a friendly-fire accident wounded two SOF TACPs who had been supporting Karzai, they needed to be replaced immediately. Minyon was selected because of his extensive SOF experience, but the circumstances were not ideal. Linking up with a team already in the field meant he was not only walking into a new group, he also missed the in-depth mission preparation done before going into the field. Instead, he got six hours' notice to meet a plane, and he literally got his intelligence brief and drew ammunition at the back of a C-130 while it kept its engines running.

The "hurry up" movement to join the team was not without incident. The C-130 took him to link up with an MH-53 that then dropped him and an air force combat controller at night onto a "hot LZ," that is, a hostile landing zone. The helicopter took off immediately, and only then did Minyon realize no one from the team had come to meet them. There they were in the middle of hostile territory, at night, looking for a team they did not know in a region for which they had not done the normal mission study. After thirty minutes they started formulating an escape and evasion plan to find friendly forces on their own. At this point a small pickup truck, the kind everyone in that region drives whether enemy and friendly, approached their position. The two did not know what to expect, so they were preparing for the worst, when a bunch of guys in the truck yelled out in English, "Is anyone here?" Having taken cover and with their weapons trained on the vehicle, the two orphans exchanged passwords with the truck's occupants and found this was their ride to their new home.

Minyon joined Karzai's forces only three days after arriving in theater and just as Karzai's assault stalled on the outskirts of Kandahar. Within hours of his arrival, he found himself being awakened by someone telling him that Karzai was resuming his advance and needed Minyon to provide CAS assistance. Minyon soon learned that Karzai's force was stopped on the north side of the Arghandab River separating them from Kandahar, and that Karzai had tried earlier to take the bridge across that river, only to be repulsed. The bridge was defended by at least one tank, a number of APCs, triple-A pieces, trucks of various sorts, and a large number of infantry. The new plan called for Minyon to move up with a SOF team and call in airstrikes to weaken those forces prior to Karzai's attempting another ground assault. Minyon describes how events unfolded: "That morning I move up with the team to an OP where we had eyes on the bridge and the Taliban, and tried to take out the Taliban forces without taking out the bridge. This lasted for two and a half days of pulling up a little bit, moving back. . . . The first night we utilized an AC-130 and had them pretty much hitting anything south of that bridge. . . . The next day I had probably six sets of F-18s. I actually had an F-14 FAC/A [airborne forward air controller] that marked targets with rockets and then the F-18s would roll in and hit the targets for me. . . . The third day more F-18s and F-14s. . . . Finally [on the third day] we moved up enough and attrited enough of [the enemy] forces where they surrendered to Karzai."

The airborne forward air controller Minyon spoke of was another adaptation to fit the unique circumstances. Though not always available, airborne FACs can be more than just another set of eyes looking for targets. The same ROE requirements that often sent TACPs moving extremely close—sometimes too close—to positively identify a target as hostile could in some circumstances be met by pilots specially trained to PID targets from the air. They can look in spots where the ground controller cannot see, report what they see back to the TACP who, being with the ground commander, can verify that there are no friendly troops in that area and that striking the target fits in with the ground commander's scheme of maneuver. At that point the TACP can clear the pilot to engage the enemy. Air FACs can also mark targets with small rockets, as the one working with Minyon was doing, and in other ways help the TACP orient other aircraft to the ground situation, but aircraft and delivery of weapons remain under the TACP's control. Minyon speaks to the benefits he found in relying on this particular air FAC: "That F-14 FAC/A became one of my best friends. It seemed like he would always be out there when I needed him, and he was always the same guy. I could talk him onto the targets really well."

The force that surrendered to Karzai was just the force guarding the bridge, so their surrender only gave the Northern Alliance a toehold across the river just north of Kandahar. Karzai then moved forward under light resistance to the outskirts of the city and established a fire base around the former compound of Mullah Omar, the Taliban leader who had fled as the rebel forces approached. Karzai's forces set about clearing the northwest sections of Kandahar, meeting surprisingly light resistance.

The biggest part of the Kandahar story involved Gul Agha Sharzai's efforts. One reason Karzai encountered so little opposition taking Kandahar was because while he was moving in from the north, Sharzai and his forces were moving in from the east, and the Taliban were putting up a tremendous fight to keep the Kandahar airport out of Sharzai's hands. A

SOF team had earlier linked up with Sharzai, and with them was a combat controller who used the call sign Texas 17. Combat controllers, part of the air force's SOF community, primarily control air traffic into and out of airfields and landing zones in hostile territory, but many get training in controlling CAS for emergency situations. Texas 17 had a lot more CAS experience than most because he had been a TACP for several years before becoming a combat controller. That CAS expertise came in handy and helped break the back of Taliban power in their last remaining stronghold. Texas 17 has since left the military, and all efforts to locate him were unsuccessful, so unfortunately his story cannot be told here. Still, he deserves credit for his part in beating the Taliban where they were expected to put up the toughest fight.

With the fight for Kandahar ended, so too was the Taliban's hold on Afghanistan. Most observers had predicted a long costly struggle to accomplish this goal; many had said it couldn't be done at all. The ingenious combination of SOF and air power, backed up by Afghan rebels, however, had defied the predictions in a matter of weeks and in the process gave a dramatic demonstration of what CAS could do on the modern battlefield.

4. Operation Anaconda

After the fall of Kandahar some Taliban and al Qaeda fighters who had come from other nations returned home. Diehards, though, fled to the inaccessible mountain regions on both sides of the Afghan-Pakistan border. Pakistan has a large Pashtun population in that area, so there was a natural affinity based on tribal identity, and some regions, most notably Waziristan, were notoriously independent of Pakistani authority. Afghanistan's White Mountains close to the Pakistan border were also a natural redoubt. The difficult terrain, coupled with innumerable cave and tunnel complexes, made for natural defenses. Many tunnels were quite ancient, but many had also been expanded and improved in modern times by mining firms and military organizations. Two primary tunnel-cave complexes were most notorious—Tora Bora and Milawa—and the new Afghanistan government and its coalition allies assumed the Taliban and al Qaeda would make their last stand there.

Afghan and coalition leaders wasted little time after the fall of Kandahar in focusing their attention on these mountain enclaves. On 8 December, the day after the city fell, the new Afghan government launched an assault on Tora Bora that drove the enemy out of the tunnels and caves, but just what it accomplished in concrete terms is still subject to debate. One thing is clear: the campaign, which lasted roughly a week and a half, did not destroy the enemy as an organized force. Weeks of bombing and bloody assaults by Afghan forces obviously inflicted a number of casualties and deprived the Taliban of significant stores and ammunition, but the prey slipped through the snare. One widely cited reason was that sympathetic troops and commanders among the Afghan and Pakistani blocking forces let the enemy escape, so the assaults simply pushed the quarry deeper into the mountains and across the border into Pakistan.

Another factor, though, was that the Afghan generals followed their previous tactic of alternating assaults with negotiating sessions aimed at getting the Taliban to surrender. While U.S. leaders claimed this repeated easing of pressure bought the enemy time and allowed them to slip through the pursuers' fingers, Afghan military leaders countered that the Taliban wanted to surrender, but that the Americans wouldn't accept the terms proposed. Either way, the enemy escaped, and over the ensuing weeks regrouped farther south. Combing through caves and tunnels afterward turned up treasure troves of information about other al Qaeda operations and planned terrorist attacks, but it also illustrated the determination of the enemy—they had huge stockpiles of food, supplies, and ammunition, and entire families were living with their family members fighting for al Qaeda and the Taliban.

Remnants of the enemy began to congregate in the Shah-i-Kot Valley roughly sixty miles southwest of Tora Bora. Over the course of several weeks in February a plan to deal decisively with this buildup began to emerge. Known as Operation Anaconda, the plan came together in piecemeal fashion and didn't emerge in its final form until days before it kicked off on 2 March 2002. The continual changes, coupled with the unique circumstances in Afghanistan made Anaconda the most controversial campaign of the entire war.

Perhaps the most consequential effect of the war's unusual circumstances on this operation concerns its personnel and how they came to be included. The unit most often associated with Anaconda is the 10th Mountain Division out of Fort Drum, New York, but to call Anaconda a 10th Mountain operation is a misnomer. Elements of 10th Mountain had been brought into theater to provide airfield security in Uzbekistan, but because U.S. officials did not want military forces to give the appearance of being an occupying army, they set a strict cap on the number of troops 10th Mountain could bring. Only selected units of the division actually deployed, and only a portion of the division staff went with them. In one of the most critical decisions on who should go and who should stay, the division commander, Maj. Gen. Franklin L. "Buster" Hagenbeck, opted not to bring any of the TACPs attached to his unit, officer or enlisted. The 18th Air Support Operations Group commander, Col. Mike Longoria, responsible for providing TACP support for the entire theater, felt strongly that this was a mistake. In fact, unable to change the army's mind on this point, Longoria claims to have bent the rules to make sure 10th Mountain would have what he knew they would eventually need. "I bailed them out because I sent [Lieutenant Colonel] Bochain to the location where 10th Mountain was, and I cheated and I sent them more ETACs without being tasked. And lo and behold they used them all—wanted more—like we told them they would." In the end, when Hagenbeck found himself going into war, he would have TACP support available, thanks, in large measure, to Longoria's foresight.[1]

This was not the end of the personnel issues regarding Anaconda, though. A major portion of the troop strength came from the 101st Airborne Division, out of Fort Campbell, Kentucky. Like 10th Mountain, the 101st had sent a number of units into theater to provide airfield security, first in Pakistan, and later at the Kandahar airport. Together, units from 10th Mountain and 101st Airborne would provide the blocking force for Anaconda and thus avoid what many saw as Tora Bora's fatal flaw. The drivers who would flush the quarry and push them into the waiting arms of the blocking force would be made up of SOF teams from the United States and six coalition partners, working with an Afghan force led by Gen. Zia Lodin. In the midst of this basic plan, other SOF and OGA assets would be contributing in various tangential ways. As if this odd mix wasn't bad enough, Hagenbeck's real authority over the Afghan forces, who would play a critical, and as things would turn out, fateful role,

1. Operation Anaconda has become a lightning rod of controversy, and General Hagenbeck has been at the center of that controversy from the start. For this reason I felt compelled to give him the chance to respond to accusations made by others against him. Attempting to extend that courtesy, however, has been a surprisingly frustrating exercise. I began coordinating for an interview early in the summer of 2004 and by late July had obtained the necessary approval from army public affairs to contact General Hagenbeck's staff. General Hagenbeck's public affairs officer responded right away and told me he would put me on the general's schedule but that the general was very busy and so he didn't foresee an opportunity for at least several months. Seven months later, with the book approaching completion, I still had not heard back from him to coordinate a time and date, so I decided to make one last effort and called General Hagenbeck's public affairs officer directly. He was very apologetic, assured me that they regarded this as their fault, I had "slipped through the cracks," and that the general would like the chance to respond. The general was still a very busy man, however, so a time could not be arranged in the foreseeable future, and when the general declined a telephone interview, the public affairs officer suggested I submit some written questions for the general to answer. This I did the very next day. Unfortunately, the public affairs officer was offended by my questions—he called them among other things "whacky"—but he did say he would forward them to General Hagenbeck. A couple of days later I received General Hagenbeck's answers, which indicated, to me anyway, that he too may have been put off by my questions. More to the point, his answers did little to address or quiet the charges made against him. For example, General Hagenbeck stated flatly that 10th Mountain's battalions brought their ALOs and ETACs, but he offered no details and made no attempt to explain or counter the points raised by others as I had asked. This accusation, as well as others addressed in this section, have been largely corroborated by an in-depth analysis of Operation Anaconda written by Sean Naylor, an award-winning journalist with *Army Times* who was with U.S. forces during Anaconda. In his book, *Not a Good Day to Die,* published by Berkley Publishing Group, Naylor characterizes General Hagenbeck as "patrician"—my experience with the general and his staff suggests this characterization may be an understatement.

amounted to little more than persuasive authority. His authority over some of the SOF and OGA elements was little better.

Disparate force structures in today's era of coalition warfare are nothing new, and an acknowledged challenge of modern warfare is the need to "synch-up" the various components of such coalitions. But in this case, the piecemeal order of battle was going to be aggravated by piecemeal planning. Some components were brought into the planning process early, others later, and some, such as the Afghans, not at all. Furthermore, several elements had dramatically different visions of how the operation should unfold. The most damning reflection of how the planning process broke down is that, according to Sean Naylor's analysis, several key components marched into combat with radically different ideas of what was to happen and who was to do what. The combination of odd force structure and irregular planning created a very challenging context for this operation before the first shot was even fired.

Another legacy of the unique circumstances characterizing the war is that up to this point it had been waged by an unprecedented combination of Afghan rebels, Coalition Special Forces, and air power. With Anaconda, Americans were conducting their first major conventional ground operation. The United States still had not moved the conventional theater-level ground force infrastructure into theater, though, so a division commander with an incomplete staff was going to lead a brigade-size force made up of units from two divisions, Special Forces from a number of different nations, as well as Afghan forces that still had much of their "warlord militia" character. Moreover, their close air support was going to be coordinated by a handful of airmen working as an ASOC—a situation reminiscent of Bochain's group at Task Force Dagger. This combat mix meant that when the shooting started there could be a lot of different organizations wanting to shoot a lot of different weapons in a lot of different directions at the same time.

Since air power had been a big part of the formula in Afghanistan up to this point, one would expect it to play a big role in Anaconda. The man responsible for integrating air power was Maj. Pete Donnelly. An ALO with the 20th ASOS, Donnelly had been brought to Afghanistan about three months before by Longoria in his effort to get as many 20th ASOS people into theater as possible. Since the 20th normally supports 10th Mountain, its people would be the best choice to have on hand should Hagenbeck decide he needed them. Up to this point Longoria had kept Donnelly busy handling pop-up missions around the theater, including a stint with his regular boss, Lieutenant Colonel Bochain in TF Dagger Headquarters. The varied tasks meant Donnelly was more aware than most where problems in the system existed and how to overcome some of them.

Notified around 18 February that 10th Mountain needed him to help with Anaconda, he arrived around the twentieth. This left him about a week to get up to speed before Anaconda was set to begin. The main features of the plan were already in place by the time Donnelly arrived, so rather than helping to integrate CAS into the plan as it took shape, or advise on how to build a plan that could take maximum advantage of air capabilities, Donnelly could do little more than work air in around the margins. In addition, he and his team had to get an air cell up and running from scratch in short order. The problem of cobbling together an ad hoc ASOC had been hard when Bochain did it to support a handful of SOF teams; now Donnelly was given a week to do the same in support of a major conventional operation. When weather forced postponement of Anaconda by two days, Donnelly greeted the news as a godsend—it gave his team, as well as the 10th Mountain staff, some badly needed extra time to exercise their procedures.

The command and control structure for CAS also presented challenges, and Donnelly felt he needed to make changes prior to commencing Operation Anaconda. The arrangement first put in place to coordinate air support had evolved by this point. Now instead of TF Dagger headquarters coordinating all CAS for all of Afghanistan, a second coordination cell had been established when the 101st set up at Kandahar airport, and the two centers effectively split the country between them. Neither center, however, was collocated with the ground commander in charge of the operation—a major tenet of standard CAS procedures—so Donnelly decided he had to set up an operation at Bagram that would better serve Hagenbeck's needs. Once again, though, an ASOC is a service normally provided at corps level or higher. Donnelly had spent several weeks working with Bochain, so knowing the roles and responsibilities this entailed wasn't a problem—the problem was that as with Bochain and TF Dagger, a handful of TACPs, this time led by a major, were going to do the work of a corps level staff normally numbering dozens, as well as provide the routine functions of a division air support staff.

Donnelly also had to contend with problems at the combined air operations center. Tasked with coordinating all air operations within theater, not just CAS, they would play a major role in planning and executing such a large conventional operation. For example, they were responsible for scheduling all the noncombat support aircraft that would be needed in greater numbers—AWACS, JSTARS, air refueling tankers, just to name a few. More important, they handled all the non-CAS-related air attack requests, such as preassault strikes against known targets, and they handled scheduling enough sorties to provide adequate CAS availability throughout the battle. These last two areas require close coordination with the ASOC, which meant Donnelly. Once again, the dearth of CAS experience, let alone expertise, at the CAOC created needless headaches. Donnelly only had a few days to make contacts and arrange for what he needed. He did get the information he needed and coordinated what he needed to coordinate, but the many, and often unnecessary, difficulties in doing so took time he couldn't spare and increased friction between his team and the army staff he was supporting.

The biggest problem those planning Anaconda faced, however, was intelligence and their expectation of what the enemy would do once the attack began. Early intelligence estimates put the number of enemy in the region at quite a low figure—only a couple hundred. The closer they got to D-day, though, the more opinion began to vary, with some observers beginning to suspect a much higher number. More important than numbers is what they expected the enemy to do, and here Anaconda planners were headed for their biggest surprise. One key factor shaping American expectations was what had happened with Tora Bora. The standard U.S. interpretation of Tora Bora's failure was that when faced with a major assault, the enemy fled and sympathetic blocking forces allowed them to escape. From this, U.S. military leaders deduced that if pushed again the enemy would run again, and that if American troops were put in the blocking positions, the enemy would simply surrender and all the blockers would have to do is round them up. One young airman stated that his unit, assigned to be one of the blocking forces, went in on the first wave carrying signs telling the surrendering enemy where to go to be processed. The only problem with this scenario is that by all accounts, those who were still in the fight by this point were hardcore, and from the beginning hardcore elements had proven to be tenacious fighters. Yes, they had shown that if the odds appeared to be against them and they had an escape route they would use it and regroup to fight another day, but if there was no escape route, there was every reason to believe they would fight like hell—as they had done before.

The First Day

The opening assault finally kicked off before dawn on 2 March, but before anyone had even fired a shot the operation scored its first success, albeit a very minor one. Nonetheless it underscores the effectiveness of air power in this war. S.Sgt. Brian Wilchenski, normally with the 20th ASOS, was augmenting the SOF TACPs. He relates the following encounter as his SOF team moved into position: "When we pushed the team up we had this Afghani guy come running across this field. . . . He probably ran about five hundred meters and he is out of breath and gets to the truck, he goes, 'Don't bomb us! Don't bomb us! My brother runs this area and he is not helping al Qaeda at all and I got lots of weapons, mines, and RPGs. I will turn them in to you right now, just don't bomb us! Don't bomb us!' So the team went up to this compound and they had a whole flatbed full of mines, RPGs, mortars, the whole truck full of stuff and they gave us everything they had."

Shortly after that small victory, the other side of air power's impact was seen. As another SOF team moved into position with its Afghan allies on the south end of the valley, an AC-130 crew operating overhead notified them of a group of people and vehicles that looked like it was massing in a position to block their forces. It looked like a military force, and it was reported by the gunship crew to be right where intelligence had predicted they might encounter enemy resistance, so the commander ordered the AC-130 to fire. The AC-130, a modified cargo plane, is packed with the most sophisticated sensors and carries heavy firepower. Its sensors are normally among the most accurate and reliable in the U.S. inventory. What nobody realized was that this AC-130's sensors had developed a problem that introduced a five-mile error into its navigation system, and what the aircrew thought was a buildup of enemy forces was actually another SOF team leading General Zia's forces into position on the north end of the valley. There was even an ironic twist to this tragedy: the AC-130 crew backed up their assessment by using terrain association— manually comparing the terrain they saw in their scope with what their maps said the terrain should look like in the area where they thought they were aiming. This did not avert the accident because the terrain surrounding the friendly location roughly matched what the map showed for the intended target area.

The immediate consequence of this friendly-fire incident was the death of one American soldier, CWO Stanley L. Harriman, and several Afghan soldiers. The long-term impact was far worse. As soon as they came under attack, everyone ran for cover, assuming it was enemy fire. In fact, the initial reports on Harriman's death stated that he had been killed by an enemy mortar round. Zia's forces had already encountered a number of problems up to this point, but the AC-130 incident was the severest blow; Zia decided to pull his men out of the fight, and several days of U.S. persuasion could not get him to rejoin. The plan calling for the Afghan contingent to play hammer to the American anvil was suddenly turned on its ear. Forces meant to be one half of the plan, and the stationary half at that, now found themselves facing the full brunt of enemy forces in that area.

Before any ground forces actually closed with the enemy another controversy emerged. The CAOC conducted some preassault airstrikes on predesignated targets but not many, and far less than some had expected. Days earlier, shortly after learning of the plans for Anaconda, Donnelly had recommended an ambitious array of airstrikes on suspected enemy positions in the hours before troops moved in, but Hagenbeck opted to keep them to an absolute minimum hoping to maintain the element of surprise. In his book, Naylor states that on the day before D-day, new intelligence revealed enemy forces in several of those positions, which prompted Hagenbeck to change his mind and request more airstrikes with less than twelve hours before those strikes would have to take place. Such last-minute air requests have long been controversial in air-ground circles—ground forces often believe fervently that such requests could take place if the air force was at all inclined to help, but aircraft cannot be got ready for combat in only a few hours. Meeting such short notice requests often means retasking sorties dedicated to other combat tasks scheduled for the same time, which often requires cutting into those reserved for CAS support once troops are actually in the fight. The context within which these requests took place didn't help either, because many Americans at higher headquarters considered the war all but over and had started winding down their efforts. The staff planning Anaconda had not helped matters because up to this point they had been anticipating little resistance. Hagenbeck made his request to Central Command, the headquarters running the entire war, and it voiced immediate opposition. But, according to Naylor, CENTCOM said they would do what they could. What they actually sent out the next morning was judged inadequate by most people actually involved with Anaconda. What had happened to Hagenbeck's request is still lost in mutual recrimination at this point, but Donnelly's attempt to arrange more airstrikes days before was now looking like a golden opportunity lost.

While these preassault airstrikes were going forward, other pieces of Anaconda's plan were put into motion. In the lead helicopter of one part of the initial wave of blocking forces was S.Sgt. Stephen M. Achey, an ETAC with the 20th ASOS attached to Charlie Company, 1-87 Infan-

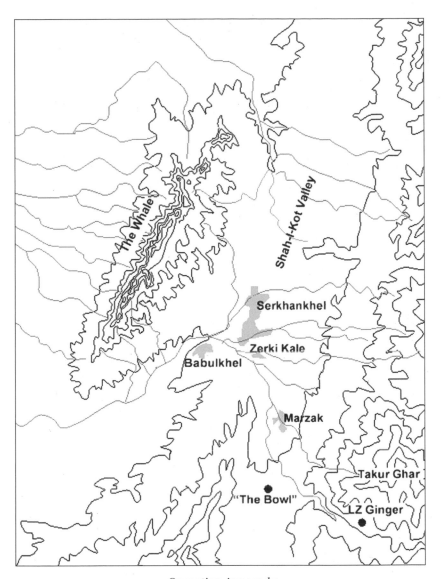

Operation Anaconda

try Battalion of 10th Mountain Division. Charlie Company was assigned one of the blocking positions known as point Ginger. They were supplemented by members of the battalion staff going in to set up a battalion command post near Charlie Company's position. According to Achey, the first fire they took was as their chopper flew over the town of Marzak, but it didn't amount to much. After they landed, though, things were eerily quiet. He describes those initial moments:

> Everybody was trying to get organized, the helicopters flew off. We had just got into our formations, and started moving. We noticed some guys on the ridgeline to our right, so they asked the Australian LNOs [liaison officer], "Are these guys friendly or not?" They said, "They're not our guys," "Well that's the only people that's supposed to be around," so this guy started shooting at them. . . . Then we started taking fire from the east. That's where it all began.
>
> Everybody dropped their rucks. I was under the impression [the order had meant], "Drop your ruck, get behind it and face the enemy and fire back." I wasn't watching the people behind me. I'm watching the dudes around rocks and taking potshots at them. I catch a burst of machine-gun fire and I turn around and look—they're all gone. "Whoa, hey, where did everybody just go to?" So I tried to contact the Apaches [AH-64 attack helicopters] and that didn't work. Tried to just call any aircraft on the common air frequency; that didn't work either.

Unbeknownst to Achey, the others had taken cover in a natural depression they came to call "the bowl." Also in the initial wave, but in the second helicopter, was T.Sgt. John E. "Vic" McCabe, another member of the 20th ASOS. McCabe had recently become the E-BALO for 1-87, making him responsible for CAS planning, coordination, and execution for the entire battalion, and he went in with the rest of the battalion staff. As soon as he got off the chopper he moved to link up with the battalion commander, and as McCabe said, "that's when the shit hit the fan." One of those strange episodes that sticks in a person's mind when under fire occurred to McCabe almost immediately:

> It was just slow motion. [I'm] walking fast 'cause they are shooting at us, and just out of the corner of my left eye I see this slow-moving projectile, this cylindrical object and it's just way too big for a bullet. I mean, your mind plays games with you. . . . It was the weirdest thing— an RPG—and it's in slow motion and it just seems to be like cartoon- ish, if you will, but just slow and it's like, "This is going to hurt!" Your mind's processing, "Do I keep moving forward because that's where we're going, or do I just stop and let it explode?" I'm like, "Just keep going Vic, just keep going!" [It] landed ten feet between us and sure as shit—it just kind of fizzles out.

The bullets, RPGs, and mortars started raining down on the small group, barely bigger than a platoon. Eight CH-47s had been planned in the first wave, but because of the fierce firefight only the first two landed. Add- ing to their desperate straits many in the first chopper had had to leave their rucks on the landing zone in their scramble for cover and couldn't

S.Sgt. Stephen Achey was an ETAC with the 20th ASOS during Operation Anaconda in Afghanistan.

T.Sgt. John "Vic" McCabe was an E-BALO during Operation Anaconda. He and Achey were pinned down with their unit and together brought considerable aid through calling in CAS.

go back for them without exposing themselves to murderous fire. After finding cover, McCabe was surprised to see Achey trapped out in the open. The two conversed by radio, and McCabe advised holding tight till they could provide some aerial cover fire. Achey agreed, but now had to survive in that exposed position till help arrived. "So I sat there and waited. . . . A guy pops out from behind a rock, starts shooting, I shoot at him, duck back behind my ruck. . . . A mortar round or something, some kind of explosive went off right behind me and threw me off to the right—I thought I was dead. I said, 'Yeah, I'm toast.' I didn't want to look down; maybe I was gone, didn't know, didn't want to know. Just kind of laid there and looked up."

Like Achey, McCabe couldn't get through on his radio to call for air support, but the battalion fire service officer managed to contact the six AH-64 Apache helicopters supporting Anaconda, and two raced to help. They provided the cover Achey needed to join the others in the bowl. "The Apaches started their attack and started drawing all the fire. They made one pass, drew a lot of fire, then I was just hoping they would come back around again 'cause that was my plan to run. They did and as soon as they did I just hauled ass. Come over the top of the bowl there's Sergeant McCabe and everybody else."

The helicopters did a great job of sending the enemy ducking for cover, and this gave others besides Achey the chance to better their position, but the Apaches were met with a fusillade of fire that inflicted considerable battle damage. They soon had to withdraw and were unable to return for the remainder of that day. More helicopters would arrive as reinforcements, but for now it was up to McCabe and Achey to bring the heavy firepower. As McCabe would later say, having Achey there to help "turned out to be a blessing in disguise." Together they began trying to establish communications with the ASOC to request air support. Whether because of their location or the terrain, they were unable to reach either the ASOC or the CAOC, and couldn't even raise AWACS. Finally they contacted a tanker aircraft who relayed their request. McCabe describes what followed:

> The first aircraft to work the target area was a B-52, call sign "Blade"; they had twenty-four Mk-82s. I started to work up our position and the enemy mortar location that was still firing into our position. I had Achey reconfirm our location and the mortars to our east, about five hundred meters we thought. I briefed the B-52 crew on our situation on the ground—it wasn't pretty. Within ten minutes they were set up to drop all of the ordnance on board along the ridgeline to our east. I

told everyone to get down and take some sort of protection because it wasn't going to be pretty with twenty-four five-hundred-pound bombs exploding that close to us.

The bombs started to drop and then the earth started to tremble from the bombs exploding. Earth and debris was coming down all around us. It was silent for awhile after the first B-52 strike. Everyone started to locate at the bottom of the bowl and then began digging fighting positions. It was probably within the hour the mortars and bullets stared to fly again. . . . The enemy had us pinned down pretty good now and also knew where we were. They had the high ground and we were stuck in this bowl with nowhere to go. . . .

That bowl was the quickest, closest place to take cover. So when everybody rolled into it essentially you had eighty-six guys. The only people that actually left [were the] 120-mm mortars. . . . They set up two tubes to our south about two hundred meters [away], and they were able to get a couple of rounds out before they were taken out. The one thing we did find was the al Qaeda/Taliban were very good with the mortars.

I got on the radio again and requested some more CAS. I gave this mission to Achey to control. . . . We could see some of the Taliban and al Qaeda moving around and some of the army guys said they could hear them taunting us. Our next set of fighters were a couple of F-15Es carrying GBU-10s and GBU-12s, and Achey had them hit the ridgeline to our east. After that mission I took over for the rest of the day controlling every hour on the hour. We just couldn't get a fix on the mortars that kept pounding us. Later . . . the scouts were able to make it part way to their objective, so we used them on a couple of strikes to hit a cave complex that the scouts had "eyes on."

The "eyes on" problem was only partially solved by the scout team's efforts because they had no way to get accurate grids to the ETACs, and Achey describes the problem they all faced trying to direct pilots to where they wanted the bombs dropped: "All we had was, 'Yeah, they're over there on that ridgeline someplace.' It was just guesswork. I mean we could see some of them, but where we were in the bowl we couldn't see the enemy." Some aircraft could, and did, come in low enough to see the enemy, F-15Es and F-18s mostly, but with many aircraft, such as bombers, this was not a practical solution because they wouldn't be able to see any better even if they did come in low. To help solve the problem Achey decided to move out onto the ridgeline himself. "After a while it was like, 'Okay, this isn't going to work.' So I took the radio and scurried up the ridgeline. . . . You were fine until you got to the top—that's where all the rounds were hitting. Then I started taking fire from other sides. At one point you're just sitting there and rounds are hitting this side of the rock, and after a while rounds are hitting underneath you, and you see all these guys moving around the other side. So you say, 'Okay I'm going to go back down now.' I never actually got over to where the enemy was or where [the scouts] were."

In addition to the difficulty of locating accurate coordinates to pass to aircraft, the other big problem was that the enemy had cemented the mortar base plates into preselected positions, so the rest of the mortar could be removed and set up again quickly without having to go through the laborious process of zeroing them in. So every time the crews heard aircraft approaching they would detach the tube, scurry into a nearby cave, ride out the attack, reemerge, reattach, and resume firing. This along with the continual small arms fire made for a very long day for those pinned down in the bowl, as McCabe relates:

> We were in contact from the time we landed to forty-five minutes before exfiltration later that night. Achey had kept himself busy while I was controlling or in between missions. He had assisted me with converting [army grid references into standard latitude and longitude coordinates], helping with the wounded; [he] gathered their unused ammo and distributed it to the "shooters"; he returned fire himself, and even assisted with the medevac later that night. That kid was awesome! Then night came and I was exhausted. I handed my radio off to Achey and instructed him to work the first AC-130 mission, and I would take over from him. Once the first AC-130 showed up and I heard the 40-mm and 105-mm rounds impacting around us I wrapped up in my sleeping bag and got some rest—I think I may have actually fallen asleep.

The AC-130 gunship is one of the most effective close air support aircraft in the world. But it is big and slow, and to be effective in the CAS role it has to fly very low and in slow circles to provide a stable platform for its aiming sensors. This makes the aircraft a sitting duck during the day. Therefore AC-130s operate only at night where the cover of darkness is their only defense. By holding out until nightfall the beleaguered men in the bowl finally got a CAS aircraft that could loiter overhead waiting for the enemy to emerge from their caves, target them, and send down very effective firepower. This turned the tide of the battle. Achey recalls what a difference the AC-130 made. "When night time came that's when the real good stuff started happening. . . . The AC-130 showed up and just literally killed everything. It was just awesome. . . . We told them there were cave entrances over there on the side of that ridgeline, so they looked around and said, 'Okay, I found one. I'm going to put a 40-mm into it and see what happens.' He did, and people came out of everywhere and the good times rolled! . . . He just couldn't shoot fast enough."

The AC-130 broke the siege, and although Charlie Company would remain there for a few more hours, Hagenbeck thought it safe enough to bring in helicopters to evacuate the wounded. Casualties had mounted throughout the day, and some desperately needed medical attention that lay beyond the resources of the battlefield medics. The medevac choppers' arrival brought the enemy back to life, but as McCabe explains, it was quickly dealt with. "I awoke to the battalion commander yelling at his guys to shoot. The medevac helicopters had landed . . . and I could see tracer rounds across the south and west of our position [where the helicopters had landed]. . . . Achey had the AC-130 hit that position, which turned out to be a heavy machine gun the Taliban had just moved into position. It was a good thing we had AC-130s—they found several mortar positions and numerous guys running around to our east on the ridgeline." A few tense, cold, but relatively uneventful hours later, the rest of Charlie Company was evacuated by helicopter, and what some were calling the "eighteen-hour miracle" finally came to an end. The miracle was that despite the desperate situation and a number of serious wounds, no one died.

While the miracle at point Ginger was unfolding, another conflict developed, this one in Hagenbeck's headquarters back at Bagram. According to Major Donnelly, this issue poisoned the atmosphere of teamwork between the army and air force staffs and may have set the stage for an ugly episode of interservice rivalry played out in the media months later. One modern marvel that has helped revolutionize the air-ground battlefield in recent years is the unmanned aerial vehicle, a drone that can loiter long over any given spot and give a real-time view of events below. This remarkable view of the battle has also led to problems, though. One is the powerful tendency to mistake the view through the UAV's lens at any given moment for the "big picture." In reality, a UAV gives observers a microscopic insight into events at one small area at one moment in time—what many have likened to watching the world through a soda straw. Another problem is the compelling urge to fixate on what appears on the screen. Troops in Afghanistan dubbed this phenomenon "predator crack" in reference to the addictive quality of the pictures sent back by the most commonly used UAV, dubbed Predator. This "predator crack" can lead to problems if observers get so caught up in what they are seeing they lose sight of what is happening elsewhere. Staff Sergeant Chris Spann, a SOF TACP, relates one such instance witnessed by his SOF team captain at Hagenbeck's headquarters while Anaconda was under way. "When [Chief Harriman was killed] our team leader had to escort the body back. [The bodies of fallen U.S. service members are kept under constant escort on their journey home, usually by someone close to them, as a sign of respect.] He said that when he was at Bagram it was stomach churning to watch these guys watching the battle on [the screen showing the] Predator feed and cheering like it was a football game. He was just getting sick, 'cause he had been in the valley the day before. Now he's at Bagram watching these colonels and whoever else cheer the battle on Predator feed while they are sipping their coffee."

When the two problems combine—when people in headquarters get sucked into Predator's tiny view of the unfolding action and insist they have a real lock on the battle and try to influence events based on that view—it can lead to some unfortunate, even unprofessional, confrontations as different observers argue over what needs to be done where and when. It can even jeopardize the lives of soldiers in combat. During the U.S. Civil War generals on both sides complained about politicians trying to micromanage the war via the new technological marvel of that era, telegraph, and many battles in Vietnam saw several echelons of commanders hovering over the battlefield in their helicopters, each trying to run the battle according to what he saw from his vantage point. The first day's fighting during Operation Anaconda saw what may be considered the latest version of this longstanding problem.

Late in the afternoon of the first day, a Predator reconnoitering an area in the mountains outside the immediate area of the battle discovered a small pickup truck that appeared to be dropping off men, materiel, or both along a narrow mountain trail at the bottom of a ravine. According to Donnelly, just how many men or what sort of materiel, whether they were related to the battle, or whether anything was being dropped off at all was unclear because of the grainy nature of the imagery. Still, Hagenbeck and his senior leadership determined that that truck needed to be destroyed right away. Donnelly relates what transpired from that decision:

> We're in a troops-in-contact situation [soldiers in a serious firefight], he points to what the Predator feed is showing him on the screen, and it's a vehicle driving around, dropping guys off at locations and [Hagenbeck] said "Kill it." So I rolled a set of F-16s toward it and they couldn't find it. . . . It's hard to see a truck moving through a ravine in a very steep mountain pass. So they ran out of gas, turned around to hit the

tanker, and I sent another set in there after them. I managed it so we didn't pull anybody off [supporting the troops], but it became an issue and at one point the debate was, "Sir, if we give what you want after that truck we'll have to pull it off troops in contact," and he said, "do it." I said, "Okay," but I didn't do it, I just said, "Okay." I mean, we hadn't hit [the truck] in three or four hours, so my personal decision [was] I didn't reroll those guys off the troop-in-contact because [the troops] were no-shit getting shot at.

I tried to explain to the chief of staff that we are not providing close air support when we're going after a truck that's over here driving through a ravine—that's interdiction. He was complaining that we're not responsive. He said, "You mean to tell me it's going to take you four hours to get air support to one of my guys bleeding out there?" I said, "No sir, we responded within five minutes to every single call for fire and we got in there and killed the enemy and saved your guys' lives. What you're talking about is rerolling assets off a CAS mission to go and do an interdiction on something that they had no coordinates for and it's a hunting expedition." He goes, "Every time I talk to you it's another excuse—blow up that truck!" And I said, "Yes sir." And we sent more shit after it. We couldn't get it—we never got it.

There was a historical irony to this last exchange. For all the decades that the air force resisted doing CAS, one of the arguments its leaders put forth was that using aircraft to kill the enemy once they were in contact with friendly forces was "inefficient," a misallocation of scarce resources. Far better, they argued, to kill those enemy forces before they got into contact with friendly forces—a mission known as interdiction—because that way each aircraft could kill more enemy and have a greater impact on the outcome. This argument would send the army into fits because it essentially said guys getting shot at were on their own because aircraft were going to be sent after more lucrative targets. Now in America's first conventional war of the twenty-first century, we find an airman arguing against taking CAS aircraft away from troops in contact to send them on an interdiction mission, and army leaders screaming mad because the air force doesn't want to do this. Without a doubt, if that truck were dropping off reinforcements it would be ideal to get it before it completed its mission so those troops and materiel couldn't get to the fight. But to do so at the expense of troops who were fighting for their lives and where CAS was the primary fire support keeping the enemy at bay puts that ideal in a much different light.

Even the circumstances of this particular confrontation bear out the ironic reversal of roles. When the air force would stress the superiority of interdiction over CAS, army leaders would argue that it was absurd to think aircraft could find everything the enemy sent out. When an air force chief of staff claimed in the nineties that the air force would soon be able to "find, fix, track, target, and engage anything of military significance on the earth," ground power advocates guffawed and began pointing out all the times the air force couldn't find something. Now senior army leaders were fuming at an air force major's claim that repeated efforts to find one small truck in a vast mountain range had failed.

Rather than an isolated incident or one moment's heated exchange, the first day's confrontation became a running battle. For one thing, it seemed to alter the dynamics of the army–air force relationship built up between members of the staff running Operation Anaconda. Again, as Donnelly relates: " [Earlier] we felt like, 'Wow, what a great job we did!' Well, within a very short period of time, when that vehicle showed up, we went from the heroes to the goats because we couldn't blow that thing up. . . . That really tore up the relationship in there." Just how bad that one truck had affected the senior leadership became apparent on the second day, when once again in the midst of a desperate troops-in-contact situation Predator found another truck. Donnelly describes what happened:

> Then that happened again. A stake bed truck was driving through the next day—[the chief of staff ordered] "Blow that up." [Donnelly replied], "Okay, we have troops in contact, [and you want me to] blow that up. . . . Sir, CAS is what we're doing, [supporting the troops in contact] is what close air support is. [The truck] is an emerging target, fleeing target, interdiction target, whatever you want to call it," but he would not listen. He said, "What I'm going to do is I'm going to put a piece of paper up next to your station and I'm going to put the time I point to something on that screen and I'm going to put the time that you kill it, and that's how you're going to be judged." It was a stake bed truck, flat sticks sticking out the back with nothing on it. So maybe there was one, or two, or three guys in the cab. So what? Probably some guy trying to go to the market or something. . . . We are going after this worthless piece of rusted-out crap going through this ravine. Another situation similar to the previous day. But why? For what reason? It was pulling assets [off troops in contact].

After the battle Donnelly learned these episodes were not going to end there, that Hagenbeck was going to elevate the issue to higher channels. Through an army contact he learned about a report Hagenbeck's staff was preparing: "Now the army leadership is drafting a memo to the four star that says, 'The air force is not supporting us. Their CAS takes four hours. . . .' I have been [traveling to various headquarters] since I got back responding to these allegations that CAS was not responsive, and it's based on the fact that we couldn't kill that truck."[2]

The Second Day

Other units had moved into position on the first day, and though some, like those at Ginger, could not reach their objectives, others did. The larger problem was that the temporary pullout of Zia's forces left a gaping hole in the original Anaconda plan. Without a driving force, all the blocking forces were left hanging. Hagenbeck shifted gears and devised a new plan. The blocking forces would now move down into the valley and sweep it of enemy forces. SOF units would be moved into the surrounding high ground to act as spotters and call in airstrikes if they saw enemy groups moving into or out of the valley. With one of those teams was Staff Sergeant Chris Spann out of Fort Lewis, Washington. Spann was a SOF TACP with the same team as Chief Harriman who had been killed in the AC-130 accident. Chris Spann was also a cousin of Mike Spann, the first American killed in Afghanistan. Spann and his SOF team were now given new orders to take up one of those observation posts. "Our mission now changed—the 101st and the 10th Mountain guys now became the primary offensive guys. . . . Now they were actually doing the mission and we were basically a blocking force, but we didn't have enough people to be a blocking force. We were really just observers, and we would put in OPs and collect intelligence. Actually my OP captured the first prisoner of Anaconda. After the 101st got in there, they were soaking up all the air, so the majority of our calling CAS after that became nominating targets and waiting for the B-52 to come hit it because the 101st and the 10th Mountain guys were real busy."

Another part of the change in plans was that Hagenbeck decided to commit his reserve, battalion 1-187 of the 101st, (not to be confused with 1-87 of 10th Mountain). With the battalion was a senior NCO and

2. I addressed this whole episode in the questions I sent to General Hagenbeck. I asked if these two episodes took place and if they had any impact on the relationships within his staff. Of the first part—whether these episodes took place—the entirety of the general's response was, "The Joint team did have to work through issues related to destroying a number of moving targets." Of Donnelly's assessment that these two episodes affected the army–air force relationship on his staff, General Hagenbeck said simply, "The success of Operation Anaconda was directly related to the combined joint teamwork shown by all members of the staff and all the disparate units, and countries, involved." The general did not elaborate further.

S.Sgt. Christopher Spann was a SOF TACP during Operation Anaconda.
He was in a unique position to witness the SOF elements of that battle.

long service TACP who asked not to have his full name used—he will be known as Master Sergeant Larry. Larry had started his air force career as a graphic artist; how he came to be a TACP provides not only an interesting story, but also a poignant comment on the current fight against terrorism. People often talk about how fighting terrorism only creates more terrorists, but little is thought about the other side of this equation: "Back in '83 I was helping the base photography [office], and I had to do the forensic photography on the marines that were killed in Beirut. I took, oh, probably close to ten thousand pictures of the marines while we were doing the identification of their remains, which basically led to my feelings that I would rather be on the giving end than the receiving end. It was a life-changing experience, I can say that much. Believe me I remembered during Anaconda, I remembered, 'For the marines!'—it was something."

Initially Larry's unit was to be inserted along the eastern ridgeline north of where 1-87's Charlie Company had gone in the day before. As Larry explains, however, this new point was no better than where Charlie Company had gone in, and they encountered a similar reception.

We started to fly into the valley and as we get the thirty-second call that we're going to land, the helos suddenly turned, and as they turned away from the LZ you can see mortar rounds landing on the LZ and going off and they looked like raindrops. The whole LZ was just exploding with mortar rounds. So they decided to abort that insertion 'cause obviously we're landing right on top of a hot LZ.

We flew back to Bagram and waited about eight hours and then we inserted again into another LZ that was farther north, and the battalion commander decided we would walk in [from there]. And so we had about a fifteen-kilometer walk. . . . We swept the eastern side of the valley going from the north to the south until we finally got down to approximately the southern third of the valley and we assumed our blocking positions there. . . . We landed initially about midnight or so, I don't remember the exact time . . . and we got into our blocking position a little after noon, so we had been moving about twelve hours sweeping the valley and we hadn't had any enemy contact up to that time.

We got to our blocking position, I was with the [battalion] TAC, I was talking with the battalion staff about CAS and how close we could drop, and things like that, and then all of a sudden we receive machine-gun rounds bouncing all over our heads and through our position and we start taking small arms fire. It was coming [from] about three hundred meters to the south of our position. . . . We were engaged for about five minutes with our small arms . . . and I heard the [commander] yell, "Air force I want CAS now," so . . . my counterpart, put his rifle down and started requesting CAS and I put mine down and got behind a rock and started working up my nine-line. . . . The CAOC immediately pushed a B-52 to me, which had JDAMs on it, and because of the close proximity . . . I was extremely concerned about fratricide at that distance, especially with the [two-thousand-pound warhead] on the JDAM. But [the commander] said do it anyway, so I had a B-52 come across and drop two JDAMs, which impacted about fifty feet from each other and the battle was over. They annihilated the enemy and we received no more small arms from them at all.

Maybe three or four hours later [the commander] was talking to [headquarters] on his TACSAT and told me he had a target of two, three hundred personnel at the south end of the valley, which was our area of responsibility, to hit them with CAS. So I requested immediate CAS for that, and then I had ten or twelve aircraft of all types show up.

There was one problem: though this force was only about a kilometer away and would be a serious threat if it was hostile, it was on the other side of a line of low hills and Larry could not see it. Here was another PID problem, so unless he or someone in the air could verify they were hostile, or unless those forces attacked, Larry could not clear aircraft to engage them. Larry opted to have aircraft look for him, and here he got a stroke of good luck, which combined with his own quick thinking, turned a potential enemy counterattack into a lopsided rout.

> The first aircraft I had were two A-10s that showed up, and they said they saw the enemy in the open, and as far as I know they were probably massing for a counterattack. One of the A-10s . . . accidentally used the call sign of "Misty," which we realized is an air FAC call sign. So realizing that, I quickly confirmed with them that the lead pilot was an air FAC-qualified person, and once he confirmed that, it changed how I was going to use the aircraft. 'Cause at that time we also had F-18s and F-14s checking in. Since [the air FAC] could see the target . . . I let the A-10s work the other fighters on the target and move the bombs around, which worked well.
>
> At that time we also had a Predator show up. . . . The Predator [operator] had come up on my UHF frequency, and [he] was giving me real world immediate feedback as we were having them sweep the valley looking for the enemy. . . . I had all types of aircraft checking in; I had A-10s, 14s, 18s, I had a B-52, and eventually we got an AC-130 overhead. . . . It had gone to dark ops [when] we finally had the AC-130, a Predator, and a pair of A-10s. . . . They're all talking to each other identifying targets, and the big part was they would identify a target, I would confirm it with the battalion commander . . . and say, "Is it a good target? Is it not a good target?" If it was, I'd tell them they're authorized to engage and clear them hot; and then they would kill it. . . . I'd never trained to do [this]; I knew the capability was out there, but let's be honest—it's not that we ever get all three different types of platforms available, but just flexing with the battle as things were going on.

The end result was that air attacks cleared that area of enemy forces, which appeared to be preparing a major attack, but they never got off so much as one shot at Larry's unit.

The Third Day

During the course of the second day Hagenbeck decided to have SOF teams placed on observation posts high in the mountains overlooking both the Shah-i-Kot Valley and the mountain passes al Qaeda forces were using to move into and out of the battle. It seemed certain after two days of combat that Taliban and al Qaeda personnel were coming and going with ease. Part of the concern with this movement was that the forces Anaconda was to have captured or killed were escaping the trap as had happened at Tora Bora, but another concern was that the opportunity to fight Americans was drawing sympathizers throughout the area, especially nearby Pakistan. Thus the enemy was getting a steady supply of reinforcements. Several SOF teams moved into commanding positions with little trouble and enjoyed some success calling in airstrikes on enemy movements. One team, however, was inadvertently inserted right on top of an enemy stronghold, which started a confusing chain of events leading to one of the most heroic and controversial engagements of the entire war.

Headquarters picked the peak, known as Takur Ghar, because it had a 360-degree view of the valley to the west and the mountain passes behind it to the east. But it was also just above point Ginger—the spot where Charlie Company, 1–87, had spent eighteen hours pinned down on the first day. Though it had been a hornet's nest on the first day, subsequent reconnaissance showed no sign of enemy presence. A navy SEAL team had been given the assignment, and they were moved into position aboard an MH-47 Chinook helicopter using the call sign Razor 03. Chinooks had been performing yeoman's service in Anaconda, primarily because the altitude of terrain around the area was too high for smaller, more nimble helicopters. The Chinook, though, is a large and lumbering aircraft, two characteristics that were now to help determine the fate of dozens of men on that remote hilltop.

The SEALs approached their LZ about 3:00 A.M., and as the helicopter came in for a landing the SEALs prepared for a quick departure. The ramp was down at the back of the chopper and the men were standing ready to jump off. With the helicopter still several feet off the ground, however, a fusillade of fire, including heavy machine guns and RPGs, broke out from several locations around the LZ. Razor 03 took immediate damage; the pilot aborted his landing; and somewhere in that sequence the helicopter lurched, sending the first SEAL in line—PO1C Neil C. Roberts—tumbling out. The pilot, unaware he had a man overboard, had all he could do to get the crippled chopper away from the ambush and keep it off the ground, but he managed to limp to a relatively safe spot on the valley floor. Meanwhile, Roberts survived his fall and was now surrounded by enemy directing all their fire at him. Armed with an M-249 squad automatic weapon, he fought ferociously for upward of thirty minutes before being killed by enemy fire.

Roberts's fate was unknown at the time, and this would be critical to subsequent command decisions. Upon learning that Roberts had fallen out of the helicopter, headquarters ordered a Predator moved to the area to monitor the situation. The picture fed right into the command post and showed Hagenbeck and his staff some of the firefight. Though it was grainy and did not capture Roberts's death, it did show what looked like Roberts being dragged into a tree line. It appeared entirely possible Roberts was still alive but in the hands of a notoriously cruel enemy.

What happened next has become one of the biggest controversies surrounding this day's action. Shortly after the crippled helicopter landed safely it was joined by another Chinook, Razor 04, which, after dropping off a team at another location, came to pick up Razor 03's crew. Word of Roberts's situation quickly spread among all personnel on the scene and, though they knew nothing of Roberts's actions on the ground, they strongly wanted to launch their own immediate rescue attempt. There were two key reasons for this. First, in keeping with a longstanding American military tradition, Special Forces vow never to leave a man behind. To some, this tradition seems a senseless waste of life, especially when it is known that those left behind are certainly dead. To others, however, it is a hallowed trust that goes to the heart of why soldiers will fight and die for each other, even in the face of daunting odds. The marines, for example, feel this promise is central to maintaining their unique esprit de corps, and fliers, who routinely fly deep behind enemy lines, take great comfort knowing that enormous efforts will be exerted to rescue them should they be shot down. The other consideration prompting these men to go after Roberts was the knowledge of their enemy and the thought that Roberts just might be alive. Chechens were known to be among the al Qaeda ranks, and in their long wars against the Russians they had earned a reputation for subjecting their captives to some of the most extreme forms of torture and execution. The thought that their comrade could at that moment be in the hands of such an enemy was enough to make every SEAL present ready to do whatever it took to recover Roberts, dead or alive. Hagenbeck, having seen the Predator video of Roberts being dragged away, approved their request and even ordered a quick reaction force—a team of Rangers standing by at Bagram air base to handle quickly developing emergencies such as this—to aid the rescue attempt. Even though it was on alert for immediate action, however, this QRF would take some time to prep for takeoff, and Bagram was more than an hour's flight away.

Razor 04 now had the SEAL team on board, but it also had the flight crew from Razor 03 as well as their own. Each crew consisted of eight crewmembers, and together this was too much load for the MH-47 to reach the high altitude of the ridgeline, so it first had to drop off Razor 03's flight crew in the nearby town of Gardez. Razor 04 then headed back with the SEAL team, unaware that the QRF, which was even then prepping for takeoff, was on their way to help. Around 5:00 A.M. Razor 04 landed at nearly the same spot Razor 03 had been ambushed, and amid a hail of fire the SEALs stormed off the ramp, and the helicopter took off again.

The team had begun returning fire before they even got off the ramp, but the enemy was in well-protected positions. Almost immediately, two SEALs were wounded and an air force combat controller attached to the team, T.Sgt. John A. Chapman, was killed. Their small numbers, coupled with these casualties, forced the SEALs to give way, and they began falling back down the hillside. Expecting Razor 04 to come back and pick up the team was unthinkable, so the team began working its way down the steep, icy, treacherous mountain all the while carrying two wounded comrades and fighting a running battle as the enemy pursued them. Chapman would later be posthumously awarded the Air Force Cross, the service's second-highest award for valor.

The SEALs' landing, assault, and repulse occurred while the QRF was en route to assist them. Two Chinooks, call signs Razor 01 and Razor 02, with a twenty-one-man Ranger team made the long flight from Bagram. Attached to the team was air force TACP S.Sgt. Kevin Vance and three members of a search and rescue team deployed to Bagram. They included a combat controller, S.Sgt. Gabe Brown, and two pararescue jumpers, T.Sgt. Keary Miller and Sr.A. Jason Cunningham. PJs are Special Forces personnel who specialize in rescuing trapped or downed forces and are extensively trained in emergency medical care.

The team arrived over Takur Ghar around 6:15 A.M., well after sunrise, which meant they no longer had the advantage of darkness. Razor 01 attempted to land at roughly the same spot the first two choppers had, while Razor 02 waited at a safe distance. As soon as Razor 01 came in to land the enemy opened fire, and while the chopper was still about fifteen feet off the ground an RPG knocked out one of its engines. The aircraft fell to a hard landing and was disabled. On board the downed craft were nine Rangers, the four air force personnel, and the eight crewmembers. Razor 01's two machine gunners returned fire with their 7.62-mm miniguns as the army–air force team stormed out the back, but one of the gunners was quickly killed by enemy fire and the other severely wounded. Three Rangers were also killed as they charged down the ramp, and several others suffered wounds of varying severity. Other members of the chopper crew were also wounded, most seriously the two pilots. As the remaining Rangers and Vance attempted to secure a perimeter, the two PJs and the chopper's medic began tending to the wounded, and Brown began establishing communication with aircraft to call in CAS. With the casualties they had sustained, retreating down the hillside was not possible.

Razor 02, having lost contact with 01, landed at Gardez, but once they learned what had happened they took off again and dropped off their half of the Ranger team on the hillside about two thousand feet below Razor 01's wreckage. These Rangers began climbing to get to their friends as quickly as possible, but it was a steep treacherous climb made worse by cold, snow, and sporadic fire. It would take more than two hours to reach their beleaguered colleagues. Thus began a desperate seventeen-hour siege in which an exposed handful fought against an entrenched enemy while they worked frantically to keep the wounded alive till help arrived.

The crash survivors found themselves in a dire situation. Fire was coming from all directions, but there were several strongpoints. In the opening minutes, team commander Capt. Nathan Self, Vance, and two other Rangers tried to rush one of those strongpoints at the base of a tree, but soon realized it was a bunker and withdrew; fortunately none of them were hit in the effort. Vance and Brown then set about working as a team to bring CAS in to help. Vance, fighting beside Self, conferred with the commander and relayed instructions and guidance to Brown, who then relayed the information to the pilots over the radio.

The first aircraft on scene was a two-ship of F-15Es loaded with GBU-12s and 20-mm machine guns. Those five-hundred pounders would have been just the thing to take out the bunker and the other enemy strongpoints, but they were so close to friendlies no one in the air or on the ground wanted to risk it. Both aircraft made gun passes, though, and they were quite effective at suppressing enemy fire for as long as they lasted, but after awhile they ran out of ammunition.

By this time another two-ship was on its way, a couple of F-16s, and while the F-15s buzzed enemy positions until the F-16s arrived, they briefed the incoming aircraft so they would be able to get right to work once on station. The F-16s employed guns as well, and with Vance and Brown moving their gun runs around to various enemy positions, they brought considerable relief to the hard-pressed U.S. position. While the enemy elsewhere seemed to be pushed back to relatively safe distances, the strongpoints still remained a serious problem. Self, Vance, and Brown, conferring on the ground with the aircrews overhead, decided on a relatively safe approach to putting bombs on those strongpoints—together the air and ground team would "walk" the bombs onto the target by dropping one bomb at a safe distance and direction, then steadily moving bombs closer as the ground controllers gave corrections over the radio. The approach worked great, and by the third bomb they had shacked the bunker, splitting the tree above it in the process.

Taking out the bunker took considerable fight out of the enemy, though the team was still getting steady fire from other forces above them and farther away. The half of the team from the first chopper knew they could not advance until they drew more strength, and they hoped the other half of their team was trying to join them. Until more help arrived, however, they had to hold their position and tend their wounded. A steady stream of aircraft kept a presence overhead, striking at whatever threats the ground controllers could see—it was now a matter of time.

The second half of the Ranger team finally made it up to their friends, and with these reinforcements, coupled with damage done by airstrikes, Self decided they could finally take the fight to the enemy. They assaulted the ridgeline, which they took with relative ease and no casualties, and then overran the enemy's base. Their situation was now dramatically improved, and though they were still taking sporadic fire, it was from a considerable distance away. Now, it seemed to Self, they could talk about evacuation under relatively safe conditions. They radioed headquarters that the LZ at their new location was cold, that is, safe for landing. After the day's previous attempts to land helicopters on that hilltop, though, and fearing the enemy was sending more troops to that location, Hagenbeck was unwilling to risk another daylight Chinook landing. Despite repeated and forceful pleas from various members of the group perched on the hilltop, including one from Self personally with his assessment that without immediate medevac some of the wounded would die, headquarters opted to wait until cover of darkness to send helicopters in to pick up the team and its wounded.

Shortly after this radio exchange a small group of enemy fighters attacked the U.S. position from two directions. The ensuing firefight was short but sharp. Small arms and machine-gun fire dealt with the brunt of the assault, but the ground controllers had navy F-14s drop bombs on positions surrounding their location, and this brought an end to that engagement. During this action, however, two Americans, the chopper's medic and Sr.A. Jason Cunningham, were hit. Cunningham's wound was serious and required surgery to stop the bleeding. Though he hung on for several hours, he ultimately died from loss of blood about two hours before medevac helicopters arrived. Cunningham was posthumously awarded the Air Force Cross.

That assault was the last serious enemy threat the Americans faced, though their fight to save their wounded comrades occupied the rest of their time on the mountain. As temperatures dropped at sunset, those who could move searched for anything to keep the wounded warm, even stripping insulation from the interior of the downed helicopter. Only days before the PJs had secured the right to carry blood supplies into combat with them, and now that blood was being used to help the wounded hang on. Despite the team's repeated request for evacuation and assurances that the threat was minimal, the first choppers did not arrive to begin the evacuation until shortly after 8:00 P.M. In honor of the SEAL who had fallen at the outset of this day's fighting, U.S. troops dubbed this hilltop Roberts Ridge—with the arrival of those helicopters the Battle of Roberts Ridge was over. The final toll was seven dead, and almost everyone was wounded to some extent.

Winding Down

The first three days of Operation Anaconda broke the back of al Qaeda and Taliban strength in the Shah-i-Kot Valley but it did not end the battle, nor the enemy's determination to attack when and where conditions favored them. In fact, for the next few days friendly troops found themselves the target of sporadic, but steady, harassing fire that was very hard to deal with effectively. The enemy, now working in small groups, would come out of caves, lob mortar rounds or fire heavy machine guns, and if aircraft showed up they would scamper back into their caves before the bombs fell. This all changed, though, thanks to the experience and insight of one old TACP.

Since his air battle against the enemy force massing to counterattack on the second day of Anaconda, Master Sergeant Larry (who asked that his full name not be used) had seen light and intermittent enemy fire. These were not direct attacks, still he would try to put CAS strikes where he thought the attacks were coming from, but they wouldn't end the attacks for long. After a few days of this cat and mouse game Larry got to thinking. . . .

Most of [the fire] was coming from either the west side of the valley or from Roberts Ridge. . . . I pounded [Roberts Ridge] for four or five days. Every time they'd shoot at us, we'd call in aircraft, we'd blow up the mortar position or come close to it, kill them, they'd have more guys come out and do the same thing. . . .

After about four or five days of this I finally asked [the battalion commander] for his permission to get a couple of fighters to do a little reconnaissance in that area. I told him it's either somebody or something that they're protecting up there, 'cause we had been beating it for days on end and the enemy refused to leave that area. So he finally agreed, "Yeah, go ahead." So I requested through the ASOC that I wanted to get two fighters with sensor pods [sensors that could take a closer look at the ground] and LGBs. They said the standard line, "You don't request [specific] aircraft and ordinance," and I explained to them what I wanted to accomplish. The [CAOC] interrupted and said, "Okay, if you can wait about an hour, we can get that to you." I said, "That's fine."

Waited about an hour and a pair of F-16s show up with LGBs and LANTIRN [low altitude navigation and targeting infrared for night] pods. I explained to the pilots what we were looking for, whether a bunker, an ammo supply, something was up there that the enemy was defending and we wanted to see if we could find it. Well, [the pilots] made about four passes, hitting different things that the aircraft had seen without much results, until finally Number Two says, "I think I see a bunker down there." Rolls in, drops an LGB on it, and the whole top of the mountain just explodes. Huge secondaries that burned for like two and a half days after he dropped the bomb on it. That was obviously their ammo supply that they had been protecting and it changed the entire pitch of the battle after that.

Before when we would drop bombs like up on Roberts Ridge, the enemy would run away. After we blew up their ammo supply they came out and it reminded me of a hornet's nest we'd stirred up—they'd come out and they really started shooting and mortaring us real heavy. They were spraying DSHK rounds and dropping mortars all over the place. But when we called in CAS they wouldn't run away, they were staying there and engaging until either we killed them or they ran out of bullets. That lasted for about three hours. It really stirred everything up, but actually it was good because when they didn't run, if we missed them on the first pass, we didn't miss them on the second pass. . . . The enemy definitely stayed and fought and died.

Apaches were able to come in and make multiple passes and [the enemy] really stayed in position and paid for it. . . . I'd get words from the brigade . . . that helos were inbound and we would "check fire"

the CAS [cease CAS attacks] until the helos had left the valley so we didn't have any problems with air space. We kept [the interval between Apaches and CAS] down within a couple of minutes; I don't think there was a serious point where we didn't have fire available.

The aftermath of this three-hour surge was decisive. It marked the last Taliban—al Qaeda attacks of Operation Anaconda. After that, according to Larry, "They stopped engaging us and we had to go find them. After that spike the . . . majority of what we did [i.e., CAS] was over. I don't think I controlled many more sorties after that." Anaconda continued for roughly another week and a half after Larry bombed the ammo bunker, but that period was basically characterized by what military leaders call "mopping up." One insight into this phase is presented by Staff Sergeant Spann who, with his SOF team, conducted operations across the spectrum. "[We] spent the next two weeks just gathering intel on the valley; we were doing sensitive site exploitation [combing through enemy areas looking for useful information] and securing the valley . . . kicking in the door, making sure nobody was there and the site was secure; then move on to the next house. After that, as far as close air support, the majority of what I did was calling in either AC-130 to scout ahead and look at spots at night or we had Cobra helicopters come in during the day and scout for us and I had them blow up some weapons caches." With that, Operation Anaconda—the largest "conventional" operation of the Afghanistan war—petered out.

5. Just Another Day in Afghanistan

Usually, the major battles get all the attention. But for the average soldier, sailor, airman, or marine any day can bring moments where one is walking the narrow line between life and death. Politicians and the media may not call it war, but for the guy getting shot at it sure feels like war. This has been the case with Afghanistan since the major combat ended; after the fall of the Taliban regime, in between headline-grabbing operations like Anaconda and Tora Bora, the U.S. military, along with its coalition partners, settled into the task of stabilizing the new Afghan government and hunting down extremists who sought to either bring down the new regime or lash out at the West. This was the real dirty work, and much of it fell to SOF and Rangers forces. Every day has been a harrowing grind of security details, reconnaissance patrols, intelligence gathering, attempts to grab high-value persons, and a host of other duties, any one of which could, with very little notice, find a small team confronted with a very nasty situation beyond the scope of its organic firepower. For this reason, TACPs, both SOF and conventional, have continued as a mainstay with forces working in that theater. Most of the time the TACP is just another member of the team, which means he could be kicking down doors and clearing rooms, or helping the medic treat illnesses and injuries in a village. Sometimes, though, he gets called on to employ his primary training, and having that level of CAS control expertise on hand at a moment's notice can save the day.

One particularly intense example of TACPs unexpectedly coming in handy occurred near the town of Khowst as Operation Anaconda was winding down. S.Sgt. Brian Wilchenski had been a conventional TACP with the 20th ASOS before 11 September, and when they couldn't find enough SOF TACPs to meet the needs of the SOF ramp-up for Afghanistan, Wilchenski volunteered to go through the crash course to become an augmentee. Wilchenski was accepted, trained, and deployed to Afghanistan around mid-December 2001. He worked at TF Dagger headquarters for awhile, and finally joined a SOF team in early February.

While with this team he pretty much ran the gamut of SOF duties. Most of it was quite routine, even boring, but Wilchenski was looking back on it as one of the most rewarding experiences of his career. His tour was nearly over when, as often happens, he had his closest brush with death.

This was right around the third week in March at the tail end of Anaconda. We all went to sleep [on our] third or fourth night back in Khowst. . . . About midnight all of a sudden things start exploding. We had mortar rounds and automatic weapons fire coming in from four different directions. . . . As I'm heading out of the building, frickin' tracer rounds start bouncing off the wall right in front of me. . . . My body armor and helmet were already turned in and locked up 'cause I was going to leave in a couple of days. [Amazingly, this is standard practice—two or three days before troops redeploy home they turn in all their equipment, including protective gear, which then gets packed up and sent to the shipping terminal.]

As I get up on top of the roof . . . I hear a snap, snap. There's different sounds you hear when you're in battle. A zing is, you know, it's close, it could be a couple yards away. A snap is a near miss. You heard a round snap, what it's doing is breaking the sound barrier over your head and it's usually only a couple of inches away. A round snaps here and a round snaps there and I'm like, "Oh damn!" I got no helmet and no body armor on and I lay on my back, "Oh, this sucks!"

I get on the radio and I just happen to say, you know, it's like calling God, "Hey, is there anybody out there?" and all of a sudden an aircraft checks in and he says, "Yep I'm here." And it was just a big, "Phew, yeah!" He goes, "I'm a B-1B, and I got . . ." I'm like, "Oh man, let me guess, you got like twenty-seven Mk-82s and eighteen JDAMs." "Yep, that's what I got." I go, "Hold on, they're way too close to us. We're right in town and I really can't have you dropping bombs." . . . "What do you need from me?" he asks, and I go, "Listen, I need you to do a flyby. . . . I need you to come down as low as you possibly can. I need you to [kick in] your afterburners and pop flares," you know, so the people attacking us would know that we're certain to do business. "All right, I'll be in there in thirty seconds."

He comes down and he's just rocking the whole compound 'cause the B-1B hauls ass. . . . And he comes rolling in and frickin' all of a sudden kicks in afterburners right over my head. Wooooshhhhhhhh! You know, and the building shook and everybody's screaming, "Yeah! Wooo!" Everybody's pumped up. And as he's pulling up his afterburners are freakin' flashing the [compound]. He probably got down to five hundred feet, I mean, he got right down. He popped flares as he pulled off and everything got quiet—for about a minute. It didn't last very long.

"How was that?" he asked. "Fucking awesome! It was awesome! That did the job!" Everything's quiet for a couple seconds, then they started firing again. He's like, "All right, what can I do for you now?" "Listen, since you have direct [communication] with the AWACS, I need to know when the [AC-130] can get here. I need the gunship because these guys are in close. I got guys within two hundred meters right now shooting at us." He says, "All right, stand by. . . . He'll be here in fifteen minutes."

Then he asked, "Well what do you want me to do till they get here?" "I need you to do another flyby." He did another flyby just to keep their heads down till the gunship showed up. He did [a third] flyby and by that time, the gunship showed up.

I got on the radio with the commander . . . and I tell him, "I've got a gunship showing up . . . I need to know where you want the fires." . . . We had a prison just to the north of us and we were getting the majority of our fire from the prison. He says, "I want the northwest corner of that prison taken out." "All right, I'll have rounds down in about a minute. . . ." I called the gunship, "Listen, I need you to find our position. We're halfway up the airfield on the north side, in the compound." And he goes, "All right, I got your position. . . ." "All right, I'm going to sparkle [designate the target with the laser] the [prison] 150 meters away." He said, "Okay, I got your sparkle. . . ." "All right, good, now I need you to go to the northwest corner and tell me what you see." "Yeah, I got at least twenty guys in the corner, looks like they're shooting. What do you want me to do?" I go, "Stand by," and I get with the commander, "All right sir, I got twenty guys in the corner [of the prison] compound. I'm ready to lay fire, are you ready?" "Yep." "All right, tell everybody to get down," and I told [the gunship], "Fire for effect! You're cleared to fire!"

And all of a sudden they put down twenty-five rounds of 105, fifty rounds of 40-mm, and it was like fireworks! And all of a sudden the whole compound, the 101st [Airborne Division] guys, the SF guys, everybody was screaming, and I'm up on top of the roof, "Yeah! Hell, yeah!" We're all pumped up. I mean everything was just like lighting up in the corner of that compound. We had rocks and stuff hitting the front of our compound. And then things got quiet. Pretty much the attack stops. . . . The commander got on the radio and said, "Ski, that was an awesome job. You probably saved a lot of lives tonight."

Shortly after this episode Wilchenski went home.

Once the heavy combat phase ended the "normal" operations of Special Forces came more to the fore and have predominated since. This normal mode is just as much what puts the "special" in Special Forces as their combat tactics and equipment, for a key part of the SOF mission involves the teams' immersing themselves in the indigenous culture, community, and lifestyle wherever they operate. This approach is far better than just spreading around American dollars when it comes to gaining the trust of locals and achieving the desired results, thus it has been one of the most important factors in the success of Special Forces.

One of the most effective ways SOF teams win the trust and support of local populations is by providing meaningful and practical assistance of a nonmilitary sort. Usually within hours of a SOF team's arrival in a village they set up a clinic—sometimes in very makeshift circumstances—and start taking care of the local community's injuries and illnesses. These services can range from the routine—infections and dental care—to the traumatic. Quite often this latter extreme involves those caught in the cross fire of war. A good example of both sides of this SOF mission is provided by Staff Sergeant Brian Murray. Like Wilchenski, Murray is a conventional TACP who volunteered to augment the SOF TACP force. Hailing from Chicago and stationed with the 9th ASOS at Fort Hood, Texas, Murray began his first SOF rotation to Afghanistan in August 2002. Operating in eastern Afghanistan, near the Pakistan border, he took part in many patrols and more than a few intense confrontations, but one episode made a lasting impression upon him.

> The times that do stand out in my mind from there—I mean, there was nonstop training, I learned every job while I was there, I got to pull a tooth on a guy that was working for us, a local guy. I got to give him anesthesia, the medic on my team taught me how to do it, put staples in people, pulled staples out. . . .
>
> There was another time we lost an American 82nd [Airborne Division] guy . . . on a patrol. We rolled out in reaction to this. . . . I'm looking somewhat west, back toward the border. I see a large white plume of smoke and tapped the guy on the shoulder, "What the hell is that?" He's like, "That would be incoming." I was like, "Aw shit!" . . . Just south of us there's a couple of compounds where all these kids usually hang out and we throw candy to them and what not—well they're outside expecting candy . . . see the explosion right behind us, where those kids were. So throw the trucks in reverse, go over there, see a mom screaming, two kids laid out on the ground, giant black cloud on the ground. A couple guys from the team run over, scoop up the kids, throw them in the truck, grab the mom, throw her in the truck, tear ass to the fire base.
>
> We had a decent medical facility; you know, granted it's an old mud compound, but decent medical facility set up for stuff like this. We pulled into the medic hooch, giant pieces of steel hanging out the

back of [one boy's] skull, conscious, screaming, obviously not into the brain or anything, but into the skull. . . . No anesthetic at this point. Little kid, I would say maybe three years old, screaming. . . .

The medic pretty much just pries the metal out of the child's head. [The medic says to Murray], "Let me show you how to do a staple." So he staples the kid's head shut, we give the kid a sucker, kid just sits there happy as can be. We did the same thing to his sister . . . pull little pieces of shrapnel here and there out of the skull, out of the arm, bandage it up. Tell the mom, "Listen, here's the deal, we're going to come back in a week and check this." Mom's perfectly happy with it. And load up the kids drive them back to the compound.

Blending in with traditional Afghan life had its interesting side as well. One that surprised a lot of people, including folks back home, was how SOF forces accepted the reliance on horses that was part of life among most communities in Afghanistan. The sight of U.S. soldiers riding shaggy ponies on mountain trails put smiles on a lot of faces across America and became an enduring symbol of how that war melded the modern with the primitive. It further reinforced the image of the Special Forces as guys who could do just about anything.

Service with SOF units in Afghanistan exposed a blind spot in TACP training, even within the SOF TACP community. For decades the unspoken assumption had been that when TACPs rolled into war it would be with the conventional army where all they would be expected to provide for fire support was CAS. If things really got desperate they might have to use their M-4 or 9-mm pistol, so they trained with those weapons, but that was it. Afghanistan, however, saw TACPs dropped into an unconventional war with very little of the assumed conventional army support, and this exposed the lack of TACPs' weapons training—especially heavy weapons such as machine guns and mortars. A typical twelve-man SOF team has a great deal of firepower at its disposal, but with such a small force, any member might have to use any weapon, therefore everyone was expected to be highly trained in everything available. A lack of in-depth training in such weapons, as M.Sgt. John Knipe relates, could cause serious problems.

We had never been on a priority for heavy weapons training, mortars, and a lot of the other weapons systems that are basic soldier skills for [SOF] . . . [but working with SOF] we're expected to be able to get up on the M-240 or whatever weapons system that [was being operated by] whoever's shot or wounded and operate it. When bullets are flying is not the time to learn how to run the M-60. We could kill thousands

of people with all the latest equipment [related to] close air support, from lasers to beacons—we had quite a bit of training on that. But the focus was too much, I think, on that training and not enough on being a well-rounded [SOF team member] that has to work with the [Special Forces] on a full-time basis and has to do other things besides airstrikes. Because airstrikes can be sometimes only 10 percent of what's going on, where the other 90 percent is pulling security, or we're not going to have an airstrike for the next two weeks because we're on [patrol]. So there are other skills that you really need to have honed.

Knipe's concern underscores the main reality of life for Special Forces in Afghanistan—constant danger amid a wide variety of daily activities. Despite the Taliban's defeat, extremists loyal to either the Taliban or al Qaeda or both were still bent on bringing down the new Afghan government and doing as much harm to Americans as possible. The scope and frequency of these attacks certainly diminished with constant pressure on the enemy, but this increased the threat every American in Afghanistan faced. Compounds and safe houses provided some measure of security, but even they came under attack. More important, though, U.S. teams could not accomplish their mission by hunkering down in compounds—at some point they had to go out and confront the enemy. One didn't have to go looking for trouble either. One of the most dangerous activities in Afghanistan was simply driving down the road, which exposed troops to ambushes, hit-and-run attacks, and the IED, what earlier generations had called a booby trap.

These routine operations could quickly turn deadly. Up to this point in the narrative TACPs have been in some pretty tight scrapes, but luck was on their side and all escaped without serious injury. It was only a matter of time before that luck ran out. Like everything else they shared with their army colleagues, they shared the dangers of combat. For S.Sgt. Jake Frazier that happened on 27 March 2003. Frazier had joined the Illinois Air National Guard in 1998 as a TACP assigned to the 169th ASOS out of Peoria, but from the start he had his sights set on becoming not just an ETAC, but a SOF TACP. He achieved that goal, and in January 2003 headed for south-central Afghanistan with his SOF team. Their tour was filled with the usual assortment of patrols and direct action missions grabbing high value targets, but on 27 March Frazier and his team escorted a civil affairs team on a prearranged visit to the town of Sanjin. Americans had already built a new school and a clinic for the people of Sanjin, and now the team was following up by meeting with town elders and officials to strengthen what they thought were good relations.

M.Sgt. John Knipe rides one of the famous Afghan ponies. Knipe served in campaigns in Afghanistan and northern Iraq.

The team had reconnoitered the town and the road leading to it a couple times in advance and found it safe, so on the day of the visit they headed out in a five-vehicle convoy. After a luncheon and meetings with town leaders they wanted to head back, but at least one of the local delegation seemed to be stalling, trying to get the Americans to stay longer. Finally the team mounted up and headed out. Outside of town they drove into a well-laid trap. Officials later described it as one of the most professional ambushes they had seen—heavy weapons had been placed just right; the ambushers waited for all five vehicles to enter the kill box before opening up—and their planning paid off. The SOF team followed their training well and returned fire while attempting to speed out of the kill zone, but the last vehicle in the convoy couldn't escape and swerved off the road. The other four turned around and came back to help their teammates, but by this point the attackers were already melting away. Inside the vehicle all three occupants had been badly hit. In the backseat Frazier had been hit in the head, dying instantly, but not before he had begun calling for air support—they found him slumped over his radio. The team medevaced the two wounded SOF troops. One, Sgt. Orlando Morales, died on the way to the hospital. The third member recovered. S.Sgt. Jake Frazier became the first TACP killed in combat since the career field was officially established in April 1977. He also became the first Illinois Air National Guardsman killed in action.

A1C Raymond Losano met a similar fate on 25 April 2003. Losano, who hailed from Del Rio, Texas, was assigned to the 14th ASOS at Pope Air Force Base, North Carolina. Losano had been in the air force barely a year and a half, but as his supervisor back at Pope said, he didn't ask to go to Afghanistan, he begged to go. Having accompanied a group of army paratroopers from the 82nd Airborne into eastern Afghanistan, Losano and his team encountered a band of about twenty rebels close to the Pakistani border. A fight ensued, and Ray called in an airstrike that drove off the attackers, but not before sustaining fatal wounds himself. Losano had a wife and one daughter, with a second one on the way; he had just celebrated his twenty-fourth birthday a few days before he died.

Both Frazier and Losano were recognized in a number of ways for their heroism and sacrifice. Both men received posthumous Bronze Stars with Valor and Purple Hearts. Each was also uniquely recognized by their communities: the state of Illinois decorated Frazier with the Illinois Medal of Valor, its highest award, and the League of United Latin American Citizens renamed their Tucson, Arizona, chapter in honor of Losano. Perhaps the most touching honor, though, came from the TACP community itself. On 30 November 2004, a new tower, used by TACPs for controlling air on the range at the Joint Readiness Training Center, Fort Polk, Louisiana, was christened the Losano-Frazier Range Tower. As long as that tower stands, the airmen who use it will be reminded that like all the other Americans who died in the War on Terror, these two TACPs gave their lives that others could live free. They died true American heroes.

Part
TWO

Iraq

Kid, I hope you guys are good, because we damned sure don't
have enough artillery to do it by ourselves.

LT. GEN. WILLIAM S. WALLACE, V CORPS COMMANDER,
SPEAKING TO THE COMMANDER OF THE AIR FORCE'S
4TH AIR SUPPORT OPERATIONS GROUP

6. A Controversial Invasion in a Context of Controversy

From the beginning of the war in Afghanistan, even before the fall of the last Taliban strongholds, some in political and media circles had been advocating a decisive resolution to the lingering problem with Saddam Hussein, and the Bush administration wasted little time after bringing down the Taliban regime before turning its attention to Iraq. Fearing Hussein was developing "weapons of mass destruction" and that he was working in league with terrorist organizations, George Bush called for the nations of the world to join in a military campaign to oust the dictator. A chorus of critics opposed to an invasion, however, quickly emerged around the world and at home. One position called for more time for UN inspectors to complete their work of proving whether or not Hussein had chemical, biological, or nuclear weapons. Other critics opposed military force on any grounds whatsoever. While the diplomatic wrangling continued through the fall of 2002, Bush's anti-Hussein coalition, led primarily by the United States and Great Britain, began massing troops in the region. The diplomatic positions had not been reconciled by the time the invasion began, meaning that this war was going to be one of the most controversial military adventures since the Soviet Union invaded Afghanistan.

The diplomatic pedigree, however, was not the only controversial legacy shaping the context for this war. In military circles another controversy stemmed from Desert Storm, the earlier war against Iraq. To the public, one of the most enduring memories of that war had been the air campaign and the riveting images of laser-guided bombs hitting with unerring accuracy. The future of war seemed clear—paralyze the enemy through air power, then roll over the helpless ground forces. At least it seemed clear to the public; to military and government leaders, interpreting Desert Storm and the future of warfare became one of the chief controversies in the years leading up to the War on Terror. This controversy reached its peak in what Donald Rumsfeld considered his main agenda prior to 11 September: military transformation—the effort to reorganize America's defense establishment to take greater advantage of modern technology. This was more than a drive to get modern weapons into the hands of the military; it focused on how to use those weapons. The rapid decisiveness of Desert Storm suggested to some that modern warfare had been radically altered—what they called the revolution in military affairs, or RMA—and military reformers were determined to bring America's military structure, kicking and screaming if necessary, into that modern era. There was, of course, opposition.

Other observers argued that despite big changes in the details, the fundamental principles of war were the same, that its nature was timeless. Each side had powerful constituencies—not just the infamous military-industrial complex, or entrenched service interests, but something new that might be termed the think tank–bureaucracy complex, a cottage industry of scholars, policy analysts, consultants, government staffers—and of course lobbyists—who study in depth every aspect of government activity and advise politicians and decision-makers in their deliberations. This group has tremendous influence and thus constitutes a great shaping force not only on the military but also on all other government agencies. Hardly a governmental function at the federal, state, or local level is conducted without consulting or commissioning studies of some sort. The battles over military transformation launched countless analyses of the details, interpretations, and relative merits of the air campaign versus the ground campaign in Desert Storm, as well as various air and ground capabilities that had evolved since then. To a great extent this debate pitted the army, and to a lesser degree the Marine Corps, against the air force, and the debate was still in full swing as the last remnants of the Taliban were being chased around the mountains of Afghanistan.

The transformation debate evoked great passions and was at times extremely bitter. This fight entailed more than just the usual fighting over budgets and weapons systems; it threatened cherished notions of not only the fundamental nature of warfare but also the different services' cultures and notions of relative worth. As often happens during debates of this sort, each side presented a faulty analogy: they held up a perfect version of their own position and capabilities contrasted with a gross caricature of their opponents' position and capabilities. Character was also brought into the fight as each side's most strident partisans presented their side as the paragon of virtue and the other as the embodiment of evil.

Neither side's vision of itself or its opponent bore a perfect semblance to reality, and this was especially true with the lessons each side took away from "the air campaign" of Desert Storm. While traditionalists denied there even was an "air campaign," what both sides focused on was that phase of Desert Storm preceding the ground phase when coalition air power pounded Iraq and its army. There were two main efforts in this phase. One involved striking fixed targets such as communications centers, command headquarters, air defense installations, and other key parts of Iraq's infrastructure in an attempt to destroy its air defenses and paralyze its military's ability to fight effectively. The second effort strove to weaken the enemy's ground forces by attrition—bombing troop positions, finding and killing tanks and artillery, and hitting logistics assets and supply dumps. Those who adhered to the notion that the air phase presaged a new era in warfare pointed to the stunning collapse of the Iraqi army in the early hours of the ground phase. Thousands of Iraqi soldiers, cut off from supplies and heartily sick of the aerial pounding, surrendered en masse. Iraqi army units, cut off from headquarters and each other, either made pathetic attempts to fight isolated battles against the coalition juggernaut or melted away as troops abandoned their equipment and positions. To reformers, this was evidence of paralysis on such a massive scale as to make an enemy incapable of fighting in any real or effective sense, and their drive to transform the military was an effort to reorient America's military structure to exploit this capability.

At its heart, though, this vision looked awfully similar to America's World War II strategic bombing theory. Back then, air power theorists believed a bombing campaign aimed at the most crucial elements of an enemy's war-sustaining infrastructure would not only collapse that infrastructure but also render the enemy unable to wage war or even defend itself. You wouldn't even need to take on the enemy's ground forces, this theory's advocates often claimed. The theory became the blueprint for America's strategic bombing campaign against both Germany and Japan. But the realities of World War II quickly scaled back the expectations of all but the most ardent air power theorists, and while the bombing campaign contributed greatly to victory against both adversaries, it still took a lot of hard fighting and dying on the ground to drive that victory home.

Still, the dream did not die. After the war, air power theorists continued to speculate that if they had varied the approach in one way or another it would have worked according to the prewar vision. So close was the similarity between World War II and post–Desert Storm air power theorists that some claimed after Desert Storm that precision weapons had finally made the early dream a reality. The World War II bombing campaign failed to achieve its potential, these observers claimed, because B-17s dropping "dumb bombs" weren't accurate enough to get the kind of results predicted in theory. Now, with stealth bombers and "smart bombs," paralysis through bombing could be achieved. The affinity between old and new can also be seen in the fact that modern air campaign theory emphasized heavily, if not exclusively, achieving its effects through hitting fixed targets and vital infrastructure rather than taking on the enemy's ground forces—what some contemptuously referred to as "tank plinking."

On the other side of the debate, traditionalists minimized or dismissed outright the contributions of the Desert Storm air campaign and claimed the ground phase had been a perfect example of what armored warfare could accomplish if you combined good doctrine, training, and weapons with an enlightened war plan. Their favored term for Desert Storm, "the Hundred-Hour War" in reference to the roughly four-day ground phase, is particularly revealing of their attitude toward the air campaign: what had preceded the ground combat in Desert Storm was so irrelevant as to not even be considered warfare, or at least not part of the *real* war. The heart of the traditionalist vision was that warfare, despite superficial changes in weapons and technology, was still fundamentally the same, that it was still focused on closing with the enemy and, as Clausewitz had phrased it, "making him do our will." The mantra of this position became "boots on the ground," and through the many military confrontations following Desert Storm a steady chorus maintained that nothing decisive could be achieved until we got "boots on the ground." But right behind the core conviction that the nature of war was timeless and unchanging was the unspoken belief that the highest art of war had been achieved in that recent manifestation: heavy armored warfare.

Not all ground power advocates fell into the traditionalist camp, and an intense debate broke out within the ground power camp itself as reformers argued that even though ground combat was still crucial, it needed to radically transform if it wanted to remain relevant. The Marine Corps spearheaded one part of that debate and focused on urban warfare. Within the army, young turks argued that the days of heavy tank armies slugging it out were over and that the army had to get lighter, leaner, and more lethal if it wanted to be a major player in the future. A key proponent of this school was army colonel Douglas A. Macgregor, whose 1997 book *Breaking the Phalanx* won him a large following within the army and made him a leading voice in the transformation movement. The man, the book, and the movement, though, shocked traditionalists and engendered not only stiff resistance but also bitterness within army ranks.

This battle for the heart and soul of America's future military was conducted in the shadow of the military conflicts of the nineties, which largely centered on containing Iraq and dealing with the consequences of Yugoslavia's disintegration, and things weren't looking good for traditionalists. Maintaining constant pressure on Hussein with Operations Northern Watch and Southern Watch involved almost entirely air forces, and even such periodic escalations as Desert Fox in 1998 were almost exclusively air shows. Similarly, America's involvement in the Balkans left conventional ground forces sitting on the bench. This became particularly controversial with Operation Allied Force—the 1999 campaign to halt Serbian oppression of its Muslim population in the Kosovo province. President Clinton's flat refusal to introduce ground troops brought howls of outrage from traditionalists and actually seemed to be a rallying cry for that community: air power advocates were claiming air power had just won its first war, and ground proponents needed to counter a growing sense that they had become irrelevant. Some even went so far as to claim that what had really brought Milosevic to terms was not air power but Clinton's softening on his earlier position by hinting that he *might* introduce ground troops.

You may be wondering why delving into this sordid story is relevant to this narrative. There are two reasons. First, twelve years of acrimonious debate had, by the eve of the invasion of Iraq, bitterly divided America's air and ground services, yet paradoxically it had also resulted in an uneasy truce through a strange doctrinal amalgamation of both air and ground visions. The standard blueprint for theater-level warfare saw coequal land, sea, and air component commanders working under one overall commander. Each component commander integrated his sphere into the overall joint effort, and in many ways they complemented each other nicely. In very real and practical terms, however, a hypothetical war would see two very distinct and independent simultaneous efforts: the air campaign and the ground campaign. In the seams between these two parallel wars, where air and ground forces had to work together, existed a twilight zone that produced enough conflicting expectations and duplicated effort to create inevitable headaches and mutual recrimination in every planning session or war-gaming exercise.

Just one example of this parallel war can be seen in the line that effectively divides the two main spheres of the battlefield—the fire support coordination line. Essentially the FSCL divides the battlefield in respect to how fire support, particularly air power, must be coordinated. The area short of the FSCL is controlled by the ground commander, and any airstrike in that region must be closely controlled and approved by the ground commander responsible for the piece of ground where the airstrike will hit. Beyond the FSCL the air component commander could strike without coordination—in fact, everyone else had to coordinate with him if they wished to do anything in that area. Many people realized there were a number of problems with this FSCL arrangement, but if you ever wanted to start a real hair-pulling, eye-gouging fight in an army–air force meeting, just suggest changing it.

The other reason the post–Desert Storm debate is important is that it set the stage for one of the most fateful decisions of the war. Secretary of Defense Donald Rumsfeld was a devotee of military transformation, and he had come into office seeing it as his number one priority. Even after 11 September he remained committed to transforming the military in the midst of fighting the War on Terror. One significant influence on his thinking was a book published in 1996 called *Shock and Awe: Achieving Rapid Dominance* written by Harlan K. Ullman and James P. Wade. Good examples of the think tank–bureaucracy complex, the authors, military and policy analysts long involved in the public sector, were not only pitching a new operational concept but also offering their services as advisers in its exploration and implementation. By 1997 they had briefed then Secretary of Defense William Cohen, and with his backing, the concept known as rapid dominance began to worm its way into a number of military reviews and studies until it reached DoD's powerful Office of Net Assessment office, where in 1999 it was designated for further study as a roadmap for U.S. military transformation. *Shock and Awe* helped shape Rumsfeld's thinking, particularly its theme that by harnessing new technological capabilities the American military could exert much greater combat power with far fewer forces. This plus such army reform thinkers as Col. Douglas Macgregor convinced Rumsfeld that the planned invasion of Iraq could be done with a fraction of the number of ground troops traditionally called for, but only if they made a lightning dash on the Iraqi nerve center: Baghdad. Thus the invasion was going to be a desperate gamble resting on whether transformational capability would work according to theory.[1]

Ironically, all the theorizing and debate about transformation had missed a critical third aspect of Desert Storm—the dramatically increased effectiveness of the air-ground team. In the wake of Vietnam, the

---

1. The exact role of *Shock and Awe* in the invasion plan has become mired in controversy. Key figures minimize its influence, but Michael R. Gordon and Bernard E. Trainor, in their book *Cobra II: The Inside Story of the Invasion and Occupation of Iraq,* published by Pantheon, have traced its influence in convincing fashion.

air force started taking its CAS responsibilities more seriously. Doctrinal issues were hammered out, organizational and structural changes were made and maintained, and most important, aircraft, such as the A-10 and the AC-130, and weapons had been developed or adapted to bring tremendous capability to the air support arena. By the eve of Desert Storm the air force CAS community was in a position to render great service, and render great service it did. That service went largely unnoticed by both sides of the military transformation debate, though, and the reasons for that oversight reflect another aspect of what truly separated the two sides of the military transformation debate.

For the air force's part, even though it finally got serious about CAS, its heart was obviously elsewhere. Most of its leaders were fighter pilots whose thinking was still wedded to air superiority and "the cult of the fighter ace," where the only true measure of a man was in shooting down other airplanes. Any air leaders or thinkers who might be concerned with the theory and practice of other modes of air power were mostly enamored with the modern version of strategic bombing that got so much attention in the Desert Storm air campaign. To most air power leaders and thinkers, focusing air power against ground forces was still considered inefficient. This can be seen in some very real practical ways. The CAS role was considered secondary, or lower, in training priorities—and of course, funding—so aircrews got less training in CAS. In the intangible but very real pilot pecking order, those who flew air-to-ground aircraft like the A-10 and the F-15E were not considered full members of the "fighter pilot fraternity"—in fact, they were at times even relegated to the same status as bomber pilots. On the ground, ROMADs as a career field were largely unknown to the corporate air force, and among most fliers, an ALO tour was considered time in purgatory and was to be avoided like the plague. ALO jobs were afforded little respect; one didn't even have to be on the all-important "squadron commanders list"—the board-selected list of officers approved to command "real" squadrons—to be given command of an air support operations squadron.

Even those in the ground power camp denigrated air power's effectiveness against Iraqi ground forces, perhaps because any emphasis on CAS effectiveness in Desert Storm would detract from their claims and give that much more credit to air power. Several ground commanders claimed they saw almost no tanks killed by aircraft as they sped across the battlefield. Even though the army claimed it embraced CAS after Desert Storm, it was not seriously exploring its capabilities or how best to exploit them. The best example of this attitude is seen in how CAS was effectively barred from participating at all but token levels in the army's premier training done at the National Training Center at Fort Irwin, California, and at the Joint Readiness Training Center at Fort Polk, Louisiana. CAS was limited to only a few sorties on limited days, and even that small involvement was scored at ridiculously low BDA levels. The level of air-ground interaction and the impact air could have in ground operations didn't even remotely match experience from Desert Storm, so clearly no new direction in air-ground operation was going to emerge from this venue. An entire generation of army officers could have been working with their air force colleagues hammering out a concept of operation that fully exploited and integrated the capabilities of each component, but instead they were taught that air power's contribution was negligible and could be overlooked or excluded with impunity.

One problem that emerged early in the Iraq invasion speaks eloquently to how both the air force and the army really weren't paying attention to how TACPs operate. When they rode into combat, TACPs had two options: those assigned to mechanized units were to use the M-113, or "track" as it is often called, while all other TACPs used Humvees. The M-113 is an obsolete APC from the Vietnam era. It is much slower, and has less armor and firepower than a Bradley, but since Bradleys had never been modified for the TACP radio set, assigning Bradleys to TACPs was out of the question. Because the lead army units invading Iraq were armored, most TACPs supporting them used M-113s. The M-113s, however, couldn't keep up with tanks and Bradleys, thus TACPs and the army commanders they supported were forced into a cruel dilemma: either provide some protection for TACPs in their APCs, which would lag behind while the armored elements raced ahead, or have the TACPs ride in the vulnerable Hummers alongside the tanks and Bradleys. A few had their TACPs hitch a ride in army Bradleys jerry-rigged to accommodate their radios. The first two options are self-critiquing, and the third isn't much better—either the TACP rode inside the Bradley where he could not see to control air, or he displaced one of the Bradley's crewmembers so he could see outside.

A small group in the air power community did study CAS in Desert Storm and they made some dramatic discoveries. For example, during the air phase a little-known engagement occurred in and around the Saudi border town of Al Khafji. JSTARS, an aircraft that can detect vehicles on the ground the way AWACS detects aircraft in the air, noticed a division-size Iraqi armored force launching an offensive. The date was 29 January;

the air campaign was in full swing, and coalition ground forces were in the midst of their massive redeployment that would set the stage for the famous Hail Mary invasion plan, so only limited air and ground assets could be diverted without upsetting the grand scheme. Still, using what little could be spared from the air campaign, a small team of marines in Al Khafji called in CAS while JSTARS coordinated an air interdiction campaign against Iraqi units outside the town. Together these two efforts were more than enough to halt this assault. This episode could have been studied in depth and might have served as the nucleus for a much more integrated, and effective, air-ground approach, but with the real interest in the air power community focused on the dream of winning through bomb-induced paralysis, the notion of focusing air power on defeating the enemy's ground forces was heresy. Similarly, any effort to share these insights with the army was greeted with suspicion. The army's reaction to JSTARS, for example, focused more on emphasizing how an enemy would find ways to negate its effectiveness rather than exploring ways to incorporate its capabilities. There would be no new operational concept emerging from either side of the air-ground team aimed at exploiting this capability. At best, the air force stood ready to support business as usual and whatever would keep the army happy, while the army was determined to prove it could win without the air force.

The experience in Afghanistan was too great to ignore, however, so rather than asking *if* it impacted the military transformation debate, the more appropriate question is *how?* Conceivably, both the army and the air force could claim that since it had been primarily a SOF-CAS war any larger lessons were nonapplicable outside that context—that Afghanistan had been an "anomaly." Fortunately, and to their credit, neither service did that completely, and to a large extent both services set to work trying to mine lessons from the war. Lt. Col. George Bochain, who had been the principal architect of the air portion of the SOF-CAS approach, was kept busy for months after his return hopping around the United States briefing various Department of Defense leaders on his observations and insights; he was even kept at the Pentagon for weeks working with a focus group—what in Pentagon jargon is called a Tiger Team—tasked specifically with learning CAS lessons from Afghanistan. In a development that speaks volumes, the air force community suddenly discovered TACPs. Airmen throughout the air force were shocked to discover that members of their own service lived, worked, and fought alongside the army, and suddenly they were getting showered with medals and awards; for example, Technical Sergeant Vance not only won the Silver Star for his role at Roberts Ridge but also was named Pope Air Force Base, 9th Air Force, and Air Combat Command noncommissioned officer of the year, and was recognized as one of the air force's twelve outstanding airmen for 2002. He was even invited to be a military guest at the president's State of the Union Address in 2003.

The army too looked like it was ready to explore CAS capability seriously. For one thing, it started taking steps to finally integrate CAS realistically into Joint Readiness Training Center and National Training Center exercises. More significantly, it began exploring a new force structure concept that shifts assets away from "organic firepower"—firepower owned by the army, particularly artillery—because army leaders felt they could rely on CAS.

Fundamentally, though, the lessons of Afghanistan did not alter the old air vision versus ground vision debate. In the September–October 2002 edition of *Field Artillery* magazine, published six months after Anaconda and as the invasion of Iraq was being planned, General Hagenbeck spoke about his observations on the operation he had commanded. Those observations bear the unmistakable stamp of the old partisan debates that had characterized the twelve-year running skirmish between air power and ground power advocates: everything army worked great, but "our air force friends" let the army down when they were under fire. Considering the many planning irregularities in the days leading up to Anaconda that had led to serious miscues during the battle, not to mention his own decision not to bring his TACP personnel when he deployed to Afghanistan, it is curious that Hagenbeck would single out the air force for blame, but the most damaging attacks actually came through official military channels. Hagenbeck's public attacks were mirrored by formal complaints that set off a wave of criticism throughout the army. Perhaps Hagenbeck's critique was a public relations ploy to deflect attention from the many other and more serious problems involving Anaconda, but the way many within the army "piled on" with these charges suggests it could also have been an attempt to deflate some of the credit air power had gained in the SOF-CAS campaign that had so stunningly defeated the Taliban. In the months leading up to the Iraq invasion, concern within army ranks about "air power's failures in Anaconda" threatened to derail army–air force cooperation in one particularly key unit. Would that concern prove fatal to tapping the potential proved in other Afghan operations or would those who saw this potential be able to win over the doubters?

Planning for the Invasion

The stage was set for what could have been more than just a showdown with Iraq. It might have turned into a showdown between the visions of air power and ground power that advocates in each camp had so long sought. The invasion was going to be the biggest U.S. military operation since Desert Storm, and in a very real sense, it was going to be the army's first chance to fully show its capabilities since that war. After sitting out so many air-only operations and after years of acrimonious debate over the right direction for America's military structure, a lot was riding on the army at this point. Many within the ground power community wanted to see the army prove that it could win without relying on air power. Moreover, as events would prove, shock and awe was long on propaganda but short on reality. The promise of a small ground force surgically slicing through a paralyzed enemy all the way to Baghdad turned out to be a mirage; the invasion might have ended up an epic disaster caught live on camera by hundreds of embedded reporters suddenly stuck in the middle of a colossal Custer's Last Stand redux. And what of the air force side? What if shock and awe meant an air force resurgence in emphasizing fixed targets? Iraq had a lot more vital infrastructure than Afghanistan, which would certainly tempt the strategic bombing advocates, and media reports on the eve of the invasion indicated that this was going to be the main air effort. Was the air force's sudden attention to CAS in the wake of Afghanistan nothing more than slapping on a quick coat of "CAS paint" for public relations purposes? Were air force leaders, convinced that Afghanistan had been an aberration, looking forward to Iraq being business as usual?

Disaster was a very real possibility. All the commentators who criticized the invasion plan for having too few ground troops had a very real point—invading a country the size of Iraq with only a two-division front in any other time or place would have been madness. Moreover, if the air force had resumed its old mantra of victory through bombing fixed targets, or if the division commander running the army's portion of the invasion had kept his airmen at arm's length—as many army commanders often did—then the full potential of the air-ground team would have been seriously stunted, and the two-division gamble might have turned out much differently. Fortunately, this is not what happened.

From the beginning, two key factors helped shape one of the best working air-ground relationships in modern warfare. On the army side, the most important factor was a rare example of the right person in the right place at the right time. Army commanders have a disproportionate impact on shaping the air-ground team and determining its success or failure. Other variable are important too, but even the most dedicated airmen or generous CAS allocation cannot overcome a commander who won't bring his airmen onto his team or into his planning process, or who is openly contemptuous and distrustful of air power. Given the invasion plan for Iraq—one army division as the main effort on the west side of the Euphrates River and one marine division on the east side of the Tigris River in support—the army's air-ground team was going to be, to a great measure, shaped by one man: Maj. Gen. Buford C. Blount III, commander of the 3rd Infantry Division, the spearhead of the army's effort. Blount won universal praise from his airmen. Lt. Col. Byron Risner, commander of the 15th Air Support Operations Squadron and Blount's head airman, says of him, "From the day he hit the ground he was air force friendly. You can tell within about five minutes whether a guy is going to be air force friendly or not. It's just that simple, and General Blount was just fantastic. If you dreamed of a guy [who would work with the air force] he was picture perfect. I think a lot of it goes back [to family]—his dad was an air force colonel, so he grew up in an air force family. He understood what air power meant to his push to Baghdad. If they were going to go quick he knew that air power was going to play a big role in his success."

Risner's comments were echoed by his deputy, Lt. Col. Mark Bronakowski: "These are quotes from the Division Commander to all the brigade commanders during the rehearsals and during the planning stage: 'Here's how we're going to fight this war: we're going to kill everything with air power and then we're going to just roll over the top of them. So the first killing mechanism out there for everybody is you don't roll forward, not one person goes forward, until we kill it with air power.'"

Initially, relations between Risner and the other 3rd ID officers were not so smooth. According to Colonel Bochain, there had been trouble brewing at Fort Stewart, stemming from General Hagenbeck's accusations about air support during Anaconda. Because Bochain was the commander of the squadron tasked to support 10th Mountain Division, and thus the boss of Major Donnelly and the other airmen whom Hagenbeck felt had let him down, he had often been called upon to answer Hagenbeck's charges. But because the stakes were so high, Risner turned to him for help. Risner needed to counter the damage caused by Hagenbeck's partisan attacks and rebuild the trust between the army and its airmen, otherwise it could have meant a serious breach in the air-ground team on the eve of the 3rd ID leading the charge into Iraq. As Bochain relates, Risner asked him for his side of the story:

> Before 3rd ID was sent over to Iraq the hubbub with the General Hagenbeck saga was ongoing and the guys out at 3rd ID were buying the General Hagenbeck story initially. Byron Risner called me up and he said, "Hey Shack, every time I go to a staff meeting here I'm hearing this thing about how CAS was not effective in Anaconda, which was wrong to begin with, but can you give me something that I can go to the CG [commanding general, i.e., Blount] with here to tell him the other side of the story?" So I typed up a response to Byron to say, "Hey, Byron, this is our perspective on how things went down in Anaconda." He brought that to the CG and the chief of staff and the ADCO [assistant division commander for operations] and said, "Here's the other side of the story."

Bochain's explanation to Risner got back to Hagenbeck, who was still commanding 10th Mountain and thus still working closely with Bochain, and what ensued provides an interesting postscript to the whole episode:

> When I sent that email to Byron I thought it was going to be between Byron and myself. Byron takes that email and he shotguns it out to the staff of the 3rd ID and the next thing I know I get a phone call from General Hagenbeck's office—he wants to have a meeting with me. So I go down there to see General Hagenbeck. This takes a couple of days. I went and saw him and he says, "Colonel Bochain I saw what your response was to this ongoing story and when I first read your email I was surprised." So [he] sent it out to other people within his staff from Anaconda, most notably . . . [his] chief of staff. He reviewed my email, sent it back to General Hagenbeck, and said, "This is factually correct." So General Hagenbeck said, "I had no idea that this was what was going on behind the scenes."[2]

---

2. In the written questions I submitted to General Hagenbeck, I asked if he could confirm and expound on Colonel Bochain's account of these events. As with his other responses, General Hagenbeck's comment did not answer my question, and he neither confirmed nor denied Bochain's claims. Nor does General Hagenbeck's response offer an alternate version. His entire answer was as follows: "The successes of, and lessons learned from, Operation Anaconda helped the army, and the joint U.S. military team perform even more magnificently in Operation Iraqi Freedom, and I am certain we will continue to become more effective, more lethal, and more joint."

With Risner conveying Bochain's "rest of the story," Blount made the decisive move of backing Risner in front of his staff and thereby demonstrating his willingness to work together and to iron out differences in the wake of Afghanistan. As Risner relates:

> [Blount] basically came up to me and said, "Listen, I want you to brief the entire staff on lessons learned from Anaconda so we don't repeat those same mistakes," which I thought was a large step forward for the army to come and ask me to do that. I think they realized things didn't go right, and it was primarily an army shortfall that basically didn't include the air force in planning. So I think you're seeing leadership in the army from the two-star level. . . . I [briefed the staff] and it was amazing how many folks really did not know the truth; a lot of myth passed around—"the air force is this," "the air force is that." But I basically took pieces of what Hagenbeck put in his article and countered them with the truth.

Blount's example set the tone throughout the division. Again, in Risner's words: "[Blount's attitude] trickled down to the brigade commanders . . . right on down to the battalion. . . . The thing I was more afraid of was [the attitude], 'Hey, I'm going to be a hero, I'm going to take my tanks in there and I'm going to shoot it out with these guys versus using my airplanes.' And that never happened. They were, trust me, to the man, they would much rather be rolling over hulks of tanks and maybe picking off one or two we didn't get rather than duking it out à la NTC and not using the air—you know, a glory hound. . . . But there was not a man that I could think of that was of that mind-set."

Other commanders picked up on Blount's attitude, or they shared it themselves. One commander, Lt. Col. Eric Schwartz of 1–64 Armor Battalion, won one of the highest compliments any officer can receive when a TACP attached to his outfit—S.Sgt. Jon Pinson—said of him: "He impressed me probably more than any officer I ever met in my career. . . . He trusted his guys a lot more than most battalion commanders. And because he did that, because he treated them right, he treated them more like men than most battalion commanders I have seen treat their battle captains and company commanders, they acted that way. I was thoroughly impressed."

Lt. Col. Terry Ferrell, commander of Third Squadron, Seventh Cavalry Regiment, also came in for praise from one of his TACPs, T.Sgt. Mike Keehan of the 20th ASOS: "Lt. Col. Terry Ferrell was an excellent commander; knew exactly what we did walking in the door. [I] didn't have to worry about anything. He was probably one of the best commanders I've ever worked for. In talking with him . . . I told the whole staff if every army unit was like this more of us TACP guys would reenlist. All the guys wanted to stay and work for him, do anything for him, 'cause he respected us, knew exactly what we did, and always had time to talk with us. He trusted me to do everything where some other army commanders blow you off and then you don't want to work for them. But he knew what he was doing, so it was an excellent time." This attitude throughout 3rd ID allowed airmen to work as key members of the team. As Risner says, "Starting at the beginning [of planning for the invasion] we were always included, so that was never an issue, and they knew air power was going to be a big player in this—the big thing is we were included, and a very, very big player in the planning."

It turns out the air force, too, was serious about its efforts to capitalize on CAS lessons learned in Afghanistan. From the top, air force chief of staff John Jumper was setting the tone. His service was going to focus even greater energy and resources on CAS, including addressing many shortcomings that had turned up in Afghanistan; he also made it very clear he wanted this effort to go forward in close coordination with the army. With this sort of leadership from the top setting priorities, a lot of critical details fell into place—new operational concepts for employing air power against ground forces emerged just in time to make a real difference in Iraq, CAS expertise was integrated into critical command and control centers, and CAS allocation levels during the invasion were set so high that CAS was characterized by many as "always available" regardless of battle tempo.

One result of the air force setting a new priority on CAS was a decision to fix one of the most glaring weaknesses turned up by operations in Afghanistan. The lack of CAS expertise in the air operations center was as incomprehensible as it was dangerous, and the air force took steps to change that for Iraq. Risner describes the scope of those steps: "They learned since Anaconda that they need to have a cell in the AOC that was dedicated to close air support and would handle our needs [manned by] people who were smart in [CAS]—you know, not an F-15 guy who doesn't know what CAS means half the time. They had a dedicated cell—a joint cell—army, navy, marines, and air force guys. . . . They were a conduit into the AOC if you had any problems. . . . They were a great help and it was something [air force leadership] saw that needed to be done."

Probably the most important practical result of the air force's revamped attitude toward CAS was the development of three new operational concepts on the eve of the Iraq invasion. Each would contribute to

*Lt. Col. Byron H. Risner sits outside one of Saddam's palaces. Risner commanded
all TACPs attached to 3rd ID and thus played a critical role in planning and
executing the division's operations.*

the success of air power against ground forces in the upcoming conflict—
and each came from a different part of the air power community. New
ideas had been bounced around the air force before, but with the old attitude toward air-ground issues being at best cool, and often hostile, those
ideas invariably went nowhere. Now, however, innovative concepts were
getting a fair hearing and good ones were being adopted.

   One such idea actually came from the CAS cell within the AOC. This
new group bore fruit before the war even started when it came up with a
new tool for coordinating CAS between air and ground forces. The concept, known as KICAS CONOPS (pronounced "kick-ass con-ops"), addressed one of the biggest doctrinal problems stemming from the FSCL
issue. When operating short of this line, air commanders had to coordinate strikes with ground commanders, and on the far side, ground commanders had to coordinate their movements with the air component
commander. Naturally each side wanted as much freedom as possible.
And for each, coordinating movements with the other was time consum-
ing and interfered with smooth operations or quick exploitation of fast-
developing opportunities, so each side wanted the FSCL placed where

it would give them the best advantage. One practical problem, though, was that any territory on the army side not within range of army weapons could become a sanctuary for the enemy because airstrikes could not take place in that area without close coordination, but the army would still want those enemy forces dealt with by air power because it was the only weapon available. Various efforts in the past to deal with this problem had failed because no solution was flexible and responsive enough to meet the needs and concerns of both sides. KICAS CONOPS met everyone's concerns and worked smoothly. It would also prove to be very effective.

With this plan, the entire combat area was divided into thirty-mile by thirty-mile squares, creating a basic grid, with each square numbered by rank and file. Each square was further subdivided into nine ten-mile by ten-mile squares. Since these nine subsquares looked like a telephone keypad, they were numbered accordingly and each was known as a pad. Each thirty-by-thirty square or ten-by-ten pad on the army side of the FSCL could be opened by the army as a kill box if no troops were in it. When a pad was opened, air could then go into that kill box and strike any enemy forces it found. When ground commanders wanted to move troops into that area, shutting off the uncontrolled airstrikes was simply a matter of closing the kill box. Airstrikes could still be conducted, but they would have to be controlled as CAS under the standard CAS control rules. Opening and closing these kill boxes was quick and easy, thanks in large part to the CAS cell in the AOC. Risner gives his perspective on the effectiveness of this approach: "We knew this was going to be a very quick moving fight, so the kill box concept just facilitated that, by opening and closing and moving quickly. . . . It was really good for the army guys 'cause now they could open and close those boxes. . . . It was a heck of a lot better than the phase lines and the FSCL. [The FSCL] was still there, but the concept of using the kill boxes and the keypads was just so much simpler and so much easier for everyone in the air and on the ground to understand."

Another new concept was a more effective way for aircraft to find ground forces and direct airstrikes against them. New sensor technology has dramatically improved the ability to locate enemy ground units and hardware, but those systems have limitations and can be fooled. So when sensor systems like JSTARS or Predator find suspicious items, they still need to be positively identified as hostile before they can be attacked. This problem had been recognized before Afghanistan, but the distinctive nature of that war accentuated the need, and a new approach for hunting down ground forces by air emerged: strike coordination and re-connaissance.

In this approach a long loiter aircraft with good air-to-ground capability and the latest sensors, such as an F-15E or an F-14, was sent out to a suspected area to look for enemy forces. This SCAR aircraft either used its own sensors to locate enemy ground forces or was directed to them by another sensor aircraft such as a JSTARS—often both methods were used—and then once the enemy was located and positively identified, the SCAR aircraft could attack using its own weapons and direct other aircraft to attack as well. SCAR aircraft had not only advanced sensors that aided in finding and identifying enemy ground forces but also sophisticated communication equipment that allowed them to send target information digitally to other aircraft similarly equipped, thus cutting down on potential for error and dramatically speeding up getting multiple aircraft moving in for the kill. On top of that, the crew members of these designated SCAR aircraft were specially trained in searching for ground forces, how to evaluate situations for both tactical considerations and ROE restrictions, and how to direct other aircraft to these targets. So, the few aircraft with the most sophisticated search equipment would do the looking, send information directly to other aircrafts' computers, and then orchestrate the attack.

A good illustration of just how SCAR worked in combat and how effective it could be comes from an anonymous practitioner who describes a mission over Iraq during the invasion:

> We were scheduled for a SCAR mission on the outskirts of Baghdad during the first week when the 3rd ID stopped to let logistics catch up. Our job was to pummel the Republican Guard divisions defending the city and talk-on other formations once we ran out of bombs. Off the [air refueling] tanker, AWACS passes us to the JSTARS—we are not even to our assigned area yet. They [identify a possible target area] and say, "Investigate . . . suspect tanks." We are long of the FSCL and cleared to [identify, evaluate, and engage] our own targets. What we found looked no kidding like the Henderson, Nevada, Auto Mall: about one hundred self-propelled 2S3s [152-mm self-propelled artillery]. They are all revetted in the burbs of the big city—the mother lode. [We] unload nineteen GBU-12s between the [two aircraft in the formation] in about ten minutes . . . and then start talking in other formations and passing designation on the [data link]. We have enough gas to get four other fighter formations through the target area, and give good coordinates off of the LITENING [targeting] pod and [watch] about [sixty targets]

get destroyed. It was very cool. From the [JSTARS contact] until initial impact was about six minutes; one hour for the whole ordeal. . . . The big thing was that [the CAOC] was quiet the whole time and let us work the fight and formations after the initial tasking. We ran the show and just kept asking them to send more guys with more bombs.

SCAR borrowed on older ideas, particularly the A-FAC and killer scout approaches, but new elements, such as sensors and data links, were added, and procedures to streamline and standardize the whole approach were rushed into operation in the wake of experiences in Afghanistan. As one longtime practitioner said on the eve of the Iraq invasion, more had been done in the previous year than in all his prior experience. SCAR also dovetailed with and helped maximize the effectiveness of KICAS CONOPS. If a killbox was open, it meant there were no ground troops to find enemies and pass on their location to aircraft, so any aircraft operating in killboxes would have to find the enemy on their own, just as if they were operating far beyond the FSCL. SCAR made that search more effective.

KICAS and SCAR were great innovations that facilitated the use of air power against enemy ground forces, but something was still missing. Both operational modes were decentralized; that is, the aircraft involved were more or less on their own to scour the countryside looking for needles in the haystack. This isn't quite as bad as it sounds, for they enjoyed several advantages. First, aircraft have been hunting ground forces in similar manner since the dawn of aerial combat, and the tactic has a long history of success. For example, P-47s and P-51s roaming the French countryside in 1944 were effective enough to make it difficult for the German army to move forces during daylight and in good weather. Further, modern aircraft have advantages earlier aircraft lacked—sophisticated onboard sensors and precision weapons—that make finding and killing ground targets easier. Also these aircraft weren't sent out totally in the blind—some were following leads from such sources as JSTARS, and others were talking to airmen on the ground who could help guide them to targets. Still, as good as these operations were, they were a long way from a centrally coordinated effort that could focus on specific goals and be integrated into the ground scheme of maneuver. Two essential pieces were missing from the picture. One was a way to tap into the flood of information pouring into the many independent and insulated intelligence agencies while that intelligence was still fresh enough for aircraft to act upon. The other was a concept of operating that melded technical capabilities with critical functions such as coordination and command decision-making, and ensured that legal and ROE restrictions were met. What was needed was a way to do what the above SCAR example did, but on a theater-wide scale. Such a concept could potentially magnify effectiveness dramatically. The potential for such a concept had existed for years, but one never seemed to materialize; finally the pieces fell into place, and that part of the story came from an unlikely corner on the eve of battle.

Here the scene shifts to V Corps headquarters in Heidelberg, Germany, and to the 4th ASOG that supports it. In October 2002, only five months before the invasion kicked off, a new ALO, Lt. Col. Mike McGee, reported to 4th ASOG and his new assignment as deputy group commander for joint integration. This position tasked him particularly with trying to weld the contributions of each service into some sort of coherent plan. By his own admission, he came with very little understanding of how the army operates or how to bring air power to bear against ground forces in a coordinated campaign. This may have been a good thing actually, because it meant he did not come wedded to "the way we have always done things." McGee's background included flying F-16s, tours at the Air Force Weapons School as both student and instructor, a stint in an AOC, and a tour at the Pentagon. Within a week of his arrival, McGee began to sense that something wasn't right.

For one thing, he could see that three decades of innovation in air power gave it a potential against ground forces that wasn't being tapped. As he examined the problem, it seemed to be more a product of institutional and bureaucratic tradition than insurmountable obstacles. The invasion of Iraq was becoming more and more likely, and with V Corps tasked as the overall command element for the army's half of that invasion, McGee knew 4th ASOG's role would be critical. In his estimation, though, the group's ability to support the lightning campaign planned by the army was not good, particularly since McGee assumed Saddam would be smart enough not to employ his forces as he had done during Desert Storm. McGee approached group and corps leadership with some radical ideas to dramatically reshape not only how the group conducted its supporting air operations but also how the entire corps headquarters did business, particularly in processing the intelligence it received. Leaders at both levels liked his ideas and changes came quickly—they had to because war was looming on the horizon. Once again, it seemed the right man was in the right place at the right time. McGee describes how his plan got started:

General Hahn [V Corps chief of staff] . . . knew what the problem was; he didn't know what the answer was. And so, he was very, very receptive to finally having the capability to execute on a mass-type scale in the corps ground space. Let me also throw out [that the fire support coordinator and his deputy] were very receptive to this also. They helped mother this along through the [lieutenant colonel/colonel] level immediately to General Hahn, and then [from] that step immediately to General Wallace [corps commander] who, [being] an artillery man by background, gave the direction to the corps guys that anything and everything to implement this we will do, because now it gives the corps commander the ability to take a fire hose and put it anywhere on the battlefield at a moment's notice. So that, once it got going, [there] was a fairly immediate implementation, although there are a lot of steps that were required for that to happen.

A big part of McGee's thinking concerned the "sanctuary" problem in that territory short of the FSCL but out of range of army weapons. Because this territory was generally "owned" by corps in most theaters, it was a major concern to corps headquarters everywhere. The close coordination process and the ROE made it difficult for air to operate effectively on a mass scale in that region because someone in close contact with the ground commander had to see either the aircraft or the target and be controlling the aircraft whose pilot could also see the target. As part of the solution to this problem, McGee suggested thinking differently about "seeing" as the basis for close coordination between air and ground—could seeing targets through such sensors as radio and UAV cameras be thought of in the same way as seeing them with the human eye? "You know [the eyes-on approach] is not [just] five years old, it's ten, twenty, thirty years old, and it's the baseline for CAS: 'I see a target, I get air, and I kill a target.' Well the definition of 'see' that most have in their mind is an eyeball seeing a tank or something within visual range . . . but, the key is, and what we haven't been able to solve is, how do we do that CAS-like execution with stuff we don't see with our eyeballs but see with other sensors?"

Another area McGee knew could be greatly improved was helping aircraft find ground forces. SCAR and KICAS CONOPS were significant efforts based on aircraft finding targets on their own, but it is very hard to find dispersed forces from the air, especially since ground forces have found effective means to hide from aircraft. What McGee knew, though, was that a small army of intelligence collectors did nothing but search for enemy units through a wide array of intelligence assets and they were good at finding those units. But the main focus of this effort was not on immediately exploiting what they found. Instead their effort went to finding units, identifying those units, and then sending reports to various intelligence centers that were trying to piece together what is known as the enemy's "order of battle"—a comprehensive picture of where all enemy units are located at any given moment—and that picture is continuously updated by tracking all those units as they move about. Keeping constant tabs on all known enemy units sucks up tremendous intelligence resources and leaves little room for any other tasks. McGee suggested that the emphasis should be placed on immediately passing enemy locations to aircraft that would try to kill them right away. As sensible as such an idea might seem, this would be a wide departure from the way the intelligence world has operated for a very long time, and as the 9/11 Commission has highlighted, the intelligence world does not like changes. McGee describes what it took to make this minor miracle happen in such a short span of time:

> None of this would've happened or could've happened without the fully integrated team within the corps. . . . We changed how the corps intel functioned. This is a big animal. Had it not been for General Hahn and General Wallace going, "Whatever needs to happen, you make happen and work with Colonel McGee to develop [it]."
>
> At the corps main [command post] . . . and the [corps] tactical command post; those two changed the way they did intel. In the past . . . they would go through all the [intelligence sources] trying to find not only what was going on, but where units were, what their strength level and capabilities were, and then try and track them. . . . So they spent the vast majority of their time after they had found something tracking that unit. . . . And they went from that construct . . . [to an] essentially real time . . . process of, "When you find it you kill it." So then you don't have to spend that hundred man-hours tracking [units]; you can spend that hundred man-hours trying to find out where another enemy unit, piece of equipment, or whatever, is to kill [it]. . . . We really not only freed up a lot of intel time but it changed their whole [outlook on waging war]. . . . Now they have the capability to kill it right now.
>
> [The intel people] were initially very skeptical. . . . It really wasn't until about day three or four . . . they started to see . . ."Okay, I see this target. Boom! It just disappeared—that was pretty cool!" "Okay, where's the next one? Boom! That one disappeared. This is pretty cool!" Once they started seeing that, the intel guys were extremely excited about [the new approach]. I mean they saw immediately the ends to the effort they were putting in.

With a new approach for "seeing" as the basis for closer coordination between air and ground, and with the corps' intelligence community reori-
ented toward finding and killing enemy ground forces in near real time,
there was only one more piece needed—a human interface between air
and ground. The key link was the TACP. When it came to the close coordination required to prevent fratricide or harming civilians, TACPs were
the experts; when a particular attack called for a ground controller to talk
the pilot onto the target, that's what TACPs did for a living; and when it
came to command and control, they had always been the link between
ground commanders and air power. But setting up a procedure where
TACPs controlled airstrikes based on what they saw through a sensor's
video feed or a pilot describing what he saw took some creative thinking.
In many ways the attack would be conducted just like a traditional CAS
mission, so there would be some obvious parallels, but the TACPs would
be controlling the attack from corps headquarters using sensors they had
never worked with before. According to McGee, coming up with a work-
able approach presented a few challenges, and on the eve of war there
were still some wrinkles to iron out.

> You had to have TAC-qualified guys at the ASOC to be able to legally
> control that air. And none of these guys had ever seen a targeting pod
> before. . . . He's gonna have to talk [the pilot's] eyes on a target using
> [maps or imagery], and he can still go, "Hey, do you see the bend in
> the road? Do you see the road intersection? Do you see the clump of
> trees?" Everything else, but he's talking off an image not off of visual
> eyesight. Guys had to be trained to do that 'cause they hadn't done
> that before.
>
> The other piece is a lot of these controls would be live controls
> through a UAV feed. So they're looking at the target through a Hunter
> or Predator and then talking the guy's eyes on. Well, some of that re-
> quires an ability to interpret IR scenes and know what you are looking
> at . . . and you know, sometimes it's not as easy as you would think,
> especially for someone who's never seen an IR pod. So there's a lot of
> training. Early on I would . . . take one of our [fliers] and put him in an-
> other tent on the radio and [say to the TACP], "Okay, talk his eyes on
> this target." And he would start off talking about, "Okay, do you see the
> lake?" and it's a mile away from the target. You had to sit down and go,
> "Okay, over this target he's only seeing this piece of ground through
> his targeting pod. So, you can't talk about stuff that's sitting here, here,
> and here, 'cause he doesn't even see that in his targeting pod, 'cause
> he's looking through a soda straw."

> The [TACPs] themselves caught on very quickly, were fairly ex-
> cited, and then the war kicked off and again it was one of those out-
> of-control forest fires. . . . [One TACP], a great guy, who's very laid back,
> yet very intense, been a SOF TACP most of his life . . . the first kill he did
> through a Hunter UAV I thought he had won the Super Bowl. I had to
> tell him to go outside, calm down, then come back in. And you know, in
> a day, even guys who had been to Desert Storm and done some other
> stuff in the SOF TACP world, had killed ten times more than they had
> killed their entire career.

As one of the key architects of this operations concept, McGee can provide a valuable insight into the thinking, theory, and intent behind the
scenes, but to really see the value of this approach we need to get a feel
for how the whole process actually worked on a day-to-day basis in the
crucible of war. One of the practitioners, S.Sgt. Nathan English, was an
ETAC assigned to the 4th ASOS in Heidelberg, Germany, which supported V Corps' ASOC during the war. A seven-year veteran, English hails
from Middletown, Ohio, and attended Ohio University for a couple years.
Not sure what he wanted to do with his life, he joined the air force and
became a TACP. English describes how the process worked on a regular
basis, starting from how their interest might be drawn to a particular
area:

> We typically get some pretty good satellite photos of the area, so we
> had a pretty good starting point. . . . Either something that stuck on
> the intelligence sensors as an area of interest or a place where we knew
> that the Iraqi Medina Division was going to be at. . . . So I'd send an air-
> craft out there to [reconnoiter]. . . . Once [the pilot] started finding tar-
> gets, and we had clearance to kill those targets, he [would nominate]
> fifteen things that he thought were hostile, if we agreed that those fif-
> teen things are valid targets he was then cleared to engage those fif-
> teen things and those fifteen things only on his own accord. . . . The
> CAS aircraft absolutely fell in love with us. . . . We'd be working one set
> of aircraft that had [found] ungodly amounts of targets . . . and they'd
> check off to go to a tanker and . . . come back with six other missions
> that he just met up at the gas line and was telling his buddies what
> they were doing. They had [a mission] that fell through or something,
> and they just started showing up with our guys. . . .
>   We would send SCAR packages out just south of Karbala, before
> the divisions got to Karbala obviously, and we would have them look-
> ing for artillery tubes, we'd have them looking for just about anything,
> and they would come upon probably brigade-size elements of armor
> and artillery and we would send aircraft after aircraft—we'd probably

spent twelve hours dropping bombs on these guys. And we would have the most unbelievable BDA . . . it was just CAS control after CAS control and [we] just beat the hell out of the Iraqis. And then the Karbala fight for the [3rd ID], with the exception of some of the smaller forces they fought, was nothing like it was going to be.

As good as this new approach sounds, one element is still missing,—the command and control piece. Just turning aircraft and controllers loose on anything intel could find would certainly have yielded impressive results, but everyone "doing their own thing" would not accomplish as much as if an overarching vision coordinated it and integrated it with the ground scheme of maneuver. As McGee explains, command and control was incorporated, and the operational concept, which V Corps called "corps shaping," became a cornerstone of their entire strategy for defeating the Iraqi army. First, at the tactical level, the ASOC created a new position to oversee routine operations. "[We] created a new position: the air boss. . . . It was kinda like the CCO [chief of combat operations at the AOC] for the ASOC. . . . [The air boss] followed the targets coming up—is there going to be a factor? He had to do all the weaponeering for it, had to deconflict, he's got to keep the big picture as to who's attacking what, and how." The air boss had a great deal of responsibility in applying this concept throughout the corps' area, but so closely did the air boss and his team work with the army that V Corps leadership came to trust them implicitly and gave them a great deal of latitude.

> The priority of what got hit, when and how it got hit, all that was delegated to us. The team was that kind of tight and there was that much trust. . . . It was, "Here are the overarching targeting priorities," and we would get that twice a day at the BUB [battle update brief], and beyond that it was, "You know what the corps commander's priorities are?" "Yep, Yep, Yep." "Go execute." And, it was good that we executed that way because there was so much going on that had we done the old process of each target being vetted, we would have gotten so far behind so quickly that that process would have imploded on itself.

The other key part of the command exploitation piece was integrating corps shaping into the ground scheme of maneuver at the operational level. As with other efforts to find and kill ground forces with air power, just turning McGee and his team loose on the enemy would have yielded significant results, but coordinating it with army efforts would most effectively exploit this new capability. Normally this would mean applying the air effort in such a way that it supports the corps commander scheme of maneuver; in fact, the term "shaping" is normally understood as "shaping conditions for the main effort." For example, they could have concentrated their efforts ahead of 3rd ID's projected path or where they suspected major battles would occur. According to McGee, General Wallace, V Corps commander, went one step farther. When deep inside Iraq he actually altered his ground scheme of maneuver to shape the conditions for better exploitation of this new application of air power.

> A day or two into the [corps shaping campaign against the Medina Division] he started to see the effects of [it] happening and essentially he became very content with [waiting], establishing the LOCs, having time to get all the required logistics [in place]. . . . So, integral to this operational pause was allowing the shaping to take effect against the enemy. . . . He understood that his shaping capability . . . gave him the capability to beat these guys down before he'd send 3rd ID through Karbala up toward Baghdad.
>
> And it was after the dust storm that [General Wallace] knew they had been beaten up but wanted to make sure they were completely beaten up before we committed land forces through that area. And thus, was [born] the five simultaneous attacks. That was essentially taking every piece of combat power he had, attacking the five main cities in that area, not to take the cities, not to come into big engagements, but to force the roaches out of their holes to show themselves so we could shape, that is, kill those guys also. It is kinda rooting out the last remnants of what was left of the Medina before he allowed the friendly forces to go [on the offensive]. And after that happened he was fairly confident that they had been beat sufficiently to commit the land forces.

Wallace's "Five Simultaneous Attacks" beginning on 31 March was a conscious attempt to use ground maneuver to draw enemy forces into the open so they could be found and killed by air power. This was a brilliant exploitation of the air-ground dilemma, because even if the enemy refused to be drawn out, by remaining dispersed and immobilized they would have made themselves more vulnerable to defeat in detail by V Corps ground forces. Further, Wallace's overall pacing of his ground offensives in coordination with the air offensive are good examples of integrating ground maneuver and air maneuver to the best advantage of each. The Battle of the Five Simultaneous Attacks set up what one observer considered the most significant supporting effort of the entire war.

Assessing the value of any particular military effort during wartime has become the fodder of interservice rivalries, particularly between the army and the air force over the CAS issue, but one striking indication of how effective the corps shaping concept was comes from the army itself. According to statistics presented in a briefing given by General Wallace after the invasion, two of the main threats anticipated by V Corps, the Medina and Hammurabi Republican Guard divisions, were decimated by this new approach. After four and a half days of air interdiction the Medina Division was only reduced from 96 percent combat effective to 92 percent; after ten days of corps shaping, however, it had been reduced to only 29 percent combat effective. More impressive, AI reduced the Hammurabi Division from 97 percent to 73 percent over the course of thirteen days, but after only five days of corps shaping it stood at 23 percent combat effective. Conventional wisdom considers any military force combat ineffective when it has reached 50 percent. Probably the best assessment, though, comes from ordinary ROMADs who time and again expressed strikingly similar observations: "We kept preparing for a big battle, but once we got there, no one was around." There would still be plenty of fight left in the Iraqi army, but most of that fight would involve foot-bound infantry and Fedayeen attacking in light pickup trucks.

Innovations like SCAR, KICAS, and corps shaping would help a lot in the overall effort, but what was happening in the area of direct CAS support for 3rd ID in the traditional sense? Well, first there was the planning, training, and preparations. And where the war in Afghanistan was notable for absences in these areas, the invasion of Iraq provided plenty of opportunity for all three. As Risner relates, planning began very early at the 3rd ID, and illustrative of Blount's attitude toward air power, Risner was brought into the planning at that earliest stage. "As things went along and 9/11 [occurred]—it was very clear soon after if anything was going to happen in the Gulf the 3rd ID was going to be it. The division commander brought me in and pretty much said as much; he had a little elite crew that [he told], 'This doesn't go past you guys, but I think by the end of [a certain date] . . . we're going to be doing that.' So we started planning, just a small cell. . . . We started a year out, at least looking at it and looking at what do we need to fix, where are our problem spots?"

The 3rd ID also took an integrated approach to its training in preparation for war, and it did a lot of training. Before it deployed, the 3rd ID did training out at the National Training Center and the Joint Readiness Training Center, but the best training took place once the division moved to Kuwait. While the confrontation with Iraq was heating up, 3rd ID was taking over responsibility for defending Kuwait in the event Hussein launched a surprise invasion. This mission, which had begun in the wake of Desert Storm, had cycled through several units around the army over the course of the eleven years since its inception, and by summer 2002 it was 3rd ID's time in the box. This meant that 3rd ID, in preparing to assume that routine mission, had been preparing to fight Iraq long before the invasion was first contemplated. Moreover, the mission usually only involved one battalion, but as tensions with Iraq mounted in the early fall, an entire brigade was sent. This change meant more 3rd ID forces were being prepared earlier, and a much larger portion of the division arrived in theater sooner, so it could begin the more intensive training in Kuwait earlier. Further, because 3rd ID had just assumed the Kuwait mission, and as an invasion looked increasingly likely, most of the division's staff went to Kuwait in November, and the rest of the division's fighting units followed soon after. Taken together, one brigade of 3rd ID had six months in Kuwait to prepare, and the entire division had at least two months. During that period the division packed in so much training that, as Risner says, by the time the invasion loomed, the general attitude was, "Hey let's get this thing going because we're tired of training." And all that training closely involved the air force. As Risner recalls, "We immediately [worked on] training and integrating [army and air force]. . . . I saw it after Anaconda, the emphasis was, no kidding, 'Let's include our air force brethren and start getting better training with them.'"

For TACPs, there were two highlights to the training in Kuwait. First, the situation gave them more and better practice in controlling airstrikes. The Udairi Range, the location of the training accident nearly two years earlier, was one of the best live-fire ranges in the world, and the U.S. Air Force air wing nearby at Ahmed Al Jaber air base gave TACPs plenty of sorties to work with. For Risner this was a godsend, "We got everybody up to speed and proficient . . . plenty of air, plenty of guys getting up to speed—so I was very happy because we get more done there than we do back home."

Second, training included integrated army and air force live-fire exercises. The Kuwaiti desert provides a great open space for large unit maneuver exercises, and the Udairi Range allows for much of the maneuver drills to include live firing of every weapon from tanks to artillery to aircraft. Working together, according to Risner, the 3rd ID and the air force staged the kind of integrated training that isn't normally possible in the United States. "I've been told that that was the biggest live-fire training exercise that's been conducted since Desert Storm. We were no kidding doing the plan out there live with aircraft and tanks and Bradleys running all over the Kuwaiti desert. We probably did three of those prior to launching—brigade all the way up to, no kidding, the whole division. We walked before we ran, but we basically [trained] the way we were going to fight—the entire division." Once they got into theater, General Blount and his staff got involved in the more detailed planning for the invasion, and the closer the date for that invasion loomed the sharper that plan came into focus. Risner's deputy, Lieutenant Colonel Bronakowski, arrived in Kuwait on 13 November and was quickly immersed in hammering out what would become the final plan. In fact, Bronakowski was a member of the group that developed the KICAS CONOPS during this same period. According to Bronakowski, the plan for invading Iraq went through a number of variations before it settled on the final two-division front.

> Initially when the thing came out it was a much bigger plan with a whole different ground scheme of maneuver. As we got closer and closer to the fight it became very apparent that it was just going to be us and the marines. But initially we were talking [about] three or four more divisions [being] involved, all running abeam each other going up different avenues. The plan we executed was a much safer plan for us because the initial plan had us crossing the Euphrates River at As Samawah, going up the center corridor through all the population base of Iraq all the way to Baghdad, versus going around the [west] side like we did, and then cutting across up the north side. . . . It left all the population in the center between the Tigris and the Euphrates until the last minute, and then after the collapse of the regime we came back from north to south to clean everything up.

While the plans for the ground battle were taking shape, the detailed planning for the distribution of air power was going on at the same time, and here is where the post-Afghanistan commitment to CAS would really be judged. All air sorties for any given day would be apportioned to the various combat missions based on the theater commander's priorities, but if more weight were placed on such missions as strategic attack, less would be available for CAS. Both Risner and Bronakowski were understandably concerned about this decision and followed its developments closely. As it turned out, leaders and planners at all levels were giving CAS virtual carte blanche. This was obviously good news for Risner and 3rd ID, and because 3rd ID was taking the lead on a one-division front for the army's portion of the battle plan, they would get top priority in the army's allocation of each day's CAS sorties. Risner could almost set his own terms for CAS availability:

[Since] we were going to be the only division, there wasn't going to be a competition for allocated CAS airplanes; we were going to lead it out front—our division—no one else. [Planning] was pretty easy because you had all the assets available. All we really had to do was plan on how many guys I wanted overhead, at what time, and at what position, so we had to set up CAS to keep up with us. . . . As long as I knew the boss's plan and I knew where he was going to meet the enemy, that's where I'd have the CAS overhead. So it made that part very easy. I just told the boss, "Overhead we're going to plan on having a two-ship cap, we have enough . . . that pretty much we're going to have someone overhead 24/7." . . . And the ability to surge [was planned]; in planning we said, "Okay, 2nd Brigade is leading the way, they're going to push, and we figure they're going to meet resistance at such and such [a place] at such a time. Hey, let's adjust our CAS force so now instead of a two-ship overhead there's maybe a four-ship or six-ship stack. ". . . It worked as well as I could have ever imagined it to work—I mean, it was like a thing of beauty.

Having the aircraft available was very important, but so was having them overhead in a position where they could be available for TACPs as quickly as possible. Bronakowski, working with the interservice CAS group at the AOC, helped shape the airspace plan used in Iraq. Essentially, they planned to put all CAS aircraft into several holding patterns, known as stacks, over the battle—one for the marines and two for the army; one of these would support 3rd ID directly and the other would support V Corps' shaping operations, but would be available to back up 3rd ID if needed. These stacks would be located to minimize interference with other fires—artillery and mortars, for example—but close enough to the fight so they could respond quickly. As the battle moved forward these stacks moved too, though in a fast-moving fight that would take a lot of coordination. Bronakowski describes how the plan came together: "I was kind of amazed at all this integration, you know, three or four guys sitting around a table built this whole airspace deconfliction plan all the way up through Baghdad and it worked out well. That was exactly how we executed [it]. . . . We were always trying to put a CAS stack so you can fight a battle, and we were fighting battles in like two or three different directions out of that CAS stack."

There is an axiom in military affairs: "No plan survives the first contact with the enemy"—how did these plans for the CAS portion bear up under the realities of war? For the most part they worked exceptionally well. The 24/7 CAS presence overhead worked as advertised and had some practical benefits, as did the idea of the moving CAS stacks. One unanticipated problem arose, but as with Afghanistan, those involved found ways to work around the problem. Risner explains:

Having guys overhead—I mean no kidding, basically following us up the route there was an ALO's dream, because that's the way you wanted it if you could have it all the time. . . . Because [of the CAS stack] when [a TACP] needed air he just basically called up to the stack and said, "Okay, Hog-11 this is Advance 02, request," and the [short delay] was basically the time it took for [the TACP] to describe the target. . . . I think our longest time was about fifteen to twenty [minutes], and that was when we got into the sandstorms and they were dropping JDAMs on coordinates. As you could imagine, that coordination takes a heck of a lot longer. We were very careful on how we did JDAMS in the weather. . . . I had to chase airplanes away because we had too many airplanes in the stack. As the march went on to Baghdad and all the strategic targets were already taken out, everybody wanted to get into the CAS fight. . . . But I never heard one army guy complain, "You weren't there when I needed you. . . ."

We had made an agreement with the marines—the marines would support their side of the fight and throw whatever extra [sorties] into the JFACC [joint force air component commander] mix, but . . . down in Basra and a couple of places they got engaged very heavy when the Fedayeen attacked and they needed more air. It just happened to be that we weren't real busy and we said basically, "Sure, take our stack and take our air. . . ."

The only hiccups we had were obviously when the weather went bad, we wanted aircraft equipped with JDAM. . . . But still the response [from the AOC was], "Okay, yeah we have a JDAM-equipped aircraft; he's going to Baghdad; we're going to reroute him down to help you." . . . So [the AOC] made us the number one priority when we had troops in contact. . . . And once [air force planners] understood that when the weather gets bad, we need more JDAMs, they would look ahead and tell you what the weather forecast looked like and they would load the aircraft accordingly.

We controlled over eight hundred sorties and we had an average time of check in to bombs on target [of] less than five minutes. So it was outstanding, and that was just due to [the fact that] they were right overhead.

Decades of haggling over doctrine and visions may have soured army–air force relations in some circles, but it had not prevented innovative air-ground thinking in one part of the military community on the eve of the invasion. Still, the drive to transform the military had helped shape that invasion into a desperate gamble; would the increased ability of air power to help in the ground fight offset the danger of trying to topple the Hussein regime with a small blitz? Only time and the test of battle would tell. But despite the time and effort expended on the eve of battle, despite the effort of those in the headquarters during the battle, there would never have been enough time and no amount of effort would have sufficed if the young men who had to carry that battle were not ready—ready in their training, knowledge, confidence, coolness under fire, resourcefulness, and imagination. Even though there were tremendous differences between what TACPs did in Afghanistan and what they would do in Iraq, there was one commonality: on both occasions they demonstrated that despite being almost totally unknown for so long, they were ready to render great service providing a capability America hardly knew it had. In Iraq they would face the test of combat, many of them for the first time.

7. "Our Business Now Is North"

While the planning was going on at the various headquarters around the theater, other preparations were going on that, while very different in nature, were just as critical. Anytime military units deploy there is a certain level of organizational chaos, so once troops arrive at the new location the first order of business is to get the unit—its people and all its gear—gathered, organized, and prepared for the mission at hand.

Hurry Up and Wait

The stories that come out of this phase, in any war, are legendary and sometimes rival the war stories themselves. The U.S. military is no exception, but the unique circumstances of the TACP community—being neither in the army world nor in the air force world—adds a distinct twist that TACPs long ago learned to deal with. A lot of details tend to get lost in the shuffle, so any deployment for a TACP unit involves coming up with creative solutions for the inevitable problems. Handling these details often falls to the NCOs.

This was certainly true during the Iraq deployment, and for the 15th ASOS, the squadron that provides CAS support for 3rd ID, one of those all important NCOs was S.M.Sgt. Russell B. Carpenter. A long-service professional from Reynoldsburg, Ohio, Carpenter had been in the air force for more than twenty years, spending the whole time as a TACP. During that period he had filled a wide array of positions at division or below—jobs that usually kept him out in the field as opposed to the kinds of staff jobs that would get him promoted to the highest enlisted rank. This concession didn't bother him, for he was doing what he loved: "I'll retire when the military kicks me out 'cause I got too many years. There isn't anything I enjoy more than doing this—leading young guys, going out in the field, controlling air; it's kind of like what I was made to do and I don't much feel like doing anything different. The day I leave the service will be the saddest day of my life." Carpenter had also served in Desert Storm, and since then had pulled a number of tours in Kuwait—"too many to count," as he said—and in fact, he was hoping this invasion would put an end to the continual deployments meant to keep an eye on Iraq.

The mad scramble had started for Carpenter much earlier, when the division began preparing for war. On top of pushing units out the door for Kuwait, one of 3rd ID's brigades, 1st Brigade, was scheduled for training at the National Training Center in November and then deployment to Kuwait as soon as it returned to Fort Stewart. Carpenter describes what that meant for him.

> End of November rolls around, I'm directed to [take over as the top NCO of C Flight, which supports 1st Brigade]. . . . So I'm recovering the brigade [from NTC], meeting the guys, meeting the ALO, discussing how we're going to do business, and oh by the way, we're [packing for deployment to Kuwait]. So we're pushing that out the door. . . . There are long days, a lot of headaches involved in that, and we're moving rapidly.
>
> It's December, now we've got the C Flight vehicles out the door. . . . We're on a short stick warning order that says our deployment is imminent and the end of Christmas rolls around, a very kind of unsettled time, but we've been basically given, "Hey look, you're not going to deploy for the Christmas holidays, okay? It's not to that level yet." So the New Year comes around, the Buckeyes win the national championship—that's great, I get to watch it—and no sooner than the first day after . . . we get the word, "Hey, you're going." By 21 January we're on the plane heading over. The trucks and everything else are on the boat—all the equipment, the [storage containers] and such. So we get over there basically 21, 22 January.
>
> We get to Kuwait, they send us out to like a tent city out in the middle of nowhere, Camp Pennsylvania. The brigade is not set up to receive us, despite all the email and stuff to get us on board—they don't really know. It's a logistical nightmare and twenty guys easily drop through the cracks.

For the first fifteen days after his arrival, Carpenter served as the squadron's operations superintendent, which made him the NCO responsible for TACP issues throughout the division, but which would have also kept him in one of the division headquarters the whole time. He was happy, therefore, when the regular operations superintendent arrived and he went back to being the NCOIC for 1st Brigade TACPs. First Brigade was the last one to arrive in theater, so Carpenter not only faced the usual daunting task of getting his people ready for combat but also constantly felt like he was running out of time. He got his troops situated with quarters and learning what they could about the plan, but there wasn't a lot they could do in terms of real training until their equipment arrived. Besides being on a ship that would take much longer to get into theater, their equipment was also packed in with the last of the division's gear—if they waited for the normal logistical processes to get their stuff to them they would lose what little time they had to prepare. Carpenter wasn't about to let that happen. He explains what had to be done to make sure it didn't.

> Each day we're falling farther behind the clock as our own clocks are ticking toward this conflict. You want to get your gear, and you want to get it fitted, and it takes two and a half weeks as we sit over there to finally be able to go to the ports and get our stuff. It's an absolute disaster in terms of the army figuring out when your trucks are coming. We're running all over three different camps, which have thousands of army guys each, basically meeting trucks at the gates looking to see if our stuff is on them. So that's a real nightmare, but again, a lot of good NCOs, a lot of good airmen were on top of it, and we finally rustle up all of our trucks. And finally the last of the [containers arrives], which has all of our gear in it. We actually had to physically drive to the port ourselves, find our [storage container] sitting almost alone now, and shanghai a local national driver to grab our gear. And the "dope deal" [with army authorities] is we got to take a bunch of stuff and head a convoy back to Camp Doha, and then from there we'll get one guy that'll take our gear out to Camp Pennsylvania. We need our gear so we make the deal.

Another great American military tradition is Yankee ingenuity in modifying equipment and vehicles to meet unanticipated needs of war. TACPs are no exception. And in keeping with yet another tradition, much of this is done in direct violation of standing orders. As Carpenter relates, much of their time was taken up with not only making common sense changes normally prohibited by regulations but also coming up with creative solutions to unexpected problems.

> We start outfitting our trucks with all kinds of modifications we need to do 'cause headquarters says the vehicle can only be set up a certain way. Intelligent things like all the jerry can holders have to be inside your truck, so you're unbolting them and sticking them on the tailgate like they should be. You can't have external antenna mounts on a GPS, so we're fashioning stuff to put GPS antennas out on our trucks.

Oh, you can't have twelve-volt cigarette lighter adaptors running off of your battery to power anything 'cause it's a nonstandard [modification]. So all that goes out the window when you need to do it for real. And we're doing all these modifications . . . that should be done in garrison [i.e., during peacetime], that isn't done because [a TACP vehicle] doesn't fit the standard [air force] mold. So we're really busting [our chops], spending a couple or three days on that.

We've picked up some satellite radios, which we don't have a lot of experience with, but it's real critical to this mission because that's what the AFARN is going to be run on. Well, the biggest LIMFAC [limiting factor] we have is we don't have an omnidirectional antenna. So we got a guy from 2nd Brigade, a good NCO, that designs us a mount, has it taken over to the metal shop on Camp Doha and gets the thing made—a prototype. Gets out in the field, works sweet. This thing goes up through the middle of your Hummer, mounts on a big metal pole, and . . . mounts the antenna right on top. Works like a champ. We go down to the metal shop, we're behind the power curve, but we kind of force through a deal with the metal shop to get our stuff made.

We did what we needed to do, work long days to do it, and I mean everybody, guys installing pallets in the tracks, getting their tracks modified with gigantic brackets to hold extra water, and just any special modifications that each operator comes up with looking at other guys' stuff, what they're doing, and ideas of their own putting a vehicle in shape to take it into combat. . . . I wish all that stuff could be done in garrison, but it's just the slow grinding wheels of the headquarters apparatus and [their concerns about] standard vehicles, and dangerous modifications [like] cigarette lighter adapters, and such.

Meanwhile my attitude the whole time is catch up, catch up, catch up. We're trying to catch up to where all the other guys are, 'cause they've already been on the ground for months. So we finally get all the equipment [ready], start getting some good satellite training; it's all happening very rapidly. We get our map sets issued, we do some terrain orientation, and . . . no sooner than we get our stuff basically fitted out then out the door we go to the tactical assembly areas.

But there was still much to be done to prepare for combat. Even at this late stage Carpenter was still resolving significant problems and focusing his men on training for the fight.

We go out and basically just stake a [piece of] ground in the middle of the desert and say, "Okay, we're going to operate from here now in a more tactical mode outside your cushy desert tents and your port-a-johns. . . ." We're sitting out there for fourteen days, we're enduring sandstorms, you're in planning processes to go to war, guys are obtaining satellite imagery from every source they can get, we're getting that stuff loaded on laptops, we're doing terrain analysis, we're walking through the battle as it progresses up to Baghdad on the computers and maps, talking about choke points, possible things. . . . We're having some vehicle issues with stuff breaking, trying to get stuff fixed, those kind of things. . . .

But it's all going well in terms of by the clock, but now we're moving out of those assembly areas and now we're moving to [attack positions]. We're already knowing we're going. This is just mere days away from the breach. We're talking about how we're going to breach the berms [the defensive earthen embankment running along the Kuwait-Iraq border] and how that's going to take place. We're just a couple of short miles from the Kuwaiti side of the border north into Iraq. Everything is definitely locked, cocked, and ready. . . .

First Brigade is a huge player in the breaching operation. The [3-7] CAV is taking down the OPs out front, and those kinds of things, and we're going to blast due north, seize an airfield, and set that up for a FARP [forward arming and refueling point for helicopters] operation before we continue the drive to the west. . . . We're going to do a passage of lines as we start to swing west. Second Brigade [will move] out front; they're going to seize an objective about halfway to Baghdad. Then we're going to pass through them to lead the charge. So we're in that mind-set that we're probably not in for a super hard fight until we make the passage of lines through 2nd Brigade, and then we know we're going to be in the fight from then on. And that's where we've done the majority of our study in terms of what we're going to do for operations.

We [Carpenter and his ROMAD assistant] are driving out very near the berm to visit some of our forward TACPs, make sure they got everything. Talk to the guys and give them a final okay, tell them I wanted to kick them out of the track and send them back of the brigade TOC [he wants to take their place so he can be in the action]. We got a deal worked with the brigade commander [Col. William Grimsley] that we're going to follow him—he's a forward-operating, thinking brigade commander. . . . He likes to co-locate with his lead battalion commander, so that promises to be definitely more exciting than having to sit back in the TOC, and it certainly was. He is an awesome, very low-key guy. . . . I can remember us talking at the big meeting before the berm. . . . He's giving the kind of, you know, "This is your go to war speech"—he's so low key you can barely hear it. You've got to listen so hard. I'm thinking, "Wow, this guy isn't a very dynamic or charismatic kind of speaker." But that was his manner, cool, calm, and collected, and I'll take that from an army commander any day, because the guy, when artillery rounds are bouncing all around us, he is just as cool as he is in any exercise—clear-headed, thinking straight through like an artillery barrage is something he does every day. . . . I got nothing but good things to say about Colonel Grimsley. He had a real appreciation for air power—what it can do. He wanted to employ it often, whenever able. He had that unique sense of, you know, "I don't need to sacrifice army lives if I can beat it to death with CAS and then walk in and scoop up the pieces."

So, we get the final kickoff speech, we basically get in our vehicles and we park in these huge arrays of monstrous lines of packages that are going to go busting through the breach. . . . I can remember sitting there that night when the big Paladins [155-mm self-propelled artillery] and the MLRS launched their initial barrage. . . . That stuff erupts at like one or two in the morning and we know we're going, we know what time we're LDing, that barrage kicks off, and I just couldn't help but feel good. You know, I was deployed over in Korea when 9/11 happened, and my philosophy was if Saddam wasn't directly involved with 9/11 he provided safe harbor for terrorists. He was the kind of guy that created regional instability because that's what he was about. In that instability grows that terrorist mind-set of hurting the West, of hitting the West, of coming to America, or Germany, or England, and doing harm. And I felt like while I was sitting there, yeah it was the Taliban, but to a great extent, I felt Hussein was responsible for a lot of that and personally I was glad to be pounding him. When those cannons went off, I felt good.

A couple three short hours later we go through the berm. . . . Although unopposed, [the whole thing seemed] more like an exercise than what you'd figure the classic kickoff to a battle would be. I kind of felt like the guys on Guadalcanal—they storm ashore, they're ready for the fight of their life, and there's nobody there. It's like, "What happened? Where's this army?"

We start shooting up north to take [Jalibah airfield] so they can use that as a FARP. . . . It was an old operating base that had been abandoned by the Iraqis. . . . We're seeing some old remnants from the first Gulf War, some hulks left out there. A lot of Bedouins—the Bedouins are real good—they're showing their hands, make sure we know they're not armed. Some of them seem friendly enough, some indifferent to us. . . . We didn't even stop at a refueling-rearming point, because there wasn't a battle to burn our fuel or to burn our ammunition up, so we blew right through that, headed up to the airfield, seized that, choppers came in. First the attack helos, then we got the transport choppers once we established the FARP later that night. . . . Then we are pressing out to the west to do our further mission. . . . We hunkered down for the night. It's a beautiful night, just stars everywhere; we're away from civilization, so the stars are coming out great. . . . Catch a couple or three hours of sleep, and then we're off again.

Across the Berm

Intelligence sources predicted that when Americans invaded Iraq they would be greeted as liberators by millions of smiling, cheering, Iraqi people happy to be rid of Saddam the tyrant. Others, particularly the Iraqi government and its infamous information minister Mohammed Saeed al-Sahaf, nicknamed "Baghdad Bob," insisted the Coalition would meet such stiff resistance they would be stopped cold. The truth, as is so often the case, was somewhere in the middle; many Iraqi soldiers fled, many surrendered at the first opportunity, but many more gave the invaders a serious fight. For some members of the 3rd ID the fight they found themselves in was far worse than anything they had ever expected, and at times it seemed like they were part of an unfolding disaster. That these moments did not end as tragedies can be attributed to training, tenacious courage, and in large measure, to a lot of innovative thinking when it came to bringing air power to bear in desperate circumstances.

The first taste of combat for 3rd ID came on 21 March with a relatively minor affair at an airstrip known as Tallil air base. It was located close to the Iraq-Kuwait border near the town of An Nasiriyah. Coalition leaders wanted to use Tallil for later air operations, and before the invasion ended they were actually launching fighters from that airfield. Third Brigade got the mission, and working with its 1-15 mechanized infantry battalion was a soft-spoken airman from Birmingham, Alabama, named John M. Stockman. A staff sergeant, Stockman had been in the air force for six years.

[The] 2-69 was the first battalion in. They kind of went around Tallil air base off to the west and then cut north up to the river. They were supposed to secure bridges in there before they got blown up [by the Iraqis]. Then 1-15 went in. . . . We rolled into there in the middle of the night. We took out a couple of tanks on Tallil airfield when we first rolled through. We took all that out with army assets—couple of tank-on-tank shots and actually shot some artillery. . . .

During the night we didn't really see [anything]; we didn't catch any fire or do anything, but it got daylight and they hit us pretty hard. They hit us from three sides with a nice ambush, and the company I

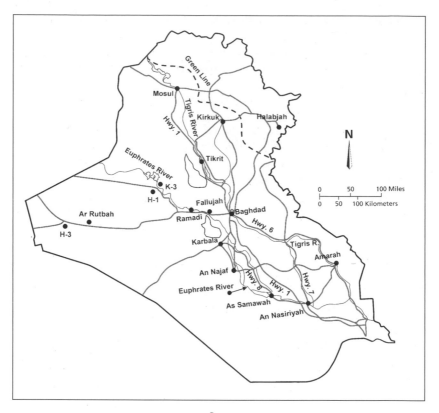

Iraq

was with was pretty spread out. We had one platoon that was a click and a half off to our east that had gone to a barracks complex and cap- tured about forty or fifty EPWs and found some suspected chemical weapons, and they were trying to get those guys and that stuff out of there when the whole company came under fire. . . . They were all dis- mounts, there were no vehicles; we were taking mortar fire—I'm not sure they ever figured out where it was coming from. . . . They hit us with some 12.7s, which is basically a .50-cal [a DSHK]; my Bradley took a few direct hits from it. There was a lot of direct [fire] from AKs and stuff. There [were] just dudes everywhere. . . . It was probably at least two platoons worth of guys, quite a company. . . . We had a couple of guys get shot up pretty bad there. . . .

We fought them with direct fire for about fifteen to twenty min- utes and pushed them back into a warehouse compound. . . . I'd say it was probably about close to two city blocks. It was fairly large; had like five really big warehouses, and probably three or four smaller office- type buildings. . . . We backed off to about a click and a half away, and that's when I got the first set of A-10s. . . . And about the time the first set was getting ready to make their first run, the second set checked on and it was kind of like a "follow the leader"—it was like, "Hey, fall in behind these guys. Just shoot what they shoot—roll with it," you know. And so the first attack was with four A-10s, and they strafed. I want to say the first pass killed twenty-five or thirty guys that were standing outside one of the buildings. It worked pretty good. We ended up dropping a total of sixteen Mk-82s, all four planes ran dry on guns, and then the first two planes were bingo and had to get out of there. The second two planes I ran dry on Mavericks—two Mavericks apiece from them—all onto that warehouse complex. We took out all five warehouses, two of the smaller buildings, but we didn't actually go into the buildings and see what was left in there or anything. They were guessing probably fifty or sixty dudes. . . .

After the attack the other platoon was allowed to pull back with their EPWs and all. Once they linked back up with us we pulled back . . . another five or six hundred meters, and we just literally sat there on the side of the road for about a day and a half before we moved out of there and went to our next objective. We didn't take any more fire [in that area] after the CAS missions. It was pretty effective.

After seizing Tallil air base, 3rd Brigade was assigned various support duties for much of the next couple weeks—it wouldn't reenter the main fight until near the end—but Stockman's battalion was transferred temporarily to 2nd Brigade; as a result he would see more action in the near future. In the meantime, lead elements of 3rd ID were approaching As Samawah. The Americans did not expect much resistance there as they approached on the twenty-second—they were in for a surprise. The 3rd ID's division cavalry was the 3rd Squadron of the 7th Cavalry Regiment, otherwise known as 3-7 CAV. The modern cavalry unit obviously has no horses, but it retains the traditional cavalry mission of scouting out ahead of an army and screening its movements to keep the enemy confused about its location and plans. U.S. cavalry units also retain much of the tradition and heritage of its Old West legacy, and none more so than 3-7 CAV: a successor to Custer's 7th Cavalry and the Little Big Horn, it maintains that tie right down to its nickname, motto, and anthem, "Garry Owen." Later in Iraq the men of this unit would wonder if the unit was also going to share the most infamous aspect of Custer's tradition.

Outside As Samawah, though, 3-7 CAV was preparing to conduct a feint. As the rest of the division moved up the west side of the Euphrates, 3-7 CAV was to cross the river at As Samawah and charge up the densely populated region between the Tigris and the Euphrates—that region

*S.Sgt. John Stockman poses in front of an A-10 after reenlisting following the
Iraq invasion. He played a key role in the fighting around Tallil Airfield
and Objective Saints.*

once known as Mesopotamia, or "the land between two rivers"—hoping
to convince the Iraqis that theirs was the main invasion force. This area
was not only the most densely populated but also the heart of the Iraqi
culture and economy, so it was a likely invasion route—3-7 CAV's feint,
therefore, would be a plausible one.

With 3–7 CAV was T.Sgt. Mike Keehan of the 20th ASOS at Fort Drum,
New York. Keehan had volunteered to augment 3rd ID as it ramped up
for war. The epitome of the professional NCO, Keehan is a quiet, serious man who thinks continually during peacetime about preparing his
men for combat. Another 20th ASOS volunteer with 3-7 CAV was Staff
Sergeant Mike Shropshire. Shropshire's professionalism and abilities
are unquestionable, but he also has an infectious sense of humor and
a mischievous spirit. Soldiers in 3-7 CAV joked about continually having to rein in Shropshire's gung ho nature. When he volunteered to help
with the invasion he was given the choice of two units; he asked which
one was likely to see the most combat. The answer was 3-7 CAV, so that's
the unit he chose. Keehan was stationed with the squadron's TOC, and
Shropshire was assigned to Charlie Troop—nicknamed Crazy Horse or
Crazy for short. For both men, their baptism by fire was about to turn
intense.

Shropshire's M-113 APC had broken down just as they crossed the border into Iraq, so he hitched a ride with a mortar crew. Approaching As Samawah, Shropshire was getting his first taste of combat, and the breakdown of his track was just the beginning of his frustrations.

[Intel] said [As Samawah] wasn't really hostile and that the people were generally friendly there. We were under the impression—this is soldier talk I guess—that they were going to give us a parade. It wasn't ticker tape they were throwing at us! So we got up there and got real close to the town. Our objective was to secure the canal bridges [outside town]. . . . We moved up kind of over the bridges and just on the edge of town. That's when we started taking 60-mm mortar fire—lots of it, and small arms fire. First round that cracked over my head, I thought someone was firing their weapon beside me and I asked the guy, "Hey, what are you shooting at?" and he said, "I didn't fire." And then some more rounds cracked and that was my first taste of what a round sounds like when it comes over your head. It wasn't nice. And then the mortar fire started coming in. We returned fire. I had a round land about five or six feet away from me. . . . It hit and it didn't go off. And all I did was stare at it for a second or two—it seemed like an eternity—but I just looked at it waiting for it to go off and blow my head off and it never went off. I just looked up and said, "Thank you, God."

We pulled back while still firing—kind of a retrograde [operation] . . . back across the dirt under one of the bridges and there were rounds hitting all around us. The weird thing was we started laughing about it. We were making jokes about, "Where's our parade?" and this and that—it just didn't seem real I guess. . . . So we pull out of their mortar range and I'm trying to hook up an airstrike. A-10 comes in the area, but the weather is so bad, the cloud cover so low that the A-10s can't get in there, but that was also when there were a lot of restrictions—a lot of [restricted operating zones], no fly zones—all around the town and inside the town. So [between the weather and the restrictions] it was almost impossible. . . . I couldn't get an aircraft in there. . . .

So the mortar crew that I was with, they were short a guy anyway—that's how I got on that track—they started lobbing rounds, and that one [crew] particularly was going real slow [because they were a man short] so I hopped up there and offered my assistance and started hanging rounds. Shot a lot of rounds, had some OJT [on the job training] while I was up there, like how to do it right. Those rounds are heavy, and you have to put them just slightly into the tube, and then when they say fire that's when you drop it; until then I had to hold it there, and luckily I'm a strapping young lad. I was okay. The rest of the time there I was hearing rounds whizzing by us—they were still trying to shoot at us. We knocked out some of their dug-in troops, some of the command control elements.

While we were firing back, they were sneaking guys up trying to fire RPGs at us. . . . A lot of civilians trafficking out of there to get away from the battle, and one time in particular we got up there and this [group of] twenty to thirty civilians with small children, some about as old as my kids, like two and three years old, were walking, and an RPG—I don't know if he was aiming at the civilians or aiming at us, but it just didn't even come close to us, and it was heading right for them. And I know they didn't understand English, but at the time the emotions set in and I just started yelling, "Get down! Get down!" They saw me yelling and saw the RPG coming and they got down in the ditch and then ran off, and one of the guys pulled a Bradley over there to try to absorb any more rounds that were going to come in and hit the civilians.

During the night, weather over As Samawah improved dramatically, but it was still a long night of little sleep and sporadic fighting. As Keehan explains, the fighting only got worse the following day.

They had taken mortar fire in this area all day, and nighttime didn't change anything. The night was long as units passed through the objective area. . . . I had intel that thirty to forty enemy soldiers had taken a position to threaten movement of forces in our area . . . they were harassing the 3rd ID guys coming in. So I . . . called in a request to the ASOC, and got two A-10s with eight five-hundred-pound bombs and [a] full load of 30-mm guns. I cleared the area and leveled the target area with the entire ordnance. . . . That was my first live control ever. It's pretty interesting to say "cleared hot" knowing you're not on the range anymore and there's actually people down there. But it felt good to actually do it and make a difference and make it count for the guys.

The next targets were the Baath Party headquarters, which took a little higher than general-level to get that one hit. Took about two hours to get approval on that. I finally got approval . . . like one o'clock, two o'clock in the afternoon. . . . I had been tasked with a four-ship of F-16s carrying four each five-hundred-pound laser-guided bombs. It was a hard building to pick out from the air, so luckily we had trained extensively in Kuwait with the CAV's OH-58 Kiowa Warrior helicopters on CAS procedures and talk-on procedures. . . . Together we got [the F-16 pilots'] eyes on the building, but to make sure, the helicopter fired a Hellfire missile into it to make a positive mark. The F-16s confirmed

T.Sgt. Mike Keehan and Sr.A. Trevor Bradford control CAS outside As Samawah.
Keehan and Bradford brought considerable help to a number of
3-7 CAV's desperate fights. Photo by Warren Zinn,

> [they saw the mark] and shacked the target, and all was well until artil-
> lery rounds started impacting two hundred to three hundred meters
> all around us. We all jumped into our vehicles and hauled ass to our
> new site.

Sergeant Shropshire was also in the area, and he gives an interesting perspective on these events.

> Keehan called in a strike on the Baath Party headquarters . . . and it
> couldn't have been more than ten minutes after that . . . they fired
> heavy artillery at us. We didn't have any intel that they had heavy artil-
> lery, nor did we know that they were putting it in place to fire on us,
> and those rounds came in . . . and they just started pounding us with
> artillery. We all grabbed what gear we could and I jumped in the back
> of a Bradley. . . . There were all kinds of vehicles all around us. . . . I saw
> [the artillery] hit these engineers, and I think a medical track. At the
> time I just ran to get cover, but [afterward] I started worrying about if
> Sergeant Keehan got out all right, 'cause he was just in a Humvee . . .
> and then some of the other guys—the army guys—I was worried
> about them. I think two guys [from another unit] were killed and some
> more wounded, but I'm not sure.

Despite the mad scramble to get out of the area, Keehan continued to fight back with CAS, and his first priority was to silence that artillery.

I was still controlling aircraft as we were driving through a field with huge ruts. Within five minutes two A-10s were overhead at five thousand feet. I just started briefing them on the situation when a SAM was launched from the city. I saw the SAM go up and quick as I could [called] on the radio, "SAM launch!" I couldn't give direction or anything because the missile was already operating. They go pretty fast when you actually see it. Luckily it didn't hit it, because at that moment I thought . . . it was going right up at him, and the A-10s were just floating around up there. . . . Another set of A-10s checked in as well, and we dropped sixteen more Mk-82s into the city and two Maverick missiles on ADA [air defense artillery] sites firing from the riverbank. . . .

That night, we pulled out of there. I continued bombing anything I could see in there. We couldn't go across the bridge—there was no way we were going to get through there; there were too many forces. . . . I guess the powers that be at division said, "Okay, we're not going to waste people going through this. . . ." Got a new change of mission, we went up ahead of everybody to go to An Najaf to go across the next bridge at Abu Sukhayr, right next to An Najaf. . . . We consolidated our forces outside the city that night, and I continued to call on aircraft to search for enemy tanks well into the night.

The CAV resumed its lead position on 24 March. Their march to An Najaf was, as Keehan relates, another intense affair marked by what he characterized as a "rolling ambush."

The bridge we would capture then cross was about eighty miles to the north. We convoyed at night through sparsely populated areas and some small towns. . . . On the way up that night we got ambushed three times within a hundred miles, so it was just a rolling ambush the whole way up there. . . . About 9:30 tracer rounds erupted from all around the convoy. We returned fire and I was quickly summoned by Lieutenant Colonel Ferrell [the 3-7 CAV commander] to get air on target. . . .

Trevor Bradford [Keehan's assistant] already had the air request formats memorized; I relied heavily on his ability with radio coordination. It was a little chaotic, both sides of the road taking fire. I had two A-10s overhead and used my IR pointer to get their eyes on the target area east of us. They strafed the entire area with 30-mm, which illuminated the area with brilliant white light. Enemy activity ceased to exist [in that area]. Then I worked the west side of the road with eight five-hundred[-pound] bombs and WP [white phosphorous] rockets. We were about seven hundred meters away when the bombs hit—everyone felt the shock waves in their bodies. I think that last strike, so near the convoy, brought us newfound respect. I think [the soldiers] had an idea of what we do. This display of sheer brute power was proof. Most importantly, as I conferred with Lieutenant Colonel Ferrell a couple of days later, we seemed to have given them an air of confidence and made them feel a bit safer. . . .

We started our march again to the north, as it must have been one or two A.M. now. We were traveling for no more than an hour up to the north when we got ambushed [again]. I had called the ASOC and told them of our situation and to keep sending us aircraft. I had two A-10s overhead in a matter of minutes with a full load of eight five-hundred-pound bombs, full guns, and rockets—standard load. The enemy positions hit us from both sides of the road, small arms and mortars. Most of the left flank enemy positions were neutralized by Bradley fire, so I concentrated CAS on the right side of the road near a long line of palm trees that lined the adjacent river. . . . I had the aircraft first strafe the area along the riverbank, making sure they had the right area that I was illuminating with my IR pointer. They were right on as they marched their 30-mm bullets up and down the banks of the river. I was then cleared in by Lieutenant Colonel Ferrell to drop the remaining bombs into that area. Huge explosions rocked our convoy on the road as the target area lit up in the predawn hours. Subsequent fires started. As the sun came up, the fires consumed an area in front of the palm trees, and it looked exactly like the opening scenes in the movie *Apocalypse Now*. . . .

After sitting for what seemed to be forever, we continued on northward to the objective, but I noticed the winds were picking up, and off to the northwest the telltale sign of a sandstorm brewing. Radio reports from 2nd Brigade confirmed it off to our west flank, as they were down to fifty feet or less visibility. We still had to take the bridge near An Najaf—the bridge across the Euphrates River. We would be the first to cross it, the first [army] unit right of the river. The sandstorm was just an eerie [harbinger] of what was to come our way.

Another group that was meeting unexpected resistance as they neared An Najaf on 22 March was 2nd Brigade. Their mission was to seize Objective Rams, a point south of the city, in preparation for 1st Brigade's assault on the city and its environs. With 2nd Brigade was air liaison officer Captain Todd Wiles; he describes what they ran into:

[We had] no contact until we approached Objective Rams just south of An Najaf. Then we started running into Fedayeen. The M-1s rolled onto the objective and about fifteen white pickups with crew-served weapons [.50-caliber machine guns] mounted on top attacked the M-1s. M-1s quickly blasted them, but they dismounted around a hundred troops in black uniforms. M-1s and Brads firing coax guns [7.62-mm machine guns] mostly at them. . . . Dismounts were said to be running all over the place and everyone kept watch around our perimeter while the brigade ran the battle, and we began requesting CAS. Fedayeen were low crawling up to tanks; Bradleys were firing straight through huge dirt berms shwacking [Iraqis] hiding on the far side. . . . The armor pulled back as [about sixty] Fedayeen regrouped and hid in a trench network.

Colonel Schwarz, 1-64 commander, said he knew where the Fedayeen were hiding, so the XO, FSO, and I worked up a plan to bring in artillery, then CAS, then launch an armor assault and root them out. [The 2nd Brigade FSO] and [the 2nd Brigade targeting officer] called in artillery. Staff Sergeant Pinson controlled the A-10s, which dropped air burst Mk-82s, but then Schwarz was afraid to let the [A-10s] drop the other half of their ordnance. Both dropped three Mk-82s a piece. Everyone loved the show. Tanks rolled in after Schwarz did a head count of all his tank crews—he was incredibly afraid of fratricide from CAS—and they continued with a huge firefight, destroying the remainder of the Fedayeen.

A positive outcome came as a result of that incomplete CAS mission. S.Sgt. Jon Pinson, a TACP attached to 1–64, had established a strong working relationship with Col. Eric Schwartz, the battalion commander. Pinson had tremendous respect for Schwartz and his willingness to listen to his people, so he approached Schwartz about Schwartz's concerns with CAS and fratricide. Pinson describes the results:

[He and I] had a couple of in-depth conversations about what I bring to the battlefield. Colonel Schwartz [had been] a company commander in the Gulf War and lost some guys due to fratricide with army aviation CAS . . . so he naturally was timid to use it. . . . So we talked about it. . . . I was like, "Sir, do you understand what goes into doing this? Like, the precautions that we take, like how we won't pass an aircraft friendly grids? Why? Because just about every targeting system in an aircraft [uses grids for targeting]. How do you tell a bomb where to go? You type in a grid. If you never give [pilots] a friendly grid, they will never type in a friendly grid. It's just common sense." And he's like, "Well how do you let them know where you are?" Things like that. It's just that he didn't know—you don't know what you don't know. And after I explained it to him . . . he opened up a whole lot. After that it was just CAS city.

Also with 2nd Brigade was a group of marines who control CAS for a living. Part of the 2nd Air and Naval Gunfire Liaison Company of the II Marine Expeditionary Brigade, they are essentially the marine equivalent of air force TACPs, and they had been detailed to augment 3rd ID. To say marines have a long history with CAS is an understatement—the single purpose of marine aviation is to provide close air support for marines, and therefore they have always taken CAS seriously. So from the moment they showed up on Risner's doorstep in Kuwait, there was never any question but that these men knew what they were doing. Though this book is primarily about air force TACPs, this marine ANGLICO deserves mention.

The 2nd ANGLICO supported 3rd ID with two supporting arms liaison teams (SALTs), which work at headquarters coordinating air support needs, and two firepower control teams (FCTs), which control the airstrikes—all were attached to 2nd Brigade. Controlling the CAS in the FCTs were Major Mark Jewell, attached to Battalion 4-64, and Gy.Sgt. William R. "Butch" Deas Jr., assigned to Battalion 1-64. As 2nd Brigade approached Objective Rams the marines were caught up in the action and Jewell relates his part.

> I was asleep [lying] next to the track on the Bradley, got my first sleep in probably seventy hours, and I woke up with a tank at a high rate of speed coming behind my Bradley and firing its gun. I woke up and I knew there was a fight, and I had no idea what else was going on— you're groggy and you're trying to get your wits back about you. Got my helmet on and got back inside the Bradley. Got on the FLIR [forward-looking infrared] and I could see commotion, but I had no idea who was who and I just kind of had to trust the tanks knew what they were doing. And about that time I saw a triple-A go off and I was able to pop a compass out and I shot an azimuth to that and I reported that on the radio to [the SALT].

A member of the SALT team supporting Jewell then used the azimuth as a starting point on a map and worked up a likely location for those triple-A batteries and passed it to Jewell. "So now I had A-10s, and [the SALT] gave me a probable location of the triple-A I had seen, and I was able to pass . . . that to the A-10s. And then as they were rolling in close I just took my laser pointer . . . and said, 'Look somewhere in that direction . . .' and [the pilot] flew down the beam to the grid I had given him and he goes, 'Oh yeah, I see them,' and rolled in and took out two triple-A sites."

Farther back in the advance with 1st Brigade, Sergeant Carpenter was also heading for Objective Rams. His drive north from As Samawah was far less eventful than 3-7 CAV's had been, but that was about to change once they did a passage of lines through 2nd Brigade and moved north to occupy an area west of An Najaf. "At this point I've been driving for twenty hours, something like that. I'm exhausted. . . . The whole time you're not in the fight you know 2nd Brigade is. You can hear some of the stuff on the radio as they're coming into [Rams]. . . . Dawn finally comes, we get some fuel. Colonel Grimsley says, 'Hey, we got some work for you,' and we basically go forward with him up to 3-69 Armor Battalion, he's going to follow [3-69]; we're going to do some CAS work as they're blasting past where the 2nd Brigaders are holding their spot. We're going to do a passage of lines and take the lead."

The 1st Brigade was headed for the spot west of An Najaf because it is the site of a long ridgeline the Americans named "the escarpment." Running mostly along an east-west line westward from An Najaf, the escarpment was a natural defensive work that extended for miles and was perfect for opposing an attacking armor force. The ridgeline had a commanding view of the plain to its south, but it was also pockmarked with caves—both natural and man-made—that the Iraqis were using to hide forces. It could have been Tora Bora all over again. Because the escarpment ran down almost to the city, which sat on the edge of the Euphrates, An Najaf was a natural chokepoint. As Carpenter explains, this chokepoint had been identified during planning as an area where they could expect a major battle.

> Basically as we are rolling north, there's three real chokepoints along our route; [one] is this escarpment. . . . And then beyond it the Karbala Gap between the town of Karbala and the lake right to the west. It's about a three-mile, four-mile opening that is a significant chokepoint. Then you spread out into a kind of a big bowl valley, and if you're driving north out of Karbala, you cant to your two o'clock and [go] about thirty kilometers [and] you start reaching some cities and the bridgeheads over the Euphrates. Those we knew were our significant fights where we could expect the Iraqis to be. . . .
>
> We got some CAS on line instantly. . . . I'm talking [pilots] in on some targets. . . . I give him the cleared hot, he's rolling in on some artillery that he's seeing, I'm hitting several missions of artillery and armored concentrations. I'm getting British [Jaguars], F-15Es, the gamut. . . . I controlled six or seven indirect missions; Captain [Jon] Chesser [the brigade ALO] is doing the coordination with the artillery folks, picking up the target stuff and then reporting our BDA back to the commander, so we're working pretty close there. We're [approaching] the escarpment . . . now my radios crap out. I'm in my Hummer, and I got a B-52 on line with some JDAMs and we're trying to get some good JDAM coordinates for the B-52 and my radio is just gone. So I go

to my second radio, I rig it up, I get like three transmissions, and it's shot. So I'm like, "You got to be kidding me!" I'm scrambling getting the portable [radio], meanwhile I hear that the other TACP in that lead battalion is snagging my B-52 and he's going to work them since my shit is in the wind, which pisses me off to no end. My 1C4 . . . does his best work of the trip. He's working hard on the radios, swapping them in and out, getting the portable on line. Meanwhile we're staring at the escarpment, we're stacked up once again in broad daylight sitting out on a two-lane road running up to the escarpment, and there's probably a thousand vehicles on this road.

The "other TACP" Carpenter mentions was S.Sgt. Travis Crosby of the 15th ASOS at Fort Stewart, Georgia. Only six vehicles from the head of the lead column, Crosby had as good a view of the Iraqi forces on the escarpment as anyone on the plain below, but since those forces were arrayed on the top of the ridge and its reverse slope, seeing just what was up there was a difficult proposition. Still, as Crosby explains, by using the pilots overhead as their "eyes," and by directing the pilots to the most likely places to look, he and Carpenter were able to control the destruction of those enemy forces indirectly. This procedure is known as an "indirect" or "type 2" control, where the pilot describes what he sees and the TACP determines if it meets safety criteria and authorizes the attack. Crosby describes what he faced:

Approaching [the escarpment] there are two marshes, one on either side [of the road], so once you get trapped in that funnel there's no turning back. . . . From looking at it, the whole escarpment, and the type of rocks, the erosion, and all this other kind of stuff, there was probably thousands of little caves, and indentions that make shadows, so basically you had to get shot at out of one of these little indentions to realize that it was more than just an earthen feature. . . . You'd get shot at and, "Okay, go kill that."

We started receiving some artillery fire then. . . . We knew what kind of artillery was coming in, and could figure out it was coming from just on top of the escarpment, a couple clicks back, and started hunting that stuff down. The A-10s found it wasn't too many, it was like three artillery pieces, and they engaged and destroyed them.

There was a complex of bunkers, and these guys were shooting RPGs, and there was a BRDM parked right beside this bunker. Each bunker was dug into the escarpment, so . . . it was hard to talk the A-10 [pilot] onto it, but I had a Mk-7, the laser rangefinder, a new piece of equipment we got, and I was able to get a pretty good grid using that. . . . She came in and took a Maverick shot at the BRDM. She could see that—she couldn't really see the bunkers—we were going to talk her on from that. She just shacked the BRDM and it was parked just to the left of the bunkers, and she noticed [the bunker complex] about the same time I was describing it to her. So she reset and came in and dumped four Mk-82s on top of the bunkers and shacked them too. And then she started picking off the fleeing vehicles and everything—her and her wingman. We saw one guy get away after the BRDM was hit. He actually—this cliff, it's probably [a] sixty- to seventy-degree incline, about eighty to a hundred feet tall—and he actually ran down the cliff when he came out of the bunkers.

Killing the Iraqi artillery and some of the forces on top of the escarpment greatly aided the U.S. advance, and now they had seized the high terrain. They could see the Iraqi forces arrayed out before them, but the Iraqis had also prepared for the possibility that their enemies might capture this valuable piece of real estate, for as Carpenter found out, they had artillery set up and ranged right on this spot they knew so well. Again, experience and ingenuity came to the aid of these men in that exposed position.

We get on top of the escarpment; they're rooting the Iraqis out of their holes. . . . There were probably three company teams of infantry up there with some antitank and some antiaircraft stuff. We get up on there and it kind of opens up into a bowl right on top of the escarpment. We kind of hunker down there trying to figure out our next move. [We start getting] a lot of registered artillery—122s, probably, maybe 152-mm—but pretty sustained barrage, definitely registered because of the area where it was hitting. It was right on the road as it crested the escarpment. I go to Colonel Grimsley, to figure out if he's got a good read on where the artillery is coming from. He didn't know 'cause his artillery radars can't range up over the escarpment . . . so he says, "They're telling me they think it's somewhere from the east," and he says, "I think it's coming from the west." Colonel Grimsley, he's calm as shit. It's like an exercise to him.

At the same time, I'm picking up a set of aircraft and I'm trying to think old Soviet-style doctrine. I know the Soviets trained the Iraqis, so I'm figuring it's a RAG [regimental artillery group] or it's a DAG [division artillery group], and either way I'm looking at the terrain [on a map] out to the west trying to figure out where [the artillery might be located]. I'm looking at the road networks and how he tactically should be oriented. I studied it quite a bit while I spent all those years [during the Cold War] waiting for the Russians to come across, so I'm looking for a [likely] DAG position or a RAG. . . . I look at a kind of a road network leading to a radio tower and think that would be a good

> spot—gives them good access. I call in a grid, pilot gets over it and he's
> like, "Yep, contact—artillery" [he sees artillery]. . . . The guy rolls in, he
> hammers the artillery.

Crosby could also see much better once he moved up onto the escarpment, and he too set to work making his contribution.

> We crested the escarpment, and I controlled two missions on two dif-
> ferent sets of BRDMs and BMPs; they were just the forward observers
> for the artillery. Then we went up a little farther and we started run-
> ning into what would later be known as Fedayeen. They would keep
> shooting at us and we thought they were army guys that didn't have
> uniforms. We actually ran into a civilian bus full of them. All of the win-
> dows were knocked out of the bus and the guys were shooting at us
> out of the windows. Had an A-10 engage that and get that off of us.
>
> We saw what would end up being called "technical trucks" later on
> in the war, you know, the little pickups with machine guns. They did a
> little drive-by on our flank over near the river and then they swung out
> in front of us. We could see their dust trails; we just couldn't see them
> because of the way the land was rolling. I had an A-10 check on station
> about the same time; . . . he went over and he found ten vehicles. It
> seemed like they were in a little powwow or meeting trying to figure
> out what they were going to do. So we cleared the A-10 in on them. He
> had come from another controller, so he only had two Mavericks and
> [his wingman] had four Mk-82s, so they went Winchester pretty quick.
> They said they at least got five of them—they couldn't tell. So that
> flight checked off. I had another one check on at the same time. . . . By
> the time I got the second set of A-10s spun up and ready to go it was
> probably five or ten minutes later, and I told them the grid of where we
> just attacked, and I said, "Let's start there, and maybe we can look for
> them." When the A-10 got to that grid and got to looking, his reply was,
> "You're not going to believe this, but there's five vehicles not burning
> and five vehicles burning." The other five guys had actually come back,
> I guess to check on their buddies or whatever, but they were in the
> exact same spot as the other five vehicles, so we went ahead and took
> care of them too.
>
> We cleared about twenty kilometers north of An Najaf. . . . Basi-
> cally when the day was done, that day we controlled air for six hours
> covering the army, and each set of aircraft went Winchester.

Sergeant Carpenter had also put in a long day, but being the NCOIC for
the brigade's TACPs he had other duties to attend to. "So now we're going
to hunker down. The escarpment kind of winds down. The objective isn't
to drive any farther that day. We've got to let the log trains and everything

catch up to us and get all of our stuff refueled. . . . The day's been won, Colonel Grimsley's happy, we take some photos with him, he's most appreciative. . . . It's a pretty good day, a pretty good time, and we kind of hunkered down there for the night and let the rest of the brigade close up on us. And that's where we spent a couple, three days."

Many people would get a few days to relax and refit before the next lunge forward, but not Crosby. Having finished the previous day's fight in the wee hours of that morning, he grabbed some sleep then went over to the TOC and got called into a whole new fight.

> Woke up, kind of freshened up, took a look around and all that, and everything seemed calm. Went into the TOC, and as I was walking out, probably about eight o'clock that morning, one of the Special Forces Humvees comes sliding in. The guy jumped out, and was like, "We need artillery, we need something." I go, "What's going on?" He said, "We have a SOF team up near Milh Lake that's about to be compromised." . . . [Near the lake] there's a kilometer-square military compound. The SOF guys took up refuge in an old mine about three or four kilometers south of that . . . but if you're coming out of [the city of Karbala] itself, you pretty much have to drive right by that mine. [The guys talking to Crosby] had gone out on a little recon mission, and when they were coming back, the [rest of the team at the hideout] called and said, "Don't come here." . . . A lot of vehicles stopped close to them and they started to get worried.

The SOF team was located outside 1st Brigade's area of operation, so with the way things had been set up for the Iraq invasion, air sent to help the SOF team would normally have been controlled by the ASOC and their corps shaping team. Since Crosby was in face-to-face contact with one half of the SOF team, however, they would make the best liaison, and since Crosby had proven his mettle earlier, the ASOC decided to let him handle the mission.

> I called up and got some airplanes on station. . . . [The pilots identified] a few vehicles and started engaging them. Had SOF guys sitting right beside me talking to their team up in the strip mine, and they were saying, "Yeah, you're hitting the right guys. These are the ones. . . ." Started ordering more aircraft 'cause approximately twenty vehicles were sitting there on the highway. Some of them were military vehicles; some of them were the old technical-type vehicles.
>
> I had a set of A-10s checked on next. I sent them to the grids; the vehicles weren't there, but they drove north and saw that compound the [SOF guys] were talking about. They spun around in the air for a

little bit, and the guy said he counted at least forty vehicles, could be more, trying to enter the compound. It was a one-lane entrance into this bermed-up compound. So with a little bit of planning, and talking about it with me, he had enough gas to do it, he hung around and waited until the last few vehicles got inside the gate and he Maverick-shot them and pretty much locked them in there where nobody could get out, at least vehicle-wise. And those two A-10s went Winchester, all except number one who had two bombs left, and he thought he saw something pretty interesting—it looked like a tank, like a fuel-type tank [it turned out to be a fuel bladder buried just below the surface.] We were twenty-two kilometers south of this area, and when he hit that tank with those two bombs, it looked like the fireball was going to reach space up there the thing shot so high. [The pilot] said he thought it shot by his airplane. Everybody got excited, he jumped on the radio started telling some of his buddies to get over there and we were doing the same.

We split up the area. . . . We had F-16s and stuff out working that compound with LGBs; everybody that had LGBs was showing up [and] we sent [them] to that compound, and A-10s were strafing the vehicles and Maverick-shooting the vehicles down by the SOF guys. . . . There's this old water processing plant near where the SOF guys were at too, and there were a bunch of vehicles running around in there. There was a Roland [French SAM system] in there too. [The plant] was a "no-hit" target, but [the Roland] kept shooting at us out of that area. . . . Took us three days to get clearance to hit that thing.

In the midst of this fight Crosby had success of a different sort that would prove beneficial as early as the next day. While in camp in Kuwait, Crosby had obtained scrolling map imagery software known as Falcon View that would automatically give ten-digit grids accurate to within one meter of any selected point—what is known as one-meter imagery. This software had the potential to allow TACPs to pull hyperaccurate grids off maps that were now loaded on their computers. It had not been tested, though, so no one knew how accurately the computer grids would match what TACPs could get off their GPS equipment. In this engagement Crosby needed to rely on his map and he was in a good position to give Falcon View a test so he gave it a try.

At [this] compound we found out we could use Falcon View as one-meter imagery. . . . We knew where the compound [was]—we had one-meter imagery of it—and off Falcon View you [could get] ten-digit grids. We didn't know if they were going to be close enough, but right before it got dark [a sandstorm] was starting to move in. On Falcon

View we looked at one of the bunkers that we knew was an ammunition bunker . . . called up grids to that [off the computer] and the guy
dropped a JDAM on it [based on the grids]. He saw the fireball and
everything else—he'd pretty much shacked it. So we had confidence
in Falcon View from [that test].

We ended up controlling that day nineteen hours straight; there
were twenty-two missions checked on with us . . . so we did pretty
good work. The army had actually planned on going in there and clearing that objective, and then we had a Predator fly over it and we ended
up bypassing it—there was no use going in there, it was pretty much
leveled.

For Crosby this day ended in the early hours of the next day—25 March.
He heard over his radio that one of 1st Brigade's battalions, 3-69, was
making a movement across the bridge spanning the Euphrates at Kifl
north of An Najaf. He had controlled air for two very long days, but still
he checked into the TOC and asked the commander if he was needed
for that movement. "Ah, shouldn't be a big deal. Take a break. We're just
going over to take the bridgehead." So Crosby climbed into his track to
get some sleep.

8. A Tale of Two Bridges

The assertion that 3-69's seizure of the bridge at Kifl "shouldn't be a big deal" turned out to be overly optimistic. After running into unexpectedly fierce resistance in An Nasiriyah and As Samawah, especially from the Fedayeen, 3rd ID decided to isolate An Najaf from outside reinforcement and resupply. This was easy enough, relatively speaking, on the west side of the Euphrates, because with the victory on the escarpment the Americans had driven Iraqi forces from that side of the river. The problem was that all 3rd ID's forces were on the west side of the river, and two bridges across the Euphrates, the Kifl Bridge to the northeast and the Abu Sukhayr Bridge to the southeast, linked the city to the most densely populated—and most heavily defended—part of Iraq. Trying to capture a city still linked to the nation's heartland sounded too much like a Stalingrad scenario, so 3rd ID opted to send forces across those two bridges and cut off An Najaf from the east as well. Those two bridges would become the scene of some of the most desperate fighting in the entire invasion of Iraq.

The biggest problem hanging over these two operations, though, was the weather. By the time lead elements moved against the first bridge, a sandstorm was in full force. This storm severely curtailed air operations since it engulfed nearby air bases from which most aircraft launched, but it also crippled several other elements of America's firepower advantage. Artillery and mortars could be used, but like direct-fire weapons were only effective as far as one could see. Essentially, the dust storm seemed to be evening the odds. But American forces still held a few aces up their sleeve.

Tasked with capturing the Abu Sukhayr Bridge south of An Najaf was 3-7 CAV and they began doing so on 25 March. After seizing the bridge they were to isolate the city from the south and east, and afterward conduct a feint by driving north through the area between Iraq's two most famous rivers. All they would have to do is ensure they held the bridge while An Najaf was being cleared, then they could begin their charge northward. Technical Sergeant Keehan, from his vantage point with the commander, gives a good overview of the unfolding operation:

> Bone Crusher [B Troop] secured the bridge early that morning with some resistance. [The Iraqis] had wired the bridge for explosives, but failed to act. Apache [A Troop] was the first in order of battle to pass through, followed by us and the TAC. My guys with both troops had armored vehicles with .50-cal. automatic machine guns aboard. Crazy [Charlie Troop] would follow us in the rear. . . .
>
> The daylight had turned into an almost indescribable orange hue. This was something none of us had ever experienced, something you might read in a Ray Bradbury book or [see in] a sci-fi movie. Visibility was fifty feet at best with heavy winds, everything was orange, and there were enemy soldiers out there set up to kill us as we drove through their city—"the OK Corral on Mars."
>
> As Bradford and I made our way across the bridge, huge explosions rocked off to our left flank. We had no idea what they were or how close, but it was close enough for me. We drove another nine hundred meters and took a left to the north at a four-way intersection; the same one Crazy would later defend. [Apache's TACP] radioed from ahead and let us know what we had to go through, a lot of small arms fire, multiple vehicles with heavy machine guns, older tanks. He was shooting away with his .50-cal. Bradford was taking pictures as he drove of burning vehicles that we could see through the dust, when we started taking heavy small arms fire from both sides of the road. We both already had our GAU-5 automatic rifles [M-16 variant used by TACPs] poised out of the windows of the Hummer and we both started shooting at whatever white muzzle flashes we could identify shooting at us. Total chaos. . . .
>
> The enemy seemed to be everywhere on the sides of the road masked by this freaky orange dust storm. Maybe that saved us as well. We halted about thirty meters up the road while [an army officer] opened up his 25-mm on a blue truck that was full of ammo. I thought at that moment we would be shot through the doors of the Hummer or fragged by the explosions of whatever munitions were located in this mystery truck.
>
> We pressed north out of this ambush area to a small cove on the side of the road, near a blown-up Astros II [Brazilian multiple rocket launcher]. We surveyed the damage and discovered a 7.62 bullet had pierced our Hummer and lodged in my second [chemical suit]. At least it protected me from something!

As Keehan and the rest of 3-7 CAV drove through this ambush and pushed up north to clear out the east bank across from An Najaf, Charlie Troop was given the task of holding the bridge. The enemy realized the significance of that bridge too, and they soon counterattacked. This assault focused mostly on Charlie Troop, and while it cut off the rest of 3-7 CAV and left it surrounded in the midst of a swirling and determined foe, Charlie Troop bore the brunt of the attack and soon they too were surrounded. For the second time in modern history it looked like a unit of the Seventh Cavalry was going to recreate a modern version of Custer's Last Stand. The first had been in Vietnam in 1965, in the battle of the Ia Drang Valley, a desperate struggle recounted in *We Were Soldiers Once . . . and Young.* The Seventh Cavalry had escaped disaster there through skill, courage, and hard fighting, but they also had clear weather, so air power had been able to make significant contributions. Now the weather seemed to preclude that key advantage. Could the Seventh CAV escape disaster a second time? S.Sgt. Shropshire, attached to Charlie Troop, found himself in the middle of this maelstrom, and he describes what it was like.

> We moved to secure the bridge. And that day it started kicking up really hard wind and the sand started blowing really hard. . . . It started getting worse and worse and worse. We pulled into the middle of this intersection and these guys just start coming out of nowhere and everywhere at the same time; I mean they're all around us and they're running trucks up to us and jumping out of the back of the trucks, firing point-blank AKs and RPGs. It looks like they're trying to get on the tanks. All around me [3-7 CAV guys are] just firing, killing these guys, and a couple guys that would slip through the holes in the [perimeter], we shot them. They gave me a . . . combat engineer with a squad assault weapon [SAW], so that helped a lot. I could cover one side with my .50-cal and the other side with [his] SAW.
>
> Then we started running out of ammo and we had to start picking up the AKs from these guys that were dead. I called up and told Keehan the situation—it wasn't getting any better, it was getting worse. First we thought it was going to be just a random attack, but they kept coming and coming and coming. It's like they were pumping guys in there from somewhere. He told me [he was] working a CAS mission . . . and at first I said, "Well, maybe it will clear up a little bit." We were holding them off pretty well, but then the darker it got, and then it started raining too, with the sand blowing, and it just made it a billion times worse—you know, worst possible scenario. You couldn't see, you were cold, hungry, tired; everything that could go bad was going bad. Guys were falling asleep at their guns at this point 'cause we had to fight all the way up, so guys had been up for quite a few hours—hours and hours and hours. I don't think anybody was prepared for this kind of

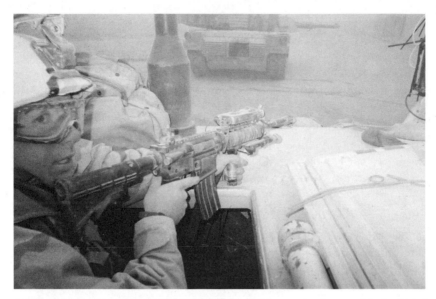

S.Sgt. Mike Shropshire, with 3-7 CAV, defends against ambushes outside An Najaf during a sandstorm. When his unit was cut off and surrounded, Shropshire's insightful use of CAS helped stave off disaster.

fight, or thinking that this kind of fight was going to come to them, because that's like right out of Vietnam—World War II kind of stuff, and that just doesn't happen any more right? But it did happen, and they kept coming, and they started taking loaded fuel trucks and trying to run them into the tanks; that was a bad thing. [We] were shooting them before they'd get to [us] but we didn't know how many more they were going to try to run into us, and they just kept using two avenues of approach, two hardballs [paved roads] to just keep running vehicles down there.

America's vaunted high-technology capabilities cannot always take the place of old reliable low tech or old-fashioned horse sense. But in the battle of An Najaf several threads of recent high-tech development came to the rescue of the 3-7 CAV's beleaguered troopers. One such area was radios: the presence TACP satellite radios in each CAV unit turned out to be a lifeline holding the squadron together. Another high-tech savior was JSTARS and its ability to see through the sandstorm when all other sensors—including the Mk-1 eyeball—could not. JSTARS was able to see and identify massive reinforcement columns streaming from all across Iraq hoping to take advantage of the storm and the trap that had been sprung on 3-7 CAV. JSTARS not only gave the troopers a heads-up of what was coming their way, it also gave them what the intelligence community calls "actionable intelligence"—in other words, they could target airstrikes based on the JSTARS picture. Perhaps most important for Charlie Troop, though, was the JDAM. Once again, this weapon that had been designed for use against fixed targets would prove to be a tremendous all-weather weapon in the CAS role. The first of these high-tech marvels to become indispensable was the radio; Keehan explains how and why:

> We got separated, and that was probably the biggest part of the battle. Crazy Troop was holding that bridge, and we went through the ambush site so far north to get out of the fire that [we] lost FM [radio] communications with Crazy Troop. . . . Lieutenant Colonel Ferrell had TACSAT to communicate to Division, but [lower echelons did not have it]. My TACP team was equipped with a gamut of radios and the best of all, we all had a [satellite] radio that worked like a champ. . . . Thank God we had our TACSAT, because we used [the air force air request net]—and hats off to [the ASOC] for letting us use [it]—to let Colonel Ferrell talk to his troop commander. . . .
>
> Lieutenant Colonel Ferrell briefed [the Charlie Troop commander] over the AFARN on defensive tactics to take, and words of encouragement. We all listened to him and I know that the only motivational object he was missing was a set of bagpipes. We were surrounded and I thought of how fitting this entire battle was. . . . We joked at the TAC nervously about Hollywood making a movie about 3-7 CAV's stand at An Najaf; nervously, because movies get made about bad battles, and 3-7 Cavalry, "Garry Owen," was Custer's unit and the same one depicted in the book We Were Soldiers Once . . . and Young, the first battle of Vietnam. Without our radios, I am not sure what would have happened to Crazy Troop. . . . That probably saved the day.

Shropshire was aware, though, that, at his end, that single radio lifeline was more tenuous than anyone at the TAC realized: "The only radio we had was my SATCOM radio, and my antenna had gotten shot up but it still worked. Thank God for electrical tape, and spit, and whatever I could do to make it work. Obviously that stuff wore off after a while, but it held up, and it did real well, and it was the only thing we had to communicate with *everyone*."

He also gave his impression of Ferrell's "motivational talk": "The squadron commander gave a pep talk to Charlie Troop commander, and basically what he told him was we had to hold that bridge—all 189 of us, we had to hold that bridge—it was the only bridge. So we fought hard. We were not going to leave that place. They would have had to kill us all before we left. . . . Matter of fact, to tell you the truth, I thought I was dead anyway, and a lot of us did. After talking to some of the guys, we thought we were dead anyway. There were just so many of them."

The desperation of the situation and the resigned but determined mood of the Charlie Troop commander came over the radio to other listeners as well. Captain Wiles with 2nd Brigade listened to the fight all night from his location over his radio and reports his impression: "Listened to [Charlie Troop] commander talk to his commander on [Shropshire's] SATCOM radio because the army had lost all communication. He was told to 'hold the bridge, son, we're gonna come for you in the morning, but hold your ground!' The commander goes on to say something to the effect of, 'They're coming for you, son, they know where you are, so use the air force's bombs . . . use all of them.' Pretty somber night. The [troop] commander sounded like he knew he was in a hopeless situation on the radio, but he simply replied, 'Yes, sir.'"

Charlie Troop was the slender lifeline for all of 3-7 CAV. As bad as things were for those at the bridge, should they fail it would have spelled disaster for the entire squadron. And as if the weather and the situation were not desperate enough already, both were going to get worse as the night wore on. Bad weather had grounded fighter aircraft at bases in the area, where most of the close air support had been coming from, but other aircraft with longer "legs"—bombers—were launching from bases outside the reach of the sandstorm, and started appearing overhead. This did not necessarily solve the CAS problem, because without the means to see the targets—either on the ground or in the air—and with sensors useless because of the weather, CAS would normally be out of the question. As Keehan observed, most would have said CAS under these circumstances was impossible. But those bombers overhead carried JDAMs, which during Afghanistan had for the first time brought all-weather bombing capability to the CAS arena. Moreover, despite the fact that JDAM had until recently not been foreseen as a CAS weapon—or maybe given the too often bureaucratic and constraining nature of doctrine written during peacetime, *because* JDAM had not been envisioned as a CAS weapon—TACPs since Afghanistan had been proving very creative as they wrote the book on how to use JDAM for CAS. But it had never been tried in a scenario like this: troops pinned down by overwhelming forces and unable to see beyond their gun barrels. Could JDAM significantly alter the stakes in this battle? Shropshire continued that innovative trend by coming up with some inspired ways of bringing this weapon to his troop's age-old dilemma, and in the process he used JDAM to dramatically even the odds.

I told Keehan that [the enemy was coming down two main roads] . . . and he said, "Hey, I recommend that the first thing you do is chunk up the roads; keep these guys from using that," and I said, "You're right, I agree with you." So that's what I did. . . . I had marked the roads on my map, sent the coordinates, triple-checked them, quadruple, six, seven times we checked them between the pilot, Keehan, myself, my [1C4], and just made sure they were the right coordinates, 'cause we did not want to drop a bomb on ourselves on accident. . . . [The bomber] releases that first bomb and I just had my fingers crossed and I don't think I breathed the whole time until that bomb hit and I was just praying to God that it was going to hit where it was supposed to—and it did. After that first bomb hit my confidence level shot way up. I was like, "Okay, now let's bring it!" . . . [It was] my first real combat CAS mission; I was there by myself and I was real nervous. But I wasn't worried about myself; I was worried that I was going to kill the army guys—I was going to kill the soldiers. I was worried I was going to kill the soldiers and I really like these guys, and that's beside the point, but I didn't want to fail them, I didn't want to fail Sergeant Keehan, I wanted to do well, and I wanted to win. So after that first bomb dropped my confidence shot way up. I chunked up the other road too, then I chunked beside them, to make sure they just couldn't get around the roads.

"Chunking" the roads brought some relief, but Charlie Troop was still getting human waves coming at them, which left Shropshire wondering what to do next.

So I talked to the [troop commander]; we were looking on the map, we're like, "Where are these guys coming from? They must be rallying somewhere and coming at us." And there was a creek bed that ran up right into our area, so I said, "Well, what do you think about the middle between the roads here?" He goes, "Yeah, I think they're using the creek bed to travel up and to hit us." I said, "Okay. . . ." [An aircraft] checked on with WCMD, CBU 103 [Wind Corrected Munition Dispenser with Combined Effects Munitions, used against armor, personnel, and equipment]. I had three WCMD to drop, and I spread them out so they would cover almost a kilometer north-south between the roads. And I kind of offset them a little bit so they had a pretty good width and length, and I had them dropped. And the fire and activity in that area dropped to nothing. . . . Tell you the truth, it was just a guess really. I have to credit most of that to . . . the [troop commander].

Tactically speaking, this was when the other shoe dropped. Just when Shropshire was thinking he and Charlie Troop could heave a sigh of relief, JSTARS reported a large column of vehicles coming out of An Najaf headed toward Charlie Troop's position. Since its radar can distinguish

tracked vehicles from wheeled vehicles, JSTARS could tell it was a formation of approximately forty tanks. The men of 3-7 CAV had been barely
hanging on when faced with waves of irregular Fedayeen whose largest
weapon was an RPG or a fuel truck—now it looked like they would be
facing an armored force. Keehan passed this information on to Shropshire, who describes his reaction: "That's when my pucker factor went
way up. I was like, 'Whoa, fighting these Fedayeen guys and a few Republican Guards was one thing, but fighting armored pieces, and you know
they're not going to just send a few, they're going to send a lot!'"

Keehan's radio gave him a ringside seat to this new threat, and for the
longest time he was powerless to do anything about it. It was incredibly
frustrating, and that frustration was readily apparent to anyone listening in on the drama over the radio. But as one observer noted, Keehan
showed an amazing ability to handle that frustration even when it came
to dealing with another person's shortcomings; despite all he had been
through and all that was weighing down on him, Keehan still managed
to keep his head. Like many Americans throughout the theater, S.Sgt. Jon
Pinson, attached to 2nd Brigade's 1–64 Armored Battalion, was following
the battle over the radio, and he relates another area where, in his opinion, Keehan averted disaster for 3-7 CAV.

> I just remember hearing Keehan absolutely amaze me on that radio.
> I can't even explain to you. . . . I guess it was an inexperienced guy up
> there [in JSTARS], or something, I don't know, but . . . [he] was kinda
> messed up in the first place . . . plus they were using all these stupid
> [code words], so nobody knew what they were talking about half the
> time. I remember Keehan getting on there and just talking to [him] . . .
> like, "Look, this is what's going on; guys are dying, you have a great
> chance to do something great for your country," you know, things like
> that, basically trying to—in a good way—slap [the JSTARS operator]
> around a little bit and tell him to, "Sense up man. Have some sense
> about you. Screw the [code words], just talk plain English. Get this
> done. If you can't do it, find a guy next to you who does know what he's
> doing. This isn't training, guys are dying down here." But in a very nice
> way he did that. And his tact doing that, I think, was one of the biggest
> contributors to the success of that battle in An Najaf and the 3-7 CAV
> not getting their butts handed to them.

Keeping JSTARS in the game was about to get a whole lot more critical,
for JSTARS was about to play a key role in dealing with the new danger
bearing down on Charlie Troop. Keehan was finally going to get a chance
to help his men.

> I [received] reports via JSTARS on military vehicles moving into our zones ... enemy forces coming south into our northern and eastern flanks. They were coming at us from all directions it seemed. . . . Because we knew exactly what was going on from the JSTARS, who was coming where, . . . I started bombing.
>
> First bomb run was ... a B-1B bomber fully loaded with twenty-eight two-thousand-pound [JDAMs]. I had permission to attack the enemy T-72s that were pushing down the highway to Crazy's position. They were utilizing a secondary road adjacent the highway to hide their movements, but we knew where they were. I mapped out several coordinates along the highway to create a stick length for the string of bombs that was three kilometers in length. Bradford was instrumental in double-checking and triple-checking the conversions to latitude and longitude. [Guys at the Division TAC] were also instrumental in helping us ensure we had good coordinates and JDAM queries. This was [my] first mission dropping JDAM munitions, coupled with twenty-eight of them! I tasked [the B-1 crew] to release half of their bomb load on the stick length prescribed. . . . I had them reattack, but this time stretching it to the south, to the edge of the city. I figured they shifted and scattered to the south to safety if any survived the initial onslaught. JSTARS confirmed they had pooled in a low area just south of the city, very near the bridge Crazy was defending. I retargeted the [latitude and longitude] and they made two more bomb runs—eight released and then the final six bombs away.

At that point, Keehan found himself once again in an incredibly frustrating position, because JSTARS was indicating that although a significant number of the attacking force had been killed, a portion had survived and moved into a populated area. Despite the fact that they were moving on Charlie Troop's position, there was nothing Keehan could do; the ROE prohibited attacks in populated areas unless the enemy was actively shooting at them from that position. These tanks were obviously moving in for attack, but they weren't shooting—yet. In his heart Keehan knew they were right, but decision-makers in a far-off headquarters, safe from immediate danger, saying no, citing legal restrictions, the ROE, rules of war, and so on, and so on, didn't help him accept that he had to sit idly by while an overwhelming force bore down on his friends. They needed another creative solution, and as Keehan illustrates, it wasn't long in coming: "With the ROE you couldn't [attack]. . . . It was too close to civilian houses etc. So what we needed was provocation—they had to shoot at us. And that's exactly what happened. Like within two minutes, we were on the radio going, 'Well, here they go, they're shooting at us!'"

Shropshire explains what had happened:

> Keehan was trying to coordinate a CAS mission before they got to us,
> but they'd mixed in with the other buildings, probably on purpose—
> everybody knows our tactics, so they know our limitations and we
> don't like to hit civilians, so they're going to mix in with the civilians.
> He couldn't get them.
>
> Then they got close enough to us where our scouting element
> could possibly see them, but they hadn't fired or anything. [The enemy]
> moved out in an open field between two fairly small little urban areas.
> And JSTARS told me, "Hey, they're right there." Then the ASOC and a
> couple of other places that were listening to the conversation weren't
> going to let me hit the tanks yet. . . . I understand the law of armed
> conflict; I understand the rules of engagement; but at that point, in all
> honesty, I could care less because these guys were taking advantage of
> the weather and were getting ready to cross that bridge, bust through
> those two Brads and one tank that we had sitting there, and kill the
> rest of us that were sitting in that intersection. And I knew that was
> what they were going to do. I think that's what everybody knew they
> were going to do. But our hands were bound.
>
> At this time our scouts went over to take a look, and [the scout
> commander] got on the radio, on our command net, and started
> screaming, "Holy crap they got T-72s! They got T-72s!" I'm like, "Oh man!
> So there's a bunch of T-72s out there," which isn't good. I mean, they're
> not the best tank in the world, but still it's got a pretty large gun and
> it'll mess up the Bradleys and it'll definitely mess up an [M-113].

Keehan was also aware of the close proximity of these enemy tanks, and
even though they could not fire the first shot, he knew the Iraqis eventually would attack, which would open the door for further air attacks—
but only if he and Shropshire played their cards right. What they most
wanted to avoid was letting the Iraqis charge into the American position so quickly that they could not call in an airstrike soon enough and
then the Iraqis would be too close to U.S. troops to risk dropping bombs.
Keehan had an idea that would avoid that dilemma—hopefully.

> The [scouts] of Crazy Troop . . . went across the bridge and that's where
> the T-72s were pooling. . . . [The Iraqi tanks] were probably six hundred
> meters away. . . . So I told [Shropshire] to hold on, do not bomb, 'cause
> I had already bombed the hell out of the whole road line . . . let them
> regroup for a while. . . . "If you start getting shot at, wait for those tanks
> to make their charge across [the bridge]. . . . At that point . . . tell your
> guys to move back. . . . I don't think they'd see [you] move back. So that
> will give you a little more space."

Shropshire agreed to the plan and briefed Charlie Troop. He had more air power on its way, it would be to him any minute, they had their plan, but they still had to wait for the Iraqis to make the first move. As it turned out, the Iraqis' move worked to the Americans' advantage.

They were giving me a B-1 and it hadn't showed up yet. . . . So [the scouts] scoot back and I said, "Okay, listen, here's the plan: [when] these guys fire at us . . . I'm going to have [the B-1] tell me when he's going to drop. I'll give you five minutes, you pull back so you don't get any of the shrapnel." They said, "Okay, no problem." They still hadn't fired at us. I was arguing back and forth trying to get [approval to bomb]—cause they were going to give me the B-1 but I don't think they were going to let me fire yet. Then [the Iraqis] sent a scouting element out—and I don't know who fired first—but the Iraqis and the scouts that we had deployed on that bridge started exchanging fire. And they said, "We're being fired at! We're being fired at!" So I got on the radio and said, "Okay, we're engaging the enemy! They fired at us, we're engaging!" I don't remember who it was, but the guy [at the ASOC] asked me, "Are they really firing at you or are you just saying that?" And I got really, really ticked off; after all that crap, I said, "Look, you want to talk to the Crazy Troop CO, I'll have him run over here out of his tank, get on the radio, and tell you that we're being fired at." There was a slight pause and he said, "Okay. B-1's on the way."

Now I'd never worked JDAMs before [that night]. The JDAM was easy to work on stationary stuff like the road, and dropping a WCMD in certain places to stop their movement, but I had to really think quick on how to use them against tanks. And I knew—cause I put myself in their shoes—if a bomb hit right in front of me I don't want to go forward into it. I'm going to try to move away from it. So I knew that's what they were going to do, or I guessed that's what they were going to do. So from the JSTARS I found out where they kind of massed, and I dropped one right in the middle of them. Then because they knew we were over here, I knew they didn't want to move toward us after that, so I dropped one 250 meters behind that one . . . almost one right after another, just like about twenty seconds behind it to give them enough time to pull back, pull back, Bam! right into the other bomb.

[JSTARS] said, "Yeah, they're moving [back]." So our scouts go back over there. . . . They see where the first bomb impacted. . . . Then a T-72 took a shot at one of the Bradleys and I was like, "Get out of there! Get out of there! Get out of there!" And they scooted back. And I said [to JSTARS], "Give me a correction off the first impact." They said, "They're 500 meters west." So I dropped another one 500 meters west of that, and then another 200 meters west of that one—you know, right where they were—and then nothing. The scouts went over there—nothing. They didn't see anything. It was totally quiet—eerie quiet. The rest of the night it was quiet too. Nothing. No more firing or anything.

So the next morning they took a look at some stuff, and they had some of the civilians bringing up pieces of tank to us and thanking us. It basically had rattled a lot of those tanks to pieces and just destroyed a bunch of them—a lot of armored vehicles, a lot of trucks, a lot of tanks. And there were just tons of bodies all around us from the firefight. And I was so tired, but I couldn't sleep. It was like that all over. And I can imagine it was like that for Sergeant Keehan and the rest of those guys too, because we'd all been fighting for hours and hours and hours. . . . This is something like seventy-eight hours of just nothing but fighting. So we were just dog tired.

I wasn't thinking about, "Thank God I'm alive," or anything like that. The two main things I was thinking about were, "Thank God we didn't lose anybody, especially because of me," 'cause I didn't want to hit any of our guys, even though the bombs started getting real close. I mean, you could feel them. You could see the glow. I mean it was just the whole track would rattle and just sway 'cause it was that close. I had a picture of my family and I just was real happy that I'm going to get to see them again—or at least I was glad I was going to live another day to see them again.

We were told, "Hey, you got to stay there another night," and I've never seen so many down faces in my life, including myself, 'cause to tell you the truth, I didn't want to stay in that fricking place. I hated it. There's nothing but death around us and I just wanted to get out of there. . . . And we had a report that there was a thousand-vehicle convoy coming right for us; so I start setting up JDAM points to start hitting them . . . but the thousand-vehicle convoy apparently never got to us and I don't know where that came from, or even if it was real. . . . So the next morning, about afternoon, we got relieved . . . and we got out of there.

The battle of An Najaf—at least 3-7 CAV's part of it—was over, and every man who had crossed the bridge before the battle recrossed it afterward. Thus another chapter in 7th Cavalry history entered American military history. The unit that is forever tied to the legend of George Armstrong Custer had survived its second brush with disaster in modern times. Like 7th Cavalry troopers in the past, they had been surrounded by overwhelming numbers, but they enjoyed one significant difference. The Little Big Horn had been a massacre, and though Ia Drang had ended in victory, it was bought at the cost of more than three hundred American lives. In the battle of An Najaf, every man survived—not a single American died defending that bridge. The unit spent a couple days resting and refitting before they reentered the fight, once again out in front performing that traditional cavalry mission—scouting and screening for the main body.

About the same time 3-7 CAV moved to isolate An Najaf from the southeast, Battalion 3-69 of 1st Brigade crossed the bridge at Kifl, north of the city, to cut it off from the northeast. As the unit approached, they realized Iraqi troops were set to blow the bridge, so they hurried to prevent it. The Americans were partially successful, but with only the lead elements of 3-69 across, the Iraqis managed to set off one charge and a section of the bridge buckled. Unsure whether the bridge was still sound, all vehicle movement across the bridge—in both directions—ceased. Shortly thereafter those elements on the east side of the river came under the same sort of Fedayeen attacks that were causing 3-7 CAV so many desperate moments. Those units on the west side of the river did what they could to help their stranded brothers, but it was clear they would need more help. Because they hadn't expected much of a fight, 3-69 did not have a TACP with them. Quickly they realized they would need one, and so only a few hours after he had turned in from his second long day controlling air, Sergeant Crosby was called for. He describes what followed.

> About seven o'clock that morning everybody started beating the panel on the side of my track saying, "Get up! Get up!" . . . When I realized the bridge had been blown, I went over to [Lt. Col. Rock Marcone, 3-69 Battalion commander] and said I'd like to go over there. He said, "Well I'm going too, so let's go." We both loaded up and took off for the bridge. It was a seventeen-kilometer sprint. We drove fast as we could go through bad guy land. They'd take a couple of potshots every once in a while at us, just two vehicles—an M-1 and a 113. . . . We linked up with the guys that were at the bridge. . . . Four tanks trapped on the other side; they had killed everyone that was over there setting the traps—it was just a bunch of infantry. . . . [On the other side is] a small town; streets aren't that wide, so the tanks had a hard time getting to where they can move their turrets around. While we were going over there I jumped on the radio and got some airplanes over that way and got them scanning the highway; there wasn't anything big over there yet. But then they started [watching] the town north of us. About thirty kilometers north of us was Al Hillah, and the planes said there were a bunch of vehicles kind of grouping up on the south side of Al Hillah. So I got them to identify a couple of military trucks south of the group. They took them out—there were six of them. As soon as they took

them out, the [other] vehicles [started] shooting back at the planes, but those planes were bingo and they had to leave. And then that's when the big sandstorm started moving in, so everything started getting interesting.

We ended up capturing their equivalent to a lieutenant colonel . . . and he said he had already made the call back to Al Hillah, and between three to four thousand people were going to be down to take the bridge back from us within the next few hours. So we spent fifty-one hours over there messing with that nice place [after] the sandstorm moved in. . . . It wasn't as thick in the beginning . . . so I had a couple of F-15s come in that had LGBs and were still able to get their laser on the ground and worked on convoys that were making their way down. Ended up killing about twenty vehicles, with those LGBs keeping everybody north of us.

The whole time we were doing this we're getting counterattacked in that town. So I'm talking on the radio, dropping the hand mic, shooting the .50-cal, mortars and stuff like that are coming in. And then our track just died on us—just shut off. We started getting probably the biggest counterattacks they had against us the whole time. The radios were still working but the engine shut off. We couldn't crank it back it up, the batteries were going dead. Shut all the radios off except the [PRC-113], which wasn't pulling that much juice and I was still able to talk to the planes. But trying to coordinate through the army to get somebody up there to [jumpstart the track]—and like I said we started getting counterattacked and all the tanks were backing up because of the mortars that were coming in and we were like left out here by ourselves for a little bit. It wasn't a real happy time. . . .

If you had a ten-minute break you were lucky. These guys were coming straight at us for fifty-one hours, so it was sporadic on the resupply. . . . Soon as you [say], "All right, pick up some ammo," guys would start loading up and they would start getting popped again. . . . These guys would drive up in pickups and shoot. You'd shoot the pickup, the pickup would flip over, they'd jump out, pick up the guns, come running at you with AK-47s.

And then finally the engineers figured out that . . . the way [the bridge] was dropped it was still sound enough for us to get the tanks back across. So we pulled the tanks back across, pushed some Bradleys over there on the other side, a platoon of Bradleys, that way we could protect the bridge a little more. . . . We had four Bradleys on the enemy side of the bridge, we pulled back to the near side of the bridge—the bridge wasn't but a hundred foot long. We were in an overwatch position. The Bradleys on the other side of the bridge were getting the close stuff and we had Bradleys and tanks strung out on the friendly side of the bridge getting everything [else]—the road [ran] pretty much right beside the river, so we could catch everything coming down there and safely shoot it from where we were on the other side.

The night before, Crosby had been able to verify the accuracy of the Falcon View map program on his laptop computer, which now proved providential. Unlike 3-7 CAV, which had some open space around them and a scout team to move around and verify coordinates, Crosby and the forces from 3-69 were pinned down to a tiny toehold on the edge of a town. Being able to pull reliable hyperaccurate grids off a map with his computer was a tremendous advantage because once the sandstorm obscured vision he could still use the precision weapons at his disposal overhead.

The town of Kifl kind of breaks up, and just in the center of the town is [a] big apple orchard. We had a Bradley kind of poke his head around the corner, and he could see that orchard and saw a lot of vehicles before the sandstorm moved in. He backed up when [the sandstorm] moved in, so we knew that was their staging area, and we got permission from higher [headquarters] that [since] it's an apple orchard even if nobody's there just go ahead and hit it. If anything, we'd blow up a bunch of apples. So we put JDAMs through the weather [on that target]. And then we started thinking about how we can find out if these guys are moving south out of Al Hillah. . . .

If you look at Al Hillah and Kifl [on the map], there's only one road you can get there by and there's . . . a Y-intersection; you have to take the northern leg to go into the town of Kifl, or if you keep going straight you're going to bypass Kifl and go toward An Najaf. [This second leg leads to the bridge that was being held by 3-7 CAV.] [This] is the same time that 3-7 CAV was in a scrap down at An Najaf. So according to what fight they wanted to get into [the enemy would go one way or the other at this Y-intersection]. . . .

I think it was six or seven hours after [the battle] first started, we finally got a hold of JSTARS, and they started working that highway coming out of Al Hillah. . . . JSTARS started reporting twenty-five vehicles moving south pretty much in a column out of Al Hillah and they were heading our way. We were going to try to stop them way up north of Kifl and some JAG officer somewhere up the chain . . . decided to speak up and say we need confirmation these are enemy vehicles and not civilian vehicles. In the worst sandstorm this country has ever seen, where you couldn't see ten feet, he or she figured those twenty-five vehicles in column formation [might be civilian]. . . .

What we had to have was confirmation from JSTARS that they were track vehicles in this convoy. The way that works, they can't see the vehicles, but they can pick up Doppler shift, which is usually returned by tracked vehicles. . . . So these were the only twenty-five vehicles on the whole highway, and they're getting Doppler shift off twenty-one of them. Everybody came to the conclusion this has got to be coming off tracked vehicles. So we got [higher headquarters] to believe that, and they cleared us [to attack]. And by the time we got that clearance they were at that Y-intersection, which actually worked out for us. Because of the sandstorm, when they got to that intersection they actually stopped to, I guess make their decisions—are they [headed for 3-7 CAV] or are they going to come fight in the Kifl battle. . . . I had F-15s on station with twenty-four GBU-12s but they couldn't drop them with laser 'cause the sand was so thick, so they just dropped them ballistically [based on grids from Falcon View]. . . . They dumped twenty-four five-hundred-pound bombs in a line up that highway starting from that intersection. And JSTARS watched it for ten minutes and got no movement out of the whole area. . . . A couple days later the army went out there and there were nineteen tanks and APCs, and then a couple of other vehicles—so JSTARS was pretty [accurate] with them. We were getting pretty low on ammo at that time, so it was pretty important that we stopped the vehicles there.

Later on more vehicles started moving down. This was the same night that Fox News and everybody had the thousand-vehicle convoy coming out of Baghdad our way, so everything JSTARS was picking up was of interest to us. So we had another ten-vehicle convoy coming down. We did the same thing with JDAMs off of B-52s—just strung them down the highway matching up with JSTARS on grids using Falcon View. . . . Just a few clicks on the laptop computer and we're bringing JDAMs through that dust. . . . From then on it was just infantry guys coming out of the woodwork, and the Bradleys make pretty good work of that. . . . Little skirmishes were still going on [the next day], but we were able to turn that area over to 3rd Brigade. . . .

We got a report back; they went and interviewed the Iraqis in that town after the war was over and right before we showed up they spotted Qusay Hussein himself trying to set up the defenses in that town. So that was his dudes. We couldn't figure out why these guys are fighting so hard for this little old town.

What had started as a hurry-up effort to prevent a bridge from being blown ended up as a prolonged battle to protect trapped U.S. forces. Thanks to the determination and courage of 3-69 Battalion, and thanks to some innovative marrying of high technology, all the men of 3-69 came home from this battle, as had the men of 3-7 CAV. They were relieved in place by elements of 3rd Brigade. By this time the sandstorm had lifted and 3rd Brigade was able to push enough combat power across the bridge to clear out the town of Kifl. Another near disaster brought on by enemy ferocity and an untimely sandstorm became part of the larger Coalition victory in the area around An Najaf.

9. Through the Gap, across the Bridge, and on to Baghdad

With An Najaf isolated, 3rd Infantry Division now controlled the city's outlying areas, which greatly facilitated capturing the city itself. Getting this far seemed, on the one hand, breathtaking in its speed and remarkably low U.S. casualties. But there had been some nasty surprises along the way—especially the Fedayeen—and the 3rd ID had had two miraculous brushes with near disaster. Were these episodes harbingers of what lay ahead for the rest of the road to Baghdad? Everyone knew Saddam had arrayed his forces in a tiered defense that got tougher the closer you got to the capital—would the rest of the journey be worse than what they had faced thus far?

This was also when the "studio generals" started sharply criticizing the invasion plans. Supply lines were overstretched and vulnerable, and U.S. soldiers had been captured, all of which prompted many observers to speculate that a massive disaster was just beginning to unfold. Critics charged that too small a force had been planned, that as a result the army couldn't sustain its momentum, supplies couldn't reach the front, and the army couldn't control the territory it had already captured. The pause at An Najaf looked like the offensive had run out of steam, leaving it stalled too deep into Iraq to pull out yet not deep enough to pose any serious threat to the regime. Everyone involved with the actual planning claimed the pause had been intended from the start, but reporters and commentators hinted this could just be the army trying to put the best face on their failed plan. Some media voices were already talking quagmire. Had the invasion force shot its bolt? Later events after Saddam's fall would certainly add credence to the charge that not enough troops had been planned for the occupation, but as events would soon bear out, 3rd ID had just begun its dramatic dash.

The army's insistence that the halt had been planned from the beginning is echoed by air force TACPs involved with the execution of the plan. Intended as a rapid thrust through what they thought was going to be friendly territory, the first phase got 3rd ID to its first planned hard fight, and now that that fight had been won, 3rd ID needed to consolidate its supply lines, refit, and prepare for the next lunge. Russell Carpenter, as a senior NCO, bore much of the responsibility for seeing that 1st Brigade's TACPs were ready for the next push, and as he explains, they too were resting and refitting, especially those who had participated in the hard fighting. Others were also actively engaged in preparing for the next battle. "Basically the Iraqis have separated from us. We have not pursued, we put out the scouts of course, the forward companies. But CAS activity is light. There's kind of a lull; we're bringing up the fuel, ammunition, all that kind of stuff, and it looks like we're going to be there a couple three days. . . . You're settling into sort of defensive [postures] against any counterattack as the rest of the log train catches up to it. . . . So, while we are doing that, the [TACPs] are reconstituting our gear, high-fiving everybody, 'Okay here's the next leap-off plan,' . . . everybody's looking now at Karbala Gap.

Though to most observers the pause outside An Najaf seemed to be a time of simply consolidating supply lines, with little action, another phase of the battle was just getting into high gear. From the beginning of the war, Coalition air power had been scouring Iraq looking for military units vulnerable to air attack. Using the KICAS CONOPS developed just before the invasion, coupled with SCAR, which had been evolving for some time, warplanes had enjoyed some success. At the same time, Lieutenant Colonel McGee was leading the effort at the ASOC to iron out the new corps shaping concept he had helped develop. There had been some growing pains, but those had been worked out, and the biggest problem now facing this campaign, as well as the KICAS and SCAR operations, was trying to find Iraqi units that had so far remained dispersed and in hiding.

Efforts to find those elusive units received a dramatic boost with the onset of the sandstorm, when Iraq began moving forces. Some were obviously set in motion hoping to take advantage of 3-7 CAV and 3-69 being trapped at the two bridges near An Najaf, but not all the units were heading in that direction. Turkey's decision to deny use of its territory for a northern invasion front had come little more than a week before the invasion, leading Hussein to feel much more secure about his northern flank. And the closer American forces got to Baghdad the more Saddam's dispersed forces had to come out of hiding and consolidate if they wanted to put up effective resistance. This is exactly what M.Sgt. Tim Stamey experienced outside Konduz, only written on a much larger scale. With army and marine forces deep in Iraqi territory, Iraqi planners felt they had a better idea of Coalition invasion routes. In fact, Iraq's assessment of the attack plan set the stage for another air power success. In the meantime, all this movement exposed Iraqi units to the view of intelligence sensors, most particularly, JSTARS, and made efforts to hunt them by air much more successful. Scouring an entire country the size of Iraq hoping to find concealed tanks is one thing, but tracking those tanks as they move to new positions is something else entirely. And larger tank formations would be much easier to find and kill than smaller ones.

The big Iraqi shuffle set off a concerted effort to hunt down those forces and kill them from the air, an effort that lasted till the fall of the regime. As late as America's entry into Baghdad, V Corps was still finding major formations, and aircraft under TACP or SCAR control were swarming on them like bees. Once a concentration was found it was a simple matter to broadcast its location to all aircraft in the vicinity, and with one central agency—the ASOC—coordinating attacks, pressure could be maintained on the enemy unit until it was eliminated. Once this feeding frenzy began there was little the enemy unit could do to alter his fate.

Thus the sandstorm, though it was cursed at the time, turned out to be a real boon for U.S. forces. Once it ended, 3rd ID was in a much better position to resume the offensive. And the Iraqis were in a much worse position to counter it as the Coalition air armada launched a storm of its own. The results of this "storm from the air" were immediate and dramatic, and as McGee attests, General Wallace, V Corps commander, was content to have General Blount and 3rd ID sit at An Najaf for a few days so they could refit and consolidate their supply lines while the air assault hammered the enemy.

Third ID's next offensive move was to pass through the second choke point, the Karbala Gap, but after seeing how effectively corps shaping was destroying Iraqi combat power, Wallace decided to modify his plan to improve chances for success in the air campaign. He had already begun to integrate his ground maneuver with his ASOC's air maneuver by pausing at An Najaf long enough to let air shape the ground battlefield; now he was using ground forces to shape the air battlefield. This thinking led to the battle known as Five Simultaneous Attacks. The heart of this plan was a 2nd Brigade feint against Al Hindiyah on the Euphrates about thirty-seven miles upstream from An Najaf. This was meant to pave 3rd ID's subsequent move north. At the same time, units from the 101st Airborne would conduct an armed reconnaissance west of Milh Lake, a feint against Al Hillah, and an assault to contain An Najaf, while the 82nd Airborne moved to contain As Samawah. This operation would keep the

Iraqis guessing about the Americans' next move: was it to be across the Euphrates at Al Hindiyah, Kifl, An Najaf, or As Samawah, or was it to loop around Milh Lake and sweep in from the west? The real intent, though, according to McGee, was to so overwhelm Iraqi defenses all at once and from so many different directions that in a panic they would start moving in reinforcements from every direction, which would expose them to American sensors and lead to their being hunted down from the air.

On 1 April, while the five simultaneous attacks continued, 3rd ID launched its offensive on the Karbala Gap. If the escarpment had been a potential choke point for the U.S. offensive, the media hadn't picked up on it, but everyone, even the media, realized the Karbala Gap had all the makings of a real disaster. The eastern end of Milh Lake, a reservoir on one of the Euphrates' tributaries, is only about eighteen miles from the Euphrates River, and in that space sits the city of Karbala—one of the holiest cities in Islam. There is more room to maneuver east of the city, but the terrain between Karbala and the Euphrates was thought to be marshy and broken. The area between the western outskirts of the city and the reservoir is better suited for armor operations, but it is only about three miles at its narrowest. Such a bottleneck was a natural place for Saddam to use his weapons of mass destruction, and many expected he would do so.

The attack plan called for 3rd Brigade to isolate Karbala from the east, while 1st Brigade screened from the west, seized bridges across the stream north of Karbala, and then launched the dash north by northeast. Sergeant Carpenter was quite surprised with the reception they got when they hit this much-feared chokepoint.

> We get the go and we start the op—it's kind of like a creep. You see 3-69 and the other battalions begin to creep to the north. We just successively kind of take some positions, and before you know it we find ourselves right south of the gap one morning. At sunset I actually see the first structure in the Karbala area. . . . We want to stay out of Karbala, we don't want to get in a fur ball in there. . . . It's a very holy city for the Muslims, so we do our best to keep all the strikes out of there. We got some extensive no-hit target lists that we don't want to touch, and we clear all our fires that way—we're very particular in terms of what we're hitting.
>
> We're prepping the [next] morning and—Bam!—we're off. It's again the funnel effect; it's a small piece of ground, it's dark, the command nets are crackling, and targets, engagements. They got a pesky ZSU in the gap that's doing some direct fire work for the Iraqis . . . keep-

ing us pinned, keeping us stopped. The terrain is kind of uneven—un-
dulating—that kind of a roly, moundy terrain. Real good for defensive work, antitank positions, but it seems to me there's only a couple
three companies defending the whole gap by now. Of course, we've
pounded them for about a week, so maybe we've given them the clue
to press on to the north.

Even without heavy defenses, the assault through the gap would have
taken longer than expected—as Crosby explains, the terrain concealed
unknown obstacles.

It was a lot slower going than what we thought. If you look at a map
you see like one or two, maybe three or four strip mines in the Karbala
Gap. But really the whole Karbala Gap is old abandoned strip mines. . . .
Trying to [maneuver] with NVGs and trying to do it in battle formation
was pretty tough. So we ended up going back to column formation. . . .
We actually had two BMPs and what looked like a school bus—could
have been just a big van—set up a road block. We had aircraft on station working my battalion and another battalion, and I just borrowed
his aircraft for a few minutes, and put down two LGBs on those guys to
clear the road for us. We lucked out with that one; got out there and
they had a few landmines, probably sixty landmines in that van—bad
looking things—and we think they were going to try to stick those out
on us. Luckily we didn't have to deal with that. As far as the whole army
goes, we engaged a bunch of infantry running through the Karbala
Gap. But aircraft really pounded them pretty hard before we got up
there. . . . There wasn't much left when we drove through the gap; [the
problem] was just trying to get through there itself.

Because it was taking so long for 1st and 2nd Brigades to push their
way through the bottleneck west of Karbala, division leadership made
a change of plan and ordered 3rd Brigade to find a route east of the city.
The terrain turned out to be better than expected and 3rd Brigade had no
problem finding passable roads, but they also found themselves with a
fight on their hands. In the lead element was 1Lt. John Blocher, an ALO
assigned to 3rd Brigade. So far in this narrative the air force officers have
all been in the headquarters. While this is the way a typical ASOS is struc-
tured, that rank divide isn't always the case; a number of officers led from
the front in Iraq and controlled a lot of air, and Blocher is one such example. An A-10 pilot from Gaithersburg, Maryland, Blocher was in a flying unit when the United States was ramping up for the invasion, and
like all A-10 pilots, he had a parallel commitment to support the army
as a battalion ALO during wartime if needed. His flying squadron was

tasked to identify a number of pilots to serve with the army, and in yet another example of entrenched air force attitudes toward CAS, the squadron commander used a simple matrix to pick those who would serve as BALOs: the most inexperienced pilots would be sloughed off to the army. Blocher, who had only been with the squadron six months, was thus identified, despite the fact that he had only the bare minimum of training and no experience. Fortunately he did not share his commander's casual attitude toward controlling CAS, and he used what little time he had before crossing the berm to conduct his own "crash course" in how to be an ALO. Thanks to this commitment he was able to bring CAS to bear at a couple of key moments during 3rd Brigade's contested passage around Karbala.

> It took us all night to clear this one route—had a couple of F-15s overhead. They actually went to the tanker probably six or seven times. Stayed with us all night long from about 10 P.M. till about midmorning. The sun had already risen by the time they went home. But they gave us top cover. [They] ended up dropping some LGBs on a couple different locations, and we had them come in and strafe. We were taking a bunch of fire from both sides of the road, a lot of small arms and . . . a whole bunch of RPGs. I was just afraid one of those RPGs was finally going to stop missing and shwack us. So we had them roll in and do some strafing. . . .
>
> The sun came up and we didn't really receive much more fire from that [point].

For all their worry about this bottleneck, the lead U.S. elements of 1st Brigade were through the gap by seven o'clock, and most important, they took no casualties in the process. Part of the credit for this stunning turn of affairs was obviously due to the successful feints 3rd ID had conducted all along the way—An Nasiriyah, As Samawah, Abu Sukhayr, Kifl, and finally Al Hindiyah had kept Saddam guessing right to the last minute as to the Americans' true route. But by all accounts, a significant part was also a direct result of the relentless pounding the Iraqis were taking from the air out ahead of the advancing army, especially during the period V Corps spent in An Najaf. Carpenter conveys the amazement, and no doubt elation, felt by many as they speed through what they had long seen as a major hurdle on their trip to Baghdad. "And then it's like all of a sudden the gap fight is over. We punched through and it opens up into a huge bowl area. It is the Iraqi [army training range]—so it's where the Iraqis do all their armored training southwest of Baghdad. . . . It opens [into] wide open flat terrain. It's got good roads, of course, to get the military traffic in and out. So we're shooting into that; we're thinking, 'They know this terrain like their backyard . . . you know, they can really make use of this [for a counterattack].' Well, they don't. And there's nobody! We just blast through. Now, I start doing some [air attacks] on the Euphrates sites—looking at a couple of bridgeheads."

Third ID didn't get much time to bask in the glow of victory after winning their second big chokepoint because almost right away came their third. Objective Peach, the code name for the bridges selected for the main crossing of the Euphrates, was their next big fight. Since time immemorial, river crossings have been the bane of attacking armies, and entire campaigns have either succeeded or failed on how they fared at bridges, so 3rd ID had obviously put a lot of thought into selecting where they would do their main river crossing. One thing going for the Americans was the location: just outside the town of Musayyib, a town so small and obscure it doesn't even show up on many maps, but it has a good bridge complex. A second factor in their favor was 3rd ID's many feints. These feints kept the enemy off balance, kept them shuffling their forces, which exposed them to air attack. It also forced them to keep fewer forces at more locations, meaning 3rd ID would find less resistance at Peach.

Once 1st Brigade passed Karbala they turned only slightly right and raced for Musayyib. Third ID did not intend to pause as they had after taking the escarpment, and since the distance between Karbala and Musayyib is little more than twenty-five miles as the crow (or the A-10) flies, Carpenter wasted no time getting aircraft out ahead looking at Objective Peach. As Carpenter illustrates, aircraft can shift from this first fight to the second in a matter of minutes.

> I'm working [a site on the way to Peach]—I don't know why [the Iraqis] defended it so heavily, but my pilots kept reporting heavy triple-A. It's like this guy's got something he really wants to defend here. It was southwest of the Euphrates, but not by much. I ended up pounding a lot of triple-A, some trucks, some ammunition bunkers. And then later on, when I turn the close fight air over to the 2-7 ETAC, he hammers a butt load of armor—something like twenty pieces.
>
> Now we're in trail. . . . You get all these guys on line and they're just screaming across the desert. I mean, you're driving sometimes as fast as your Hummer can go. The sand's coming up at you, and there's artillery around you, and there's tanks around you. It's just a mass—it's just like, "Go! Go! Go!" and everybody's flooring it. We're running for the Euphrates bridgeheads 'cause we want to capture the bridges. It's very quick—very fast. We got [the 2-7 Battalion ETAC] working some

close fight air, we got Sergeant Crosby working some close fight air near Peach, but it isn't like the Iraqis have come to the other side of the river to engage us heavily. We're not taking a lot of contact. We get to the bridges and as I remember 2-7 damn near takes theirs unopposed.

The fight for [the other bridge] is a little more contested. [A brigade ALO's] got a great plan: he's strafing up and down the bottoms of the bridges to keep the sappers from blowing the bridges. . . . And it works; they try to blow the bridge, they blow a hole in it, but they can't drop it. . . . [That same ALO] is working some air on the bridge. . . . They were trying to rig the damn bridge and then repair what we'd cut. Sure enough, we roll the A-10s in, shoot up these pickups . . . we get up on the bridge and they're uniformed Iraqi dudes, all of them, several pickup trucks full. . . .

It's kind of weird . . . you went from the flat desert, now you're on the Euphrates; the environment completely changes in the span of about five miles. You go from desolation to palm groves, and it looked like a scene out of *Apocalypse Now:* you got the choppers flying in low, firing off Hellfires and rockets, doing some gunning work. It's a heck of a fight.

Sergeant Carpenter, working at the brigade level, was responsible for assisting with "the brigade's fight," so he was working CAS out ahead of the battalions, but as the battalions got closer to the objective, the job of controlling CAS at Peach was handed over to them. So once 3-69 approached the bridge Crosby took over and Carpenter turned his attention to putting air on forces farther out. The "deep fight" Carpenter then became involved in was especially critical because once the Iraqis learned of the assault on Peach they immediately launched counterattacks from the north and south, and corps shaping played a big part in stopping both efforts before they could influence events at the bridges.

As Crosby neared the objective he not only took over CAS responsibility for the close-in fight but also found himself once again involved in close quarters combat that was so intense he at times had to forgo his CAS work to defend himself and his team. He describes the race to seize 3-69's bridge from his perspective:

We got about two kilometers away from the bridge and you started seeing the Euphrates River. In fact, everything started turning green. You had palm trees and foliage and everything. . . . You could imagine driving through all that desert and all of a sudden you start seeing palm trees, you start seeing some tall wire grass, and at first you're like, "Hey, it might be an okay place," and then the wire grass starts lighting up with sparks and everything 'cause there's dudes hiding in it, and it's like, "Uh-oh, it's just more places for these guys to hide." . . . When we started getting close to the green stuff and we got eyes on the bridge, we start slowing down and engaging everything. We were getting a whole bunch of radicals and everything thrown at us. Trucks were running up and down the road shooting at us with machine guns. . . .

That was where we first saw Iraqi ingenuity. The old German-type motorcycles with side cars, these guys had an antitank missile mounted on these side cars, and they would drive full speed with the motorcycles and you would see the guy lean over, and it was almost like he was lighting a fuse—he'd fire the missile. . . . They were pointed straight—that was their guidance. They were on a rail kind of thing—it wasn't a tube or anything—it was just the guy would just reach over and punch a button and they would come off the little rail. It would fly up in the air or something like that—and that was his only weapon. He's barreling down on tanks and Bradleys, he'd take his one shot, and then try to turn around and scoot out of there and of course none of them ever made it. . . . The first time I saw it I didn't even shoot at the guy for a couple of seconds—I was in awe. I was like, "Man, that's pretty neat!"

They had ammo caches all over the side of the highway; they had S-60s, these other kind of triple-A pieces lined up in a ground fire mode [the barrel depressed to shoot at ground targets] shooting them at us—it was a slug fest to get to the bridge. Once we got there, it was like, "Okay maybe they're defending the near side of the bridge," and this whole time we were working airplanes on the far side of the bridge, keeping people off the bridge. Didn't notice any armor or anything. I think I got two BMPs on the far side of the bridge, and it was like, "Maybe we caught them not defending this bridge." Definitely on the near side it was pretty hard. Couple times I had to turn the airplanes over to Sergeant Carpenter so I could work my .50-cal.

We get [up to the bridge], we sit there for probably about thirty minutes while the engineers actually go in the water to go check on the bridge to make sure it ain't booby trapped or whatever. We're defending them. . . . And when the A-10s reported to us that they got everything they could get, that's when the commander finally made the decision: "Let's go ahead!" We got across to the other side of the bridge. The Apaches peeled off; our other battalion was crossing [the other bridge] and they were in a little skirmish down there, so the Apaches went down to help them out.

Two companies go to the right and screen, and the company I'm with, we go to the left and start working this winding road around a couple canals. . . . That's when [the Iraqis'] best chance of getting anybody happened. They were actually buried—dug in, camouflaged, and everything. They had thirteen vehicles—BMPs and tanks—and they started their vehicles up, pulled out in the middle of our formation—we were in column formation. In front of me I had a friendly M-1, and in front of that M-1 pulled out a T-72, and right behind me I had a Bradley, and right behind that Bradley pulled out a BMP. . . . The army pretty much laid waste to those guys pretty quick. I think one T-72 got a shot and hit a tank in the front slope, which is like shooting it with a BB gun.

I knew we couldn't engage any of those with aircraft, but just from knowing the way the Iraqis had been fighting and from knowing Soviet doctrine they'd pounded into our heads, I figured if they were going to launch any kind of support and counterattack that's when it was coming. There's a highway that skirts the river that runs northwest-southeast, and I had F-18s there; I called them up and got them to look at that highway, and sure enough there were five vehicles headed down our way—three BMPs and two truckloads of infantry. So we engaged those guys and got rid of the counterattack that was coming, and probably five minutes after it all started, there were thirteen burning Iraqi vehicles and all of us trying to get around the burning vehicles.

We moved around, kept engaging infantry and stuff like that. . . . We cleared out a couple more kilometers. We started finding all these fighting positions with uniforms, boots, and everything just tossed to the side where these guys took and tossed their uniforms off and ran. . . . We thought we had it cleared, and that's when the S-3 [battalion assistant chief of staff for operations] and I peeled off and were headed back to the TOC. . . .

I'm following the S-3; he has a tank, and he's sitting at a T-intersection, so he takes a left and he sat there for a long time. We're pulling up behind him to take a left also. All of a sudden he snatches the turret around and points to the top of the T-intersection and I see him trying to work his gun so we stopped. He traverses his main gun kind of toward us and I told my driver, "Go! Go! Go! Pull forward so he can shoot." I didn't know what he was trying to shoot at . . . so I'm trying to get out of the way so he can take a clear shot. And I see him start waving his hands and he's shaking his head no and I hold my hands up like, "What?" And he jumps on the radio and he's like, "No, no, you got dismounts in the ditch!"

I turn around and I look and there's—I only saw two guys. When I turn around and looked they're getting ready to try and take some shots at us. So I leaned the .50-cal over toward them and pressed the trigger. It pops off two rounds and then jams. I'm like, "Oh shit!" I always got my M-4 on top; I reach over to grab it, and the strap hangs on something and I'm like, "Oh crap!" And these dudes had me dead to rights: all this time in slow motion they're bringing their shoulder rifles up, and my [assistant] is in the back of the track, and he's seen I'm try-ing to shoot in the ditch. He just leans his weapon over, he can't see out of the track . . . and he just shoots over top of them—a two- or three-round burst, pop, pop. He got those guys jumpy, 'cause they kind of took their eyes off me to look at the back of the track. I was able to bring out my pistol at that time and emptied the clip on both of them. Gave them a shot a piece, kept rotating until I ran out of bullets.

We get back to the TOC and I jump out of my track and the S-3 comes running over, he's like, "Man that was close!" And I was like, "Yeah, I didn't see them two dudes." He's like, "Two? I saw five at least." I was like, "Oh shit!" I only saw two. I never thought I would be using my 9-mm in the middle of a big armor battle. That was pretty crazy.

In the midst of the fight for the bridge and clearing out the bridgehead on the western side, Carpenter and his ALO were sticking close to the bri-gade commander, who went across with the lead elements of 3-69 Battal-ion. Carpenter gives his impressions as the battle wound down:

We get up to the bridge, Colonel Grimsley goes, "Hey [General Blount] said no soft-skinned vehicles across." Colonel Grimsley goes across in his track, I look at Captain Chesser, we're in a Hummer, and I go, "We're going! We're just going!" . . . We came under fire, I'm controlling [air-strikes], we're on the bridge, and these gunners were just opening up from a farmhouse down below us about two hundred meters. So we all get defensive and here we are sitting on top of this bridge in this soft-skinned Hummer.

That was all the fight for the bridgehead. . . . We've destroyed all the vehicles there, and you just see mass abandoning of the infantry positions where these guys have just stripped their uniforms and hel-mets off and fled the scene. There's literally hundreds of foxholes with boots and pants and helmets—they just took them off and ran. They ran down to the next town, which when we saw them [later] they were all waving at us then. We secured the bridgehead—that's a big deal for us—we get both bridgeheads across. . . . Now we're kind of con-solidating again, we're pushing units through, pushing the log trains up . . . and then we start [preparing for] the final assault for us in 1st Brigade—its charge into [Objective] Lions, up to the international airport.

S.Sgt. Jon Pinson drove through the area with 1-64 Armor Battalion the day after the battle for the bridge. He provides a graphic assessment of the ferocious fighting Carpenter and Crosby had just been through: "This place looked like the gates of hell had just opened up and swallowed it. I mean it was absolutely destroyed. It was a bad fight, you could tell. Seeing the aftermath of it, there was a lot of death . . . and the smell of it was bad and you could just tell on these guys' faces. I remember [another TACP] coming up to the track as we were rolling through. We couldn't stop and talk to him, but you could just see that he had been through it."

Now that they had a firm foothold across the Euphrates, 3rd ID took another short pause, but this one was only going to be for a couple days. In the twelve days since crossing the border into Iraq they had passed all three of the major chokepoints division planners thought would be their greatest challenges, and now they stood poised for the final phase, the assault on Baghdad. Rather than plunge right into the city, though, the division had two intermediate goals to accomplish first. One was to clear their southern flank. Second Brigade was going to pass through 1st Brigade's lines and swing south toward a key intersection—the junction of Highways 1 and 8, codenamed Objective Saints—roughly twelve miles south of Objective Peach and twenty-six miles south of Baghdad. They were to clear Iraqi forces, particularly the Medina Division of the Republican Guard, from the capital's southern approaches between the Tigris and the Euphrates. While 2nd Brigade cleared Saints, 1st Brigade would sustain its momentum by swinging north and seizing Saddam International Airport.

Second Brigade began its assault south the morning of 3 April. The five simultaneous attacks had set a trap, and now 2nd Brigade was going to close it. The feints against Al Hillah and Al Hindiyah had reinforced Iraqi notions that the Americans were crossing the Euphrates there so they could use the major arteries of Highways 1 and 8 to move on Baghdad from the south. As a result, the Iraqis began concentrating forces south of Al Iskandariyah, a city at the junction of the two highways. Corps shaping was of course pounding these forces, but if 2nd Brigade could come in behind them and seize the key intersection, they would effectively cut this force off from Baghdad, the city they were supposed to protect at all cost.

Second Brigade's lead units came under fire almost immediately. Initially resistance was disorganized, but it grew in intensity the farther south they went. Though lead elements reached Saints within three hours, the battle to take and hold the intersection lasted well into the night. Attached to those lead elements was S.Sgt. John Stockman with

3rd Brigade's 1-15 Battalion. Stockman had played a key role in the fighting around Tallil Airfield early in the invasion, and after that his battalion had been detailed to 2nd Brigade. Trying to catch up with them had kept Stockman out of the fight until now.

> I'm not sure what engineer was in charge of the terrain analysis and who chose the route that went from Peach to Saints, but it's probably the absolute worst route they could have ever picked for a mech and armor unit. . . . The route they picked for us was through all these suburban areas on the southwest side of Baghdad, and the road was like a two-lane road that goes through any neighborhood, you know—not really very wide. It's okay for two cars going past each other, but when you're rolling M-1s and Bradleys down it it's pretty tight. On one side there was like a twenty-foot drop off into this nice little muddy ditch, and on the other side was a canal. So there was no maneuver room. It was pretty much just everybody in line and going down this road.
>
> After we got about a mile, maybe two miles from the bridge, it's like they were waiting for us to come down that road. I don't know what the deal was, but we caught it from both sides really, *really* bad. I was in the third vehicle in line and when we crossed the bridge, my company was the lead company. . . . So we're hauling ass down this road, or at least as best we could, and it just opened up from both sides. Had dudes hanging out in the bushes not fifty meters away from us hitting us with RPGs and AKs and everything. Had dudes hanging out of windows of all the houses on the other side hitting us. It was one of those things, where there was no room to maneuver at all. . . . It was, "Everybody just keep hauling ass and just shoot what you can as you're going!"
>
> Since we were in such a close fight up where I was, my E-BALO [who was farther back] . . . had airplanes on station, A-10s, so he pushed them out in front of us a few clicks and was strafing the sides of the road, especially on the canal side and the bushes and the trees. He had them running down with the gun, say thirty or forty meters off the side of the road just strafing the shit out of it. . . .
>
> [The Iraqis] would roll off any little side streets that would come out of these little neighborhoods. They'd roll out in like a Nissan Sentra–type car hanging out the windows lighting up the lead tank with their AK-47s and [the tank driver] wouldn't even slow down, he'd just roll right over them; he wouldn't even bother to shoot. . . . I went through the better part of two combat loads [two standard issues of ammunition] that day with my M-4. . . .
>
> Once we got in close to Saints, like within a click or two, the terrain really started to open up. . . . [The fighting] continued. . . . It wasn't

as bad because the terrain opened up and we were actually able to maneuver and get into formations, set up positions, and stuff like that. . . .

[The fighting that day] lasted for about thirteen straight hours, I believe. . . . We got to Saints and fought pretty much till dark. I'd say we got to Saints by early afternoon, and my company . . . went right at the intersection of [Highways] 8 and 1. We took that southern road and we went down probably three to four clicks and set up a blocking position, and the other companies did the same thing all the way around to cut off the [other approaches to that intersection] basically, all four of them. . . . Once we set up there, throughout the day we fought. By nightfall just south of our position we probably had fifteen to twenty vehicles 150 to 200 yards [out] that we had destroyed [because they] were making runs at us and shooting at us from their vehicles . . . a couple of buses, a bunch of vans, a couple of cars.

Once everything calmed down, which was actually late that night, [2nd Brigade] came through. . . . They took off down to the south, and from what I hear, I guess they found the Medina Division. Everything was deserted but they found it.

Also with 2nd Brigade in their push for Saints were Major Jewell and the other members of his marine ANGLICO detachment. They were part of the forces passing through Staff Sergeant Stockman's battalion headed south in search of the Medina Division of the Republican Guard. Though Jewel's fight was short, it brought some intense experiences.

We were ambushed by Iraqi tanks and BMPs, and it was fairly memorable. We took two 30-mm armor piercing rounds into the Bradley. The gunner . . . hit his knee on something or something hit his knee and it swelled up a little bit. . . . We were ambushed at the same time the vehicle gun sights were down. Unfortunately for us, the mirrors in the periscopes and the sights just rotated out of position and the sights went black, so you really couldn't use the 25-mm cannon, but you could stick you head out of the turret [and] see the barrel of the 762 [machine gun]. It had some tracers, so you could . . . point it at the direction you want it, squeeze the trigger, and walk the tracers onto the target. I guess I was fortunate during that time with the RPGs coming at us that the Iraqis were not as good at firing the RPG as we were at controlling CAS and firing the 762.

I was able to get air, and the air force was very responsive. I got air and ran air on the targets. The RPGs were firing at us, and I can say that it is true—if you're nervous or if you're not very good with your weapon system you tend to fire high. There must have been thirty

RPGs that went over my head and the bridge we had passed under. I later saw that that thing was all tore up from the machine gun hits and the RPG hits. I had a lot of concrete dust down the back of my shirt and all over the top of the turret, but it was very memorable standing there hearing RPGs whiz over my head and hearing the machine-gun rounds plink off the side of the Bradley, while I was walking machine-gun fire into the muzzle flashes.

The fighting continued into the next day as 2nd Brigade cleared the area south of Saints. During this operation Jewell used CAS to kill seven T-72 tanks, six BMPs, six ammunition vehicles, and one SAM site. Jewell's experience was unique for this phase of the operation, though, because most other units reported little resistance. One element of 4-64 got into a sharp firefight, but it was with a group of irregulars using civilian vehicles. Otherwise it seemed the Medina Division had ceased to exist. One explanation for the seeming disappearance of this once-vaunted Republican Guard division was the corps shaping campaign that had been directed against it. Air assets had been searching for the Medina from the beginning of the war, but KICAS and SCAR were having only limited success. Corps shaping had been making a bigger impact, particularly after the five simultaneous attacks prompted Medina to consolidate in anticipation of meeting 3rd ID north of Al Hillah. Once they saw that Saints had been captured, though, the Medina, along with elements of the Adnan Division that had been sent to reinforce them, realized they had been cut off and tried to escape eastward around the Americans back to Baghdad. In a scene reminiscent of Desert Storm's Highway of Death, air power directed by the ASOC pummeled the Iraqis as they fled, leading to what one observer has called, "the single most destructive day of the war."[1]

After its fight for the bridge at Objective Peach, 1st Brigade took a couple days rest, but it was not idle. It had been told to prepare for an imminent assault on Saddam International Airport. As with previous pauses, Senior Master Sergeant Carpenter helped prepare for the upcoming battle by controlling SCAR and CAS missions in the objective area, "We sat there static for a couple of days fighting the deep fight south of the airport . . . hammering good armor units, dug in armor south of the airport. [Crosby] is working air, 2-7 is working air, we're working deep air. It's a target-rich environment, but we think we've got these guys beat."

1. Charles E. Kirkpatrick, "Joint Fires as They Were Meant to Be," National Security Affairs Paper, published by the Institute of Land Warfare, Association of the U.S. Army, http://www.ausa.org/pdfdocs/LWP_48.pdf.

On the same day 2nd Brigade rolled south to take Objective Saints, 1st Brigade headed north. There were a lot of reasons for taking the airport right away. First, it would give 3rd ID a base from which to launch assaults on Baghdad. The airfield would also give them an aerial lodgment into which they could fly supplies. Finally, in a reflection of the predominance aviation has achieved in modern society, taking Iraq's main international airport—and the one that bore Saddam's name—would be a severe blow to Iraqi morale, signifying to all the world just how poorly Iraq was faring in this war. Travis Crosby was once again playing a leading role in 1st Brigade's assault. It was a serious fight, especially at the end:

We thought we were going to get a little break, we were going to have other guys out in front of us. That's when the division commander wanted to seize the initiative and launched us to go take the airport. So at noon on the third, after about two or three hours of sleep, they said, "Let's go!" So we loaded up and took off for Saddam International.

We headed out to Highway One at about probably four o'clock; it didn't get dark till about six, six thirty. We were going through two little small towns, we were getting waves, people were inviting us in to eat, they were all cheering us on. After seeing the scenes from Desert Storm, everybody started feeling like, "Wow! This might be over. They might know something we don't know." Nobody really let their guard down, but everybody had a little pep in their step and smiles on their faces—soon as we hit Highway One that all changed.

Soon as we passed through that second town, we get on the main highway all hell breaks loose again. We got ambushed from two compounds on both sides of the road. . . . They were trying to charge into us . . . nothing but bullets coming from both sides of the road—bullets and RPGs. So running about thirty kilometers [per hour], my guy in the back is shooting on the left side, I'm shooting the .50-cal out the right side. The Bradley behind us is spraying everything. I'd kind of waved a tank up to our left; he was covering our left flank. . . . [A little farther down the road] we got hit again—another set of vehicles jump on us—technical vehicles, I think there were a couple BMPs and stuff. That lasted for about four hours of like eight kilometers of highway.

We get right outside Baghdad airport, about two kilometers south of the airport, and the sun's going down, so we decided to wait until we put our night sights on and attack the airport at night. . . . We're sitting there waiting on it to get dark, all of a sudden five sets of fighters show up at the same time—two sets of A-10s, two sets of F-15s, and a set of F-14s. . . . So we started working on Saddam International. . . .

There were two air FACs [in the F-14s]; didn't know they were air

FACs at the time. It wasn't real effective with me controlling the airspace and trying to get these guys in on target, so I asked the question over the radio, "Anybody up there air FAC qualified?" And of course the F-14s spoke up, so we spun them up over the top of the airport, and we basically chopped it up into four blocks, and put each set into their own respective square. . . . We worked everybody Winchester there, and then we got about three more sets of fighters in, Winchestered those guys taking out tanks, S-60s, SAM sites, and a bunch of stuff.

Once everything was set for the assault on the airport itself, 1st Brigade had a surprise for its defenders, as Carpenter explains:

We actually go through where the engineers blow a hole in the wall—it's probably a fifteen-foot, twenty-foot high wall that surrounds the airport—instead of driving through the main gate, which they looked like they have pretty heavily defended. . . . They had triple-A positions ringing the airport about fifty-eighty meters; just an amount of triple-A that was unbelievable. Some of the [Iraqis] tried to use that [in direct fire mode] and engage our guys pouring through, but very quickly we are turning an armor battalion loose [on them]. They were just pouring in and engaging triple-A, and whatever vehicles. [The Iraqis] had about six hundred, seven hundred infantry along with the triple-A. Not a lot of armor on the airport itself, but pretty tough characters.

Since this was a close-in fight, Crosby played a bigger role than Carpenter, and he describes the fight for the airport.

We were on the southwestern-most taxiway when I called up and said, "Hey there's airplanes all over the place—want to take them out?" The answer was, "No!" I got off the radio and somebody popped off a tank round and shot one of the airplanes. I jumped on the radio and called, "Hey, that wasn't an airplane! I didn't take it out—CAS didn't take out that plane!" And it wasn't five minutes after that the second one—boom!—explodes. Every article I have ever seen written about the war says, "Aircraft destroyed on the tarmac by coalition airplanes." I'm like, "That's wrong; I sat and watched both tank rounds shooting."

The northwest section of the airport had a *bunch* of bunkers—vehicle-size bunkers—and these things started emptying out. The A-10s were up there and they started noticing this through their NODs. Our tanks were engaging them, we were engaging them with .50-cal and stuff, and the A-10s were getting what they could get. The F-18s only showed up with two JDAMs apiece, and we were using them more like recce in the beginning. Then Saddam's guys had S-60s on top of near about every aircraft bunker, and they started trying to lay their guns down where they could shoot at us with these things. The F-18s were able to get a grid with their systems and drop on top of these bunkers and take these guys out for us. That was really helpful 'cause a 57-mm bullet flying makes a big noise, and you don't want that coming your way. . . .

We attacked on and that was when we found all those bunkers on the north and northwest side of the airport. . . . All these guys start attacking us down there. Turned out there's an SRG headquarters— Special Republican Guard guys. We ended up capturing a colonel and two of the generals. The generals didn't want to give up, but the colonel did.

We sat there [on the airfield] all night. About every ten minutes we had infantry coming at us. We [TACPs] didn't have [thermal sights] so we were, we called it "second to respond"—we'd see what the army guys were shooting at, we'd pick out a few targets in there and spray it with the .50-cal or M-4s. We were in the center—didn't have many shooting lanes—but it kind of saved our butt one time. We had a few guys get into our ranks, they got into our formation, but they didn't count on us being in there, so we were able to take care of them.

Although he didn't play as active a role in seizing the airport as Crosby, Carpenter did have a ringside seat and he describes how the battle wound down, particularly the telltale sign that things are well in hand: when headquarters shuts off CAS. "I could see Travis, he's targeting the different targets for [aircraft], and we're hearing the work, and [the fighting is] really kind of dying down, and I hear, 'Oh yeah, we're taking some triple-A!' And you hear Travis, 'Cleared hot!' Boom! Big detonation, these ammunition bunkers going up. We're like, 'Okay, you're done with this.' It's like, 'Listen, I think they got this under control. We got a lot of guys streaming into this airport now, and we don't want to use any more CAS,' so we cut him off and pretty much said, 'The fight's done.'"

10. The Thunder Runs

With the newly renamed Baghdad airport in American hands, 2nd Brigade securely entrenched at Objective Saints, and the Medina Division and other forces south of Baghdad largely destroyed, 3rd ID was now poised to begin the assault on Baghdad. News of U.S. forces deep in Iraq and across the Euphrates had flashed around the world and it was seen as a real blow to Hussein's regime, but "Baghdad Bob" was still crowing about Iraqi military success and denying the Americans were anywhere near the capital. Everyone knew that for most Iraqis the only irrefutable proof that the end had come for Saddam's murderous regime would be the sight of M-1 tanks in downtown Baghdad. More important, though, from the start it had been clear that Baghdad was the heart of Hussein's power, and therefore nothing short of capturing the city would suffice. Military planners before the war had assumed that taking Baghdad would involve a long, bloody, street-to-street urban battle, and no one was looking forward to it.

For years defense analysts and military experts had been studying the urban combat problem—or as the military dubbed it, military operations in urban terrain (MOUT)—and it seemed to be the toughest nut to crack, militarily speaking. It raised the specter not only of many casualties for the attackers but also of massive civilian deaths and widespread destruction. And lessons from such urban conflicts as Grozny in Chechnya suggested that those weapons that gave U.S. forces a decided advantage in other environments would turn out to be handicaps in an urban fight. Conventional wisdom in military circles held that RPGs fired from basement windows would find the relatively vulnerable spots on tanks, while shoulder-launched surface-to-air missiles would make low- and slow-flying aircraft, such as helicopters, easy targets. In addition, high-flying aircraft would be useless, as the widespread destruction inherent in airstrikes from that altitude would do more harm than good.

On top of all this, hanging over the heads of U.S. military and civilian leaders was a distinctly American nightmare: the haunting memory of Mogadishu and its aftermath. Bill Clinton's effort to resolve Somalia's chaos by stepping up pressure on the warlords paralyzing that nation had culminated in a disastrous urban street fight in the Somali capital chronicled in the riveting book *Black Hawk Down.* Aggravating the tragedy of eighteen deaths suffered in that encounter was the video footage showing jubilant Somalis dragging dead American soldiers through the streets. The outrage expressed by Americans across the country over this debacle prompted Clinton to summarily pull U.S. troops out of Somalia in what was widely seen as a humiliating defeat. No one connected with the military campaign in Iraq wanted to see that kind of controversy heaped on top of an already divisive invasion.

Still, 3rd ID's success up to this point had been nothing short of stunning. Some have said the dash from Kuwait to Baghdad ranks as the fastest armored thrust in military history, and war planners were eager to keep that momentum going. Moreover, the success of corps shaping and particularly the destruction of the Medina Division heartened military leaders and left them feeling more confident about moving on Baghdad. No one thought capturing Baghdad would be easy, but they realized that the speed of their arrival on the city's doorstep had caught Iraqi military leaders flat-footed. Therefore, they knew the longer they waited the more time Iraqi defenses would have to coalesce inside the capital, thus making it harder to capture. Military leaders realized audacity had been a key part of their success thus far, and they were looking to continue that trend with their next step.

Within this context a daring plan evolved. First, 2nd Brigade would send one of its battalions, 1-64, charging up Highway 8 to the airport held by 1st Brigade. Then 3rd Brigade, which had missed most of the offensive action thus far and was still on the west side of the Euphrates guarding Karbala, would move west of Baghdad and around the city to isolate it from the north; this would send it slicing through Baghdad's northern suburbs. Finally, after seeing the success of 2nd Brigade's drive to the airport, military leaders decided 2nd Brigade would launch another drive through the heart of the city culminating in downtown Baghdad, where it ultimately set up headquarters at one of Saddam's palace complexes. These lightning raids would turn into intense battles reminiscent of the close-quarters combat witnessed by 3-7 CAV outside An Najaf, and CAS would play a critical role. And as with the An Najaf battle, the ROMADs and ALOs involved would find themselves controlling CAS as they too were fighting for their lives in some of the most intense action of the entire war; by all accounts, these airmen performed both roles with the same ferocity and effectiveness as their army comrades.

The opening round in the battle for Baghdad began on the morning

of 5 April 2003. The plan—when viewed with detachment—was deceptively simple: 1-64 Armor Battalion was going to proceed from one secure
U.S. position, Objective Saints south of Baghdad, to another secure U.S.
position, Baghdad International Airport west of the city, by driving down
the modern divided highway separating the two positions. The only problem was that this would take the battalion through the southern and western neighborhoods of Baghdad itself, and thereby, presumably, draw out
whatever forces loyal to Saddam Hussein might be located in those parts
of the city. There wasn't much intelligence on how many forces they might
encounter, but given the poor predictions they had been given before the
invasion, few soldiers or airmen were in a mood to trust more intel predictions anyway. Clearly the Americans were hoping to strike a psychological blow, both by keeping the momentum going and by showing the Iraqi
people (and the world) that they could do as they pleased in the city.

When planning started the night before the assault, few who were
going along knew what kind of reception to expect. One person who
would help bring air power to the fight was a marine augmenting the
air force contingent with 3rd ID, Gy.Sgt. Butch Deas. Attached to Charlie Company of 1-64, "Gunny" Deas hails from Leicester, North Carolina,
right outside Asheville, and he had been with 1st ANGLICO before it had
been disbanded in 1998. Deas was one of the first to sign back on when
the Marine Corps reconstituted the ANGLICOs just before the Iraq war.
As one of the most experienced forward observers in the Marine Corps,
he used the long voyage to Kuwait to run a refresher course for his fellow
forward observers, many of whom had only just come back to the field
from other jobs. This training program proved invaluable on a daily basis
throughout the invasion, but one area would be put to use in a particularly dramatic episode. Working with an air force unit meant Deas could
actually control airstrikes, something the marines did not let enlisted
forward observers do at that time. They have since changed that policy and now, like the air force, let enlisted personnel control CAS. Deas
gives some insight into the human reaction to the news of the impending
Thunder Run—one common among many that night. "It was the night
of the fourth . . . and it's getting dark. [The company commander] pulls
us around his Bradley and he pulls out the map. . . . He's like, "Well, this
is what we are going to do tomorrow." . . . He points to where we are on
the map and he just draws his finger [from] Objective Saints up Highway
8 and all the way around to the airport. . . . And we just look at him like,
'Have you lost your mind?' And he looked at me and he says, 'Gunny, I
want you on ABC [TV] tomorrow.' I'm like, 'No problem, sir!'"

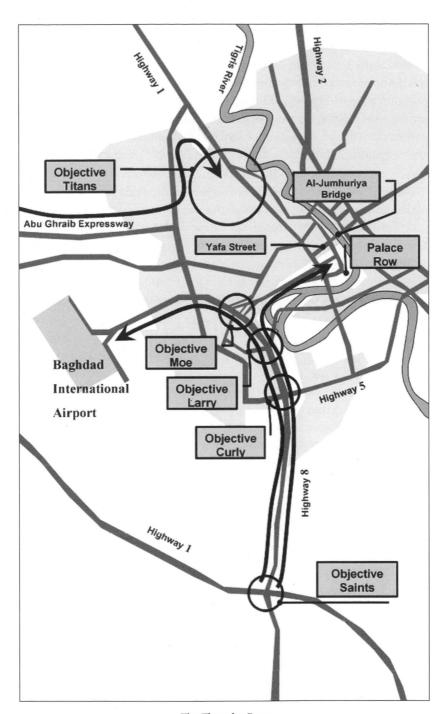

The Thunder Runs

Deas's first impression had been more prescient than his second. Preparations kept him up until almost three o'clock that night. "So I got down for about an hour's sleep. Next thing you know, a little after four, we're cranking up the vehicles and rolling out." Almost as soon as they left friendly territory they ran into a maelstrom. Saddam had stationed numerous forces in his capital, including artillery and antiaircraft units, so even though his main forces had been cut off outside the city there were significant threats, including fedayeen. The Iraqis hit them with everything, often in swarming attacks.

A big part of the responsibility for actually bringing CAS to bear fell on the shoulders of one airman, S.Sgt. Jon Pinson of Lenoir, North Carolina, the TACP with the company at the head of the column. With the entire battalion traveling down a highway, only one person could effectively control airstrikes, and from his vantage point he was in the best position to see and deal with threats out ahead of the column as they moved forward, so this young man carried a load of responsibility. Pinson describes how his day unfolded and the reception they received:

> We start rolling, and reality starts setting in and we're like, "Dude, we're really doing this! Just rolling up Highway 8!" . . . I was with the lead company . . . but Colonel Schwartz went with that company, so he was the ground commander at the time, and I was right behind Colonel Schwartz . . . a hundred meters or less from the lead vehicle.
>
> I remember I was explaining [the situation] to the aircraft . . . they're looking at stuff, and all of a sudden the sky just blacks out. It was phenomenal flak. I remember talking to aircraft numerous times . . . and they'd just say, "I gotta go," and they [would start] defending themselves against triple-A. Numerous times that happened. It may have taken a good forty-five minutes to an hour before I could even really give an aircraft a target because they were so preoccupied defending themselves. . . . I'm like, "Can you talk to me yet? Can you talk to me yet?" And they're like, "No, No. . . ." I remember this one A-10 pilot; " [I said] can you just give me a grid and maybe I can get some artillery on these triple-A positions." He's like, "Yeah, I got a grid for you: Baghdad." And I was just like, "Okay, I get the picture; now I'll shut up."

After they had suppressed some of the air defenses, Coalition aircraft were able to lend critical assistance, especially paving the way out ahead of 1-64, as Pinson explains.

> Aircraft would check in, and we attacked numerous targets right along Highway 8. Most of them were like artillery pieces, just groups, just

S.Sgt. Jon Pinson took part in the Thunder Runs, the U.S. multipronged advance on Baghdad. Here, he holds up a Glock he found during a sweep through one of Uday Hussein's palaces.

clusters—I don't know why they did it this way, but clusters of artillery pieces that they would use as direct fire weapons. A lot of 23-mm [guns], a lot of light, white pickup trucks, like little Nissans or something with 23-mm strapped to them. And the aircraft were good eyes on this stuff. . . . So, a lot of [what the aircraft were doing] was finding targets that we couldn't see. . . . They could attack it at the same time depending on where it was in relation to us. I probably said over a hundred times, "All friendlies are on Highway 8; no bombs on Highway 8." And [Colonel Schwartz and I] had kind of a basic [agreement], "Okay, keep it five hundred meters from friendlies—but if it's close, we can probably work through it." . . . There were a lot of trucks with dismounts running out around them; we would bomb them. . . .

The idea for using CAS during the Thunder Runs was to hit them before we got there. They were working ahead of us. I mean, a lot of the targets we attacked I didn't have eyes on, I just had eyes on the aircraft and the friendlies. . . . So it was basically the aircraft finding something, they would say, "Yes it is definitely enemy, I see muzzle flashes, I actually see the gun," or whatever. "Okay great. What's it near? Is it near a bunch of civilians? Are there houses, apartments, whatever?" "No." "Okay, sounds like a good target." I would say, "Stand by for ground commander's clearance," get on the mike with Colonel Schwartz, "All right sir, we got this here, yea or nay?" . . . Actually, I give more credit to the aircraft because they were the ones that were finding them. Basically, all I was doing was linking the aircraft to the man who owned the ground to get permission to attack. . . .

I was in the middle of a fight; between my rifle and the handset we were all pretty busy. [My 1C4] didn't feel comfortable up on that .50-cal unless I was covering his back at least with my rifle because he could only face one way at a time. So just to ease him, I would always be up there with my rifle, and I'd set it down to do some aircraft stuff, and pick it up [when I was done]. I had bent down [to do] some math or something on my map, I can't remember what it was I was doing, and I got back up and [my 1C4] wasn't in the hatch. . . . I asked [him] what was wrong, and he said, "Dude, I've been shot!" And I was like, "Where?" And he was like, "On my shoulder. . . ." It ended up not being a very bad wound, it was just a flesh wound right on the edge of his shoulder, and I mean it bled, but it didn't hit any bones. . . . Got the CLS [combat life saver] bag and threw a bandage or two on there. . . . He couldn't feel his arm, but he was cool with it. I was like, "Dude are you okay? Do I need to put [someone else] up on the .50?" He's like, "No, no, I got it man, just put me back up there. I can't feel this arm." It was like his arm was paralyzed for about thirty, forty minutes.

I remember one particular mission on the northern edge of [what we called] the Fish Hook. We were just getting shwacked by some artillery pieces on the north side of the road [on] a huge hill. . . . These artillery cannons were somehow just pointing right down at us. And the tanks couldn't elevate their main guns to hit them. There was only like a couple of them actually firing. . . . And I had A-10s on station, but [the target] was, I'd say, maybe 150 meters between the friendlies on the road and where this line of artillery was. The A-10s were very quick to get their eyes on it—A-10s are absolutely phenomenal. . . . So, we had them strafe that. It was an east-to-west trace right on the very northern tip of the Fish Hook, and it was like heaven to hear that 30-mm open up on those guys, it was like heaven just opened up and said, "I gotcha boys, don't worry about it." I remember a few remarks on the FM radio, on the battalion net, of guys coming over saying, "Man! Listen to that!" These guys loved that. And that was really the first strafe run I saw in Baghdad.

Not far behind Pinson was Gunny Deas, who though not actually controlling airstrikes, was assisting by looking for targets and using sensors to determine distances and grids. He was also kept busy with the same job occupying everyone else—defending the column with his personal weapons, in this case, his M-16, his 9-mm pistol, and the Mk-19 grenade launcher mounted on his track. The swarming attacks mounted by the enemy seemed almost surreal, when suddenly the danger became very real.

> A couple hours into it, I think we're up at Curly [code name for the first intersection north of Saints], and we started meeting heavy resistance. We got pickup trucks, vans, little cars, everything coming at the task force—you know, guys out in back with AK-47s just all over the place shooting. You got RPG signatures all over the place. . . . There's this one incident when it first started getting hairy; there was a white Toyota pickup, and I mean it came barreling right at us. It clipped the Bradley behind us and it ran into the back of us. There was this one Arab in it, and you know, you could tell he wanted to see Allah or something, but it was so close we couldn't engage him with the Mk-19. We're getting ready to put a couple M-16 rounds in his head and the Bradley behind us opened up with his coax. All you see is a couple sprays of glass and a little bit of red, and the truck just stops immediately and everybody just keeps going right over top of him. . . .
>
> A lot of these guys were just playing possum alongside the road with weapons beside them, RPGs especially, and once a tank or a track would go by them they'd reach for that RPG and try to shoot it in the ass end. . . . It was nothing but close engagements. I mean, everything was so close you couldn't engage the dismounts with the Mk-19. . . . And [Pinson] was probably about five hundred meters in front of us, and he got a couple of A-10s to come in and strafe the side of the road. . . .
>
> Next thing I know, I'm working a laser range finder, I'm thinking, "God! There's so much shit going on here! Where's a viable target?" I'm looking, and I turn back around toward the front of the vehicle and there's an impact, you know, something hits me in the face, it felt like a ball bat. So I'm like, "Oh man!" and then I see the blast where it knocked the track commander down. He was manning the Mk-19 . . . and I'm shaking him like, "Hey! You all right?" and I reached back just to make sure I still have my face, and I could feel it was there, but I could feel something wet, 'cause of course it was bleeding all over the place. . . . There were bone fragments and everything else. . . . For a minute I was okay but then after a couple minutes it's like, "Man, something doesn't feel right. . . ." We had an army medic in the track with us, and basically all he did was just clean it off and put the compress on my face, and tape it closed. . . . I was probably [incapacitated] for about a good forty-five minutes to an hour. . . . But after awhile it just sort of started coming back to me, "Okay, I got the bandage on my mouth, good to go."

Making it to friendly lines at the airport seemed to many like passing through a curtain separating hell from heaven, for it seemed like the fight-

ing stopped instantaneously. This sudden transition was a welcome relief. Pinson comments on how those who had run the gauntlet reacted.

> The closer we got to the airport, there was a lot of resistance because
> they were expecting us to come from the airport, but we came up on
> their backs. After we got through, we're sitting on the airport, on the
> flight line there; we ate first, and drank water, that was like the biggest
> thing. And smoked some cigarettes to calm down. [My 1C4's] making
> remarks, "Man, when I get home, I'm going to church now," everybody
> was talking stuff like that. I mean, it was like the worst we'd seen yet.
> And then [my 1C4] wasn't even going to go to the medics to get his arm
> looked at. I was like, "Dude, you can get a Purple Heart out of that. I un-
> derstand you don't want glory or whatever but at least do it for promo-
> tion points." He's like, "Nah, nah, I don't care." The first sergeant over-
> heard me and he told him, "No, you're going. You're getting a Purple
> Heart." So he walked him over there to the medics and had to fill out
> that card. And then a lot of people were taking pictures. I got a few pic-
> tures of myself at that time, and it was like, "Man, it's over!"

Once he got behind friendly lines, Gunnery Sergeant Deas went to the
aid station for an examination of his wound and found it was more serious than he had realized.

> I went out and got evaluated by the medic, actually a field surgeon
> that was there, and he looked at me and says, "Okay, well considering
> everything else that's going on, this is considered pretty mild." . . . [The
> shrapnel] went in on the septum that separates your nostrils; about
> half of that was clipped off. When it went in . . . it went in through my
> nostril, but it was so large it busted the side of it out and it just kept
> going back. . . . And once I got evaluated, [I was] like everybody else—
> everybody was just like, "Glad we made it through that! Hey, let's break
> out the chow and eat!" And at that point I was just like, "Yeah, I better
> eat something too." . . .
>
> Close to 1700 that day I finally made it to the field surgical tent at
> the brigade headquarters where they sewed me up. They looked at me
> and said, "Yeah, well this is what we can do. There's not a whole lot we
> can do about the piece of skin you got missing between your nostrils."

Battalion 1-64 left the airport that afternoon and returned to Saints by a
route that ran through friendly territory. The next day they stood in place
while they rearmed and refitted, but then the action shifted to 3rd Brigade. In a move to block outside help and bottle up defenders trying to
escape, 3rd Brigade was going to move through 1st Brigade at the airport,
head north along the western outskirts of Baghdad, then swing east

across the northern flank of the city and south down Highway 1 to a bridge designated Objective Monty. There it would take up positions occupying the northern sectors of Baghdad. This meant 3rd Brigade would have to fight its way through the northern suburbs and face a gauntlet similar to what the other brigades had faced the previous two days.

In the lead elements of this fight was First Lieutenant Blocher, and the battle would be far more intense than anything he had seen thus far. In fact, he would look back on this day as "the worst day of my life."

We LDed through our lines around ten in the morning and we probably didn't get to our final objective until about four in the afternoon. . . . Right as we did the forward passage of lines through [1st] Brigade we started taking fire, and we still had about forty clicks to go. The biggest thing we took was a whole bunch of artillery fire—everybody and their brother was lobbing whatever they could at us. And RPG and small arms fire as well. Ran into a whole bunch of abandoned tanks and APCs from the bad guys; [they weren't] shooting back at us. The people that were shooting back were the dismounts with AKs, RPGs, and then they'd run over to the artillery tubes and shoot those when we couldn't see them. The good part is the whole forty clicks I had aircraft overhead and they picked up a lot of that stuff and blew it up before we even got to it.

As we first made contact with the enemy I had a couple of F-18s overhead, as well as a couple of F-14s. F-14s [served as air FACs] and they started deconflicting aircraft from one another while I deconflicted them from the artillery and started talking them onto friendlies and where we were taking fire from. They IDed the targets and they'd roll in and kill them. We had A-10s on station. They blew up a bunch of stuff in front of us. Had a couple of F-15s check on and they started blowing up a bunch of things. . . . Basically I had at least a two-ship on station at all times. I mean I can't even tell you all the call signs and all the type aircraft. I had F-18s, GR-4s, GR-7s, F-14s, F-15Es, and a whole bunch of A-10s. . . . The A-10s took out a hell of a lot. . . . The number of aircraft I controlled during the whole war was just over a hundred sorties. That day was the lion's share of that, so probably sixty or seventy just that day. . . .

I was traveling with the lead company myself, so I was the one talking to the aircraft pretty much the whole time. . . . There were actually a couple times when my M-4 saved my life and not the aircraft overhead. It was scary and much more reactionary, and kind of just self-preservation and training kicking in rather than any thought processes or cognitive thinking. . . . When somebody shoots at you, you generally point your M-4 at them and shoot at them too, and hopefully you hit them before they hit you. Sometimes it was the fact that it was usually me and at least two other guys shooting at whoever was shooting at me, so definitely I'm not complaining about that. Also not complaining about the .50-cal that was attached to the front of my vehicle—that I very much liked.

April sixth was probably the worst day of my life. . . . Not only am I controlling all these aircraft, but really the whole time I was returning fire with my M-4 at guys on both sides of the vehicle. I pretty much had the mike in one hand and the gun in the other. I didn't bother to set either one of them down. I felt that they were both equally important. I mean, there'd be lulls and there would be major points. I can remember one specific time when we all kind of gave up the fight on the outside and dropped inside the vehicle. I couldn't even stick my head out, there was too much fire. I just basically called the aircraft and talked them onto the friendly position and said, "Hey, if you see anything other than this convoy moving north, they're bad guys and they're shooting at us. Please kill them. . . ."

Got to Objective Monty, and the big problem was that the Tigris River was the big boundary between the marines and the army, so . . . we held the bridge from this side, but couldn't go to the other side to truly secure it. At that point, after forty clicks of fighting the fight, [we] were low on gas, low on bullets, low on everything, and then we started taking some tank fire from across the bridge. By now the air force had finally gotten some respect, so the company commander actually came on the radio and said, "Hey, can I get some CAS in here? I'd really like you to blow up these guys 'cause I can't find them."

So he actually requested CAS, and that was pretty cool. The visibility, though, was so crappy you could [only] see about a mile. . . . So I requested a couple A-10s . . . [they] IDed the bridge, and then they looked off to the east side, and sure enough they saw a whole bunch of tanks and APCs. . . . They rolled in with the gun probably six or seven times each, but like I said, the visibility was so crappy you couldn't even pick up the vehicles until you were about a mile away from them. That's a pretty quick shot, pretty low angle . . . you'd pick something up, and all you'd have time for would be one quick correction to get your gun cross on it and pull the trigger real quick, and then you'd have to [pull up]. . . . But the 30-mm did its job and blew a hell of a lot of stuff up, and sure enough, by the time those guys headed home, the tank fire had stopped and we never took another tank round from across the bridge. . . .

All through that whole night we had periodic [aircraft] check on and take out some different stuff, a couple of random buildings near

**there that we'd take out because we were taking out [enemy]. . . .
[I did] a little bit of CAS [after that], but nothing huge.**

On the seventh of April, 3rd ID kept up the unrelenting pace of direct pressure on Baghdad. Like the earlier operations, this one counted on audacity and sustaining momentum, but this run was also supposed to send an even clearer message to the Iraqi people and those still holding out for Saddam's regime: this time they would go through downtown Baghdad straight for the heart of the capital and end at a potent symbol of Hussein's power—his downtown palace and government compound, a complex Americans had dubbed Palace Row.

This mission also fell to 2nd Brigade, but where the earlier plan had been relatively small and deceptively simple, this one was going to involve more forces and was, as a consequence more complex. In fact, the brigade commander, Col. David Perkins, had a more ambitious objective for this day, which brought with it a greater element of risk. Rather than a drive-by as with the First Thunder Run, Perkins hoped to set up a long-term camp in Saddam's palace, but to do so his troops would have to be able to keep a supply line open. This meant more than just driving down the highway as before; now 2nd Brigade would have to hold it and make it safe for convoy travel. Also they would have to commit greater forces to holding the Palace Complex because, unlike a raid that catches the enemy off guard and is gone before they recover, settling in meant 2nd Brigade could very likely face an organized counterattack. To accomplish all this, Perkins planned to send two battalions, 1-64, which had gone on the First Thunder Run, and 4-64 Armor Battalion to take and hold Palace Row, followed by 2nd Brigade's third battalion, 3-15 Mechanized Infantry, which would set up blocking positions on the three main intersections between Saints and the palace. Initially, the run down the highway seemed like a repeat of that on 5 and 6 April, with the greatest threat being to 3-15's effort to hold those intersections—then came the counterattacks.

On the drive to Palace Row, 1-64 led the way as they had on the First Thunder Run, and the same company that led the battalion on that day led the way again. That meant Staff Sergeant Pinson was once again at the head of the U.S. assault, but according to him, this run was less intense than the first.

**The day after [the First Thunder Run], on April sixth, we were told that
we're going back doing it again tomorrow. Everybody's like, "What?"**

Morale just sunk 'cause we thought we were done . . . but we knew
what to expect this time.

[The Iraqis] had put these huge three-foot-by-three-foot and
maybe fifteen, twenty feet long concrete tank obstacles across the
road [since the first run], and we drove right over those bad boys. I
could not believe it. . . . I told [the driver], "Dude, go around, we are not
in a big M-1!" But as I am telling him that, vroooommmm. I'm falling,
I'm just going crazy in the back of this APC, just getting thrown everywhere. But he went over it, and we were fine. All we had was a broken
sprocket. We were still good to drive but we [later] had to change the
sprocket out during a firefight.

Everything was pretty much the same [as the first], though we
turned right [off Highway 8] just north of the Camel Hump and went
up toward the [Palace Complex]. . . . The first day was the bad day as far
as having all that CAS, and they gave it to us the second day, but I don't
really remember being as busy.

Coming behind 1-64 was 4-64 Armored Battalion. The biggest action
4-64 had seen up to this point was in clearing the area between Saints
and the Tigris River. They had run into a couple of nasty ambushes, but
nothing serious enough to require CAS. The battalion's task this day was
to help capture and secure the Palace Complex. With 4-64 was T.Sgt. Mike
Green from Plattsmouth, Nebraska, just outside Omaha. Green grew up
in the shadow of Offutt Air Force Base. He joined the air force in 1986 and
spent the first fourteen years as a vehicle mechanic. That is a long time to
be in one career field and cross-train into another, but Green had been
close to the action in support of such units as Special Forces and Red
Horse teams, which are something like air force combat engineers. This
left Green with the desire to get more involved in combat, so about four
years before Iraq he decided to become a TACP.

Green almost didn't get the chance to go on the Second Thunder Run.
The night before, battalion leadership decided not to take their air force
team. According to Green, "They said, 'No, we're not going to take the 113
[APC] and we're not going to take you [TACPs] in.' And I'm like, 'What
are you going to do if you get stuck there? You don't have your mortars
or stuff to protect you. What are you going to do for heavy fire support?'
And we talked our way into this battle. I think they were concerned that
we'd be too easy to target because of the 113." It was a good thing Green
talked his way into the fight, because when they set out the next day they
were within twenty-four hours of finding his services to be a real lifesaver.

Green gives his impressions of that day's drive for Saddam's palace: "We met resistance all along the way. I guess the biggest part was [Highway 8] before you made the turn onto the Matar Saddam al-Dowli. . . . There were people behind walls, on overpasses, in the buildings, and they were firing a lot of RPGs. . . . We watched an RPG fly just a few feet above the head of our battalion commander, and we're kind of looking at each other thinking, 'Ooh, that was kind of close.' They were just jumping up firing and hiding; a lot of times they weren't even aiming."

Bringing up the rear was 3-15 Mechanized Infantry Battalion, which was given the task of securing the highway as a supply line to the forces holding Palace Row. The battalion commander stationed one of his companies at each of the three highway intersections—code named Moe, Larry, and Curly. The battalion had been one of the first American ground units to cross into Iraq at the start of the invasion, but since then they hadn't seen a lot of action. While waiting in the Kuwaiti desert they had trained extensively for their main objective—clearing out the Republican Guard divisions south of Baghdad. This would have pitted them against mostly tanks and APCs; what they encountered while holding the highway this day looked a lot different from what they had trained for. Attached to 3-15 was T.Sgt. Jim Rigney from Gautier, Mississippi. Rigney had been in the air force for fourteen years and had spent the entire time in the TACP career field. Rigney had been attached to 3-15 during Desert Storm and had served alongside the commanders of both 3-15 and 1-64, who had both been company commanders in 3-15 at the time. Like his unit's training in Kuwait, all Rigney's years working with CAS hadn't quite prepared him for what he would face this day; he describes what took place.

> We moved out that morning about 6 A.M., went up through the south of Baghdad clearing it out. . . . On our left they had businesses where guys were hiding out shooting at us, and then on [the right] side of the road there were houses, but they were farther off the road than on the left; they had people hiding in those shooting at us. You really couldn't see them that well, but you could hear all the bullets and stuff flying by. I was taking care of that side, and my airman and everybody else . . . would shoot on [the left] side. . . .
>
> I was at the middle [intersection—Objective Larry]. . . . Once we got [there] we set up [with] guys out on each side of the overpass, and me and the battalion commander were underneath the underpass. [The company] basically sat there and those people kept coming and

coming. . . . We had three tanks—two tanks on one side, and then a tank, his Bradley, and my APC on the other side of the road underneath the underpass and that is basically where he did everything. . . .

Our TOC was at the southern overpass. They had like five [tractor trailers] full of ammo and [fuel] get destroyed; they had a big fight down there. . . . One thing that was bad was [that company's TACP's] Humvee had broken down, so when the TOC came up he got left at Saints. . . . If I could have been down where our TOC was getting attacked we could probably have used [CAS] there.

You had people coming up in cars and trying to either come up our way or come up the overpass and try to get past us. We had some buildings that were [under construction] about two or three hundred yards north or northeast of us on the side of the road. They had some guys that would try to get in there, and they were shooting at us. So we had the tanks take those guys out. . . . We had a couple of close calls there with the building next to us. Matter of fact, the commander wanted me to call in an airstrike and I'm like, "Uh, no sir, that's a little too close to be trying to take that building out." Probably about two hundred yards or so—way too close. It was like a [row] of buildings, and people are up on the roof shooting RPGs and stuff at us, and we tried to take a couple out with TOWs [vehicle-mounted antitank missile] but we couldn't. . . . [Later we sent] infantry guys out and they were doing searches throughout those buildings. . . .

The fighting at Larry, Curly, and Moe lasted all day long, but as the day wore on the attacks tapered off. Moreover, 3rd ID was able to move reinforcements in to help the beleaguered 3-15. Still, it was a long fight and a tense night, as Rigney attests: "It went almost all day and then I stayed up almost all night too. But they still had guys running around. . . . Yeah, that was a busy day for us. . . . I think I ended up staying there for like three or four days."

Completing the Second Thunder Run and arriving at Palace Row wasn't the end of that day's harrowing experiences for the other two battalions. After reaching the Palace Complex, the two armored battalions took up stations around the area to secure it. Though they anticipated a counterattack, and though they continued to take fire to varying extents throughout the day, leaving the highway initially brought a noticeable decrease in combat tempo. As Pinson relates, things remained at a *relatively* low intensity—that is, compared to what 3-15 faced.

After we got off Highway 8, stuff died down. There were incidents of sniper fire and also being engaged with area fire weapons from building tops or a certain story in a building. Also there were spotters for mortars in these buildings and we would find them and we'd either have an aircraft strafe it or a tank would put a [round] in the building. Small arms fire was pretty much out of the question. . . .

The targets I attacked that day were more strategic than the First Thunder Run. . . . We had attacked a couple of different military compounds, . . . groups of artillery, 'cause they were everywhere, hidden in palm trees, palm groves, and what not, and we were just shwacking them. . . . Colonel Schwartz had pulled up right beside me and we . . . were working very close, hand-in-hand with each other . . . because we had the companies and aircraft out there searching for targets.

The pace of combat was less intense, but it was no less dangerous. As Gunny Deas illustrates, though, one incident provides another example of the ingenuity needed by those who integrate air power into the ground war.

That day we just kept getting sniped at and we kept firing back and [another] platoon that was with our company, our tank platoon, hit a bunker that was about 180 meters in front of our track. . . . There were some Iraqis that were going down in the bunker, I guess to retrieve RPGs and stuff, to keep shooting at us. The tank got 'em with the thermals and BOOM! Yeah it went BOOM all right—it went BOOM for about an hour. . . . This thing must have been loaded with tons of friggin' ordnance 'cause it cooked off for about an hour. We had to batten down the hatches. . . .

We're [at the Palace Complex] for, shoot, not too long and we start taking mortar fire, and it's just impact here, impact there, a couple of impacts here, a couple of impacts there. . . . [I] see a couple mortar impacts where the battalion TOC's set up. . . . You could tell they were small caliber; they were definitely 60s [60-mm mortars]. . . . We're delivering some EPWs that we'd captured . . . and then [I] run into Dan Brown. He's out there, he's like, "Hey, come here Butch." You know, pop! here comes another mortar.

Gy.Sgt. Dan Brown was another marine with the ANGLICO, and he had been applying knowledge gained in Deas's onboard refresher course involving an arcane subject known as crater analysis—the study of bomb or shell craters to determine what type of ordnance had been used and, more particularly, when dealing with artillery and mortars, to gain clues as to where the shell had been fired from. As with many aspects of what makes the best CAS controllers, crater analysis combines great technical expertise with good old-fashioned horse sense, because if the controller is good, he can pinpoint the location, send an airstrike, and silence the barrage. That's what was needed here. Brown was no slouch when it came to being a good forward observer—he was so experienced he had helped Deas conduct some of the onboard refresher course—but when it came to crater analysis, Deas was the recognized guru. And this particular case required every bit of expertise the two men could muster, as Brown realized when he called Deas over for consultation. Brown describes what he was seeing: "The mortars were hitting real close, so I went out there . . . and the craters weren't very big because most of them were hitting the sidewalk, and the cement, and the roof, but a couple of them had hit in the dirt, and I was unsure. I had them figured out, let's say, coming in from nine o'clock, and so I started working up the data and then Gunny Deas comes up . . . and I asked him to come look at it. He looked at it and he said, 'I think they're coming from this direction,' you know, pointing mc in a different direction, which was probably more like seven o'clock or six o'clock."

What was confusing Brown was that these were not typical mortar craters. For his part, Deas was factoring a couple of other critical pieces of information into his thinking. "[Brown's] like, 'Hey, these are where these things are coming from.' I look at them like, 'Nah, they're about 180 out—look, low angle. These look like little bitty fuse-quick craters [craters made by shells with fuses that explode on impact rather than delayed-action fuses that allow the shell to bury itself before exploding].' I said, 'They're not coming in high, blowing [debris] backward; these are coming in low, blowing it forward.' So I told him, 'Yeah, you'd probably plan for about two clicks out. This is where these guys are coming from.'" What Deas had noticed was that unlike typical mortar craters created by shells lobbed in at very high angles, which is how mortars are usually employed, these craters indicated that the shells were coming in at a low angle. This told Deas not only how to properly read the crater to determine the shell's direction but also that the mortars were being fired from close to their extreme range, and Deas knew what that maximum range was from his familiarity with that type of mortar's capability. Brown still was not sure, but as he explains, he came across one more critical clue that told him all he needed to know.

> So [Deas] left, and then another one hit right after he left, and when that one hit I stood in the crater, and I looked up and I saw a hole in the [leaves of a] tree, and the hole was pointing exactly where Gunny Deas had thought they were coming from. So, I mean, it was easy; I just took my compass, pointed it at the hole [in the tree], shot an azimuth, and . . . we figured the max range of about two thousand meters. So I

took all [the information] . . . pulled out a map and I showed it to the task force XO, and he said, "Well that's actually coming out of a military compound that we haven't hit yet." So he said, "Well let me get the CO and see if we can clear this mission." So then the CO came over and said, "Hell yeah, take it out!"

Then I guess from me giving the grid to the XO, he was going up army channels too, not only for approval but they were getting ready to send artillery and MLRS into that same area, so that once the aircraft released, I guess [the army] turned on the MLRS and artillery. . . . So whether I got them or whether [the army] got them I don't know, but [the mortars] stopped.

While 1-64 was dealing with all that in the southern half of the Palace Complex, just to the north, 4-64 found much the same steady but manageable pace in their sector. Taking and holding the Palace Complex, according to Technical Sergeant Green, was relatively straightforward: "We rolled along the road [in front of] the Republican Palace . . . and it was fairly easy. There was firing here and there, but to be honest with you, it didn't seem that hard taking that part of Baghdad. . . . During the day you . . . would hear firing—little firefight here, little firefight there as they would find a new position."

As 2nd Brigade was securing its hold on Palace Row, the brigade's leadership suffered a devastating blow when its tactical operations center was hit by what most later thought was an al-Samoud II missile, similar to a Scud. Three soldiers and two foreign journalists were killed. Despite the blow and its temporary disruption, by the end of the seventh things had quieted down for the most part, and it seemed 2nd Brigade was firmly in control of the Palace Complex and the highway leading to it. The anticipated counterattack to reclaim the Republican Palace had not materialized, and that made many people nervous. All of this changed suddenly in the wee hours of the eighth as the long-expected counterattack broke loose, aimed primarily at 4-64. The Iraqis had marshaled a sizable force on the east side of the Tigris River where they enjoyed a bit of a sanctuary. The 1st Marine Division, which made up the eastern prong of the coalition invasion plan, owned from the Tigris eastward, and thus 3rd ID had to refrain, for the most part, from firing on the other side of the river. But the marines hadn't reached that part of Baghdad yet, so it became a temporary haven the Iraqis were now exploiting. Enemy forces, foot-bound and ferried by vehicles, were pouring across the Al Jumhuriya Bridge, and in conjunction with several strongholds they had established on the west side of the river, were bringing tremendous pressure to bear on the

Americans; for a time it even looked like 4-64 might be overrun, which would also compromise 1-64. T.Sgt. Green describes the battle.

> Early in the morning, all of a sudden, fire started coming from everywhere. On the east side of town they started to bring RPGs, guns, and everything, across that southern bridge north of the Republican Palace . . . and they worked their way down to our palace. Just out of the blue, it's like a coordinated attack. . . .
>
> The tanks were firing and all the radio chatter was going crazy all of a sudden. . . . They quickly started pushing [the Iraqis] from the Republican Palace up toward the government offices until they got to Yafa Street; . . . it didn't take too much to push them back. But they got to Yafa Street, and on its northwest corner there was a building . . . it was just huge. . . . Running northeast-southwest on the north side of Yafa Street and on the east side of Haifa there was a park and [the Iraqis] put in several defensive fighting positions. They dug them into the ground and built them down to help protect [that corner]. And then there was a twelve-story red building, like an apartment complex of some sort. The third location was on the north of Yafa Street and the west side of Haifa Street, a two-story building. We were taking heavy fire from all three of those positions.
>
> Now this [huge] building by the park area . . . had a room just filled with nothing but RPGs, and [the Iraqis] were running back and forth and getting more. [Enemy fire] had gotten so bad that they disabled [a couple] tanks in the sense that they could not [fire their main gun]. [The Iraqis] had them pinned down; for about an hour the tanks could not move. The firing was just that bad. And I tried and I tried and I tried to get the company commander to respond, but I couldn't get him to respond to me, so we went straight to the fire support officer and I say, "Hey let's use planes." And that's when it all of a sudden clicked to him—"Yeah, let's use planes."

This points out yet again not only the kind of ingenuity needed to make CAS work but also the benefits gained when army leaders embrace their TACPs. Some argue there should be many, many more CAS controllers, and that they should be assigned down as low as the platoon level—General Hagenbeck suggested this in his critiques following Anaconda. Such an approach, though, would bring significant problems. For one thing, there aren't enough planes, bombing ranges, or flying hours to train that many controllers to current standards. And deconflicting aircraft between dozens of controllers on a relatively small battlefield would be a dangerous nightmare. But this approach isn't necessary. Anybody can work with a TACP over the radio to coordinate CAS, but it takes practice.

This points up Lieutenant Colonel McGee's notion of "seeing" differently. If the TACP is talking on the radio to ground forces who can see the target, and if they have practiced together, they can "see" the target for him, describe the target and its location, and he can control the attack based on their description. This approach, known as a type-2 control, was used all the time in Afghanistan and Iraq, with pilots describing to TACPs what they saw. Battalion 4-64 had hit upon this idea while in Kuwait, and Green gives most of the credit to the battalion's FSO.

> He wanted to make sure we were all comfortable doing type-2s together, so he pushed it really hard. I had just gotten my certification to control as a TAC, and in January while we were [in Kuwait]. . . . there was a concern because of not [having] TACPs at every company. So we talked to the [FSO]. . . . We went in and gave him [a briefing on type-2 controls], on how to do it, what the capabilities were, and what we could do, and [he] loved it. . . . He started running us through at least two hours a night of doing nothing but type-2s with the mortar platoons, the scouts, and all the fire support elements in each of the companies. I went down to [each company] and I would work with his fire support guys and we started off with something simple . . . including simulated talking to the planes, everything over their [radio] net so that they could hear everything that was going on and they could feel comfortable about what we were doing and how well we could do it. And as we got better at doing this, we did it two, three hours a night and then debriefed another hour. . . . And after we did it a couple nights we would cut out parts so they couldn't hear the pilots talking, and then they would do it so they couldn't hear [the ETAC talking to the pilots]. Basically we got down to where they would hear exactly what they were going to hear during a combat situation. . . .
>
> [The FSO] would throw a scenario out there real quick, "Okay, this is your scenario, go with it," and he would give it to maybe the scout team and then they would send up their thing. And we did a lot of talking about [terminology] because I understood they weren't going to learn all the terminology, we just had to be on the same page. And so I says, "You tell me what you're saying and I'll confirm that this is what you mean." . . . Basically we let them use their terminology to talk to us, and then we translated it . . . talking to the planes.

Now it was time for Green to put that type-2 CAS training to work.

> We backed our track up right next to the fire support element . . . and we did type-2 [controls] from kind of a makeshift TOC using the fire support vehicle and our vehicle. It was just us two [Green and the FSO] and we started talking back and forth. Like I said, I couldn't get our

guys to answer me on the radio, so I looked at him and I says, "They're not listening to me. I need you to tell me what target they want to hit." I would listen to everything they said, so I understood everything they wanted, and I could do it. I could look at the map and actually pick out the targets. And that's how we controlled the planes on them. I heard everything they said, and I would basically give the [FSO] a thumbs-up: "I got this. This is easy."

We pulled them back about . . . two, three blocks. . . . [Enemy forces] were coming across [the Al Jumhuriya Bridge]. . . . They were driving van loads of people over. . . . [The commander] said, "We got to stop these vehicles from coming across the bridge, but we don't want to destroy the bridge." So on our side of the river we had [an aircraft] throw a Maverick on the road just to catch their attention—"Hey, coming across that road is not a good idea." And so they struck it near the base of the bridge, where the bridge and the road meet on the ground so it wouldn't do any damage to the bridge.

Then we started making runs. And I don't remember off the top of my head which we hit first, but we put a round into that big red building because they were taking fire from there. . . . I think they put a Maverick in that one; just one. . . . We weren't wanting to really destroy everything, but yet we were trying to get them to cease the firing, and it did—they didn't take any more firing [from that building] for the rest of that night. . . . And then we hit the park real hard with a lot of [A-10] gun strafing. And then the two-story building, they completely leveled it. We couldn't even see it.

This was all type-2 [controls] using our front lead elements . . . and it just came together so smooth that after it was over the fire support officer says, "You guys just saved the day. That was just unbelievable." He never dreamed that it could go as smooth as it did. . . . After that the tanks rolled right in and it was their block. . . . I didn't even hear of any firing after that.

This was the last real threat to the U.S. position at Palace Row. With 2nd Brigade now safely ensconced in the heart of Baghdad, and 1st Brigade holding the airport while 3rd Brigade blocked from the north, 3rd ID settled in for what some have called the siege of Baghdad. Iraqi forces continued counterattacking, but the Americans weren't on the defensive. They began the steady reduction of resistance in the city by slicing off section after section from unoccupied portions of Baghdad. CAS played a role during these days, but it was a diminishing role and this phase didn't last long—only a few days. It produced some memorable episodes for those TACPs involved, and even a few close calls, but for the most part, they had the same experience Sergeant Carpenter spoke of shortly after seizing the airport—CAS was severely curtailed and TACPs soon found themselves on their way home. A small TACP contingent remained in theater just in case CAS was needed, but for the most part, it was not—the mission in Baghdad quickly turned into one of ground forces trying to bring order and stability to the city in the face of a growing insurgent movement.

11. The Scud Hunt and Operations in Western Iraq

One of the most chilling memories from Desert Storm was the fear evoked by Hussein's use of theater ballistic missiles, or Scuds, against urban targets throughout the Middle East. These missiles could be used to carry chemical or biological agents, and since Saddam had gassed his own people, no one doubted he was capable of using Scuds to launch such an attack against his enemies. The most worrisome attacks had been leveled against Israel. If Israel had retaliated, as was their standard policy, it could have upset the dynamics holding together the already shaky coalition against Iraq. If Israel entered the war, even if uninvited, those Arab states arrayed against Iraq would appear to be on the side of Israel against another Arab state. This would have brought the coalition crashing down, which of course was why Hussein used this tactic. In an effort to end the threat against Israeli and Saudi cities, and to assure Israel that everything possible was being done to end the threat, Coalition forces launched a massive effort to find and destroy the Scuds. This campaign, dubbed "the Scud Hunt," soaked up a huge percentage of Coalition air power, which was diverted from the larger air campaign against Saddam's army, and yielded few concrete results. That diversion was probably the only militarily significant result of Hussein's Scud attacks.

Early on in planning a second war with Iraq, U.S. political and military leaders determined a second Scud hunt was necessary. One reason was simple force protection concern—the thought of hundreds or thousands of American soldiers dying in a chemical attack and the impact that would have on the U.S. public was enough to inspire military leaders to make every effort to ensure such an attack never happened. As the war loomed closer, and as it became clear that this war would be much more controversial and any diplomatic agreements even more fragile than in the first Gulf War, the prospect of Scuds raining down on tepid supporters or on Israel made this Scud hunt even more urgent.

The second Scud hunt was not going to be a mere repeat of the first, though, for several things had changed since then. First, American military analysts had studied every aspect of Iraqi Scud operations and capabilities and come up with a set of parameters and limitations they could exploit to assist their efforts. Instead of searching throughout the entire haystack, analysts got some pretty good clues that the needle would most likely be found in a few surprisingly small sections. Second, the United States had refined its capabilities. Some refinements were technological—sensors better able to find Scuds; others were operational—forces able to react quicker to information from sensors and hopefully within time to exploit the information.

Working together, these advances gave the second Scud hunters tremendous advantages. Of course, this all may have been moot, since evidence today, at least that released to the public, indicates that Hussein had eliminated his chemical and biological weapons, as well as most of his Scuds. But that wasn't known at the time, so the Scud hunt, which was mostly confined to western Iraq, was a high priority in the war against Saddam.

The Scud hunters had a second objective as well. Since they were going to be combing the western Iraqi desert anyway, if they located Iraqi forces, they would engage them. But this was not just a matter of attrition—that is, killing everything they could find—or a serendipitous exploitation of good fortune. There was a larger strategic goal, one that would be exploiting lessons learned in Afghanistan: to pin down as many Iraqi forces as possible in the west so they could not be used against the main effort marching on Baghdad from the south. How this objective was accomplished, with a relatively miniscule force, is a testimonial to the men involved and an illustration of what CAS and small ground forces can do together when applied with ingenuity.

As in Afghanistan, a big part of the western effort involved SOF teams that included SOF TACPs. Though they found no Scuds, at least as far as the public knows, they did find a lot of Iraqi forces, and on occasion ran into some trouble. Their efforts, though less visible, are a part of the larger story and certainly bear recounting.

One of the key figures leading operations in western Iraq was Lt. Col. George Bochain. Bochain had been a principal architect in forging the SOF-CAS operational approach early in the Afghanistan war, so it was natural that he would play a big part in an operation that relied on the closest integration of SOF forces and CAS exploitation. As Bochain illustrates, this integration was the key to making their operations work, both with the Scud hunt and in engaging much larger Iraqi forces. It was also the key to avoiding disastrous consequences if either part of the mission failed.

We had the opportunity to practice with live-flies at Nellis Air Force Base twice before the war started. My analogy is the Doolittle raid, where they practiced, practiced, practiced. We brought in all the players from three different countries, we brought Special Ops Forces, and we went from the very basic all the way up through the graduate level execution . . . to make sure we had the ability to get air on a target within minutes. Because we figured from the time we found a Scud we had a very short period of time . . . to take it out before it got its shot off. So we designed a system to make sure . . . that at any given point in time—twenty-four hours a day—if the call was made, "We found one," we could get aircraft to that point within minutes. And that was from the air side.

The ground side was also equally planned out to where we knew certain areas were likely spots where they could fire from. We wanted to make sure we had ground forces that were in a position to observe these most likely launch areas, so that if one came out from under its camo [camouflage] net and popped up, we had it covered. Now it's a huge area, and we fully understood that we'd have to get very lucky in order to catch every one of these. If he had had a lot of them out there, you know, we're not sure if we would have got them all. But fortunately we consider the mission to be a success because not a single one of them launched. Whether or not they were there or they moved just prior to us coming in will be analyzed for years to come. And what happened to the ones that we know were out there at one point, where they went to prior to us being inserted, that's another question. But the mission of strategic denial of Saddam Hussein's ability to range Tel Aviv from western Iraq . . . was successful.

That was mission number one; mission number two was to deny the use of western and northern Iraq to whatever forces he could put together to do some kind of harassment, counterattack, escape. We wanted to control all of western and northern Iraq to bottle [Hussein] up in the areas where the guys coming up from the south could engage. So it was an economy of forced effort that became even more important once we lost the access to Turkey. . . . It became a Special Operations event from the north and the west—very few guys supported by a lot of air power. And guess what—they never needed those conventional forces from Turkey because the air power tied in with the SOF guys was successful. And that was something that had been argued from early on in the fight: "You know, you really don't need to have these conventional divisions pouring in from Turkey, because if the mission is to deny and cut LOCs, why do you need to send in this huge conventional infrastructure?" You couldn't make that same argument for the south—you needed a large force to press forward into Baghdad, secure the oil fields, capture the thousands of soldiers we thought were going to surrender—but you could make that argument for the north and the west.

The integration was a great success. . . . We were given the right leadership, the opportunity to practice, and the assets to support the mission from very early on in the fight, and it was successful. We did not lose a single soldier or airman, within the group I was with, to direct enemy fire even though they had a lot of contact, because of the success of that integration. . . . We called in—I won't give you the hard number—let's call it several hundred airstrikes . . . [against] concentrations of forces, triple-A, antiaircraft sites, bridges, airfield, lines of communications, Baath Party headquarters, the whole gamut. . . . There was plenty of contact, but it was done correctly where you probe, you make contact, you back off, you bomb until either they give up or they go away. . . .

I think one way to look at the north and the west is sort of taking Afghanistan operations to the next level because it was really a similar setup where you had a huge area to cover. There were organized forces out there, but you could use an economy of force because of the highly mobile nature of the SOF guys supported by the right air power—they could be everywhere and nowhere at the same time. And the guys that were captured thought we had divisions out there because anywhere they turned they were getting hit, and they didn't know what to do. They just couldn't figure out how they could be getting pounded from all directions and not finding anybody. And they were getting pounded not only from air but [also] from guys using direct fire, but it might be a team of Rat Patrol guys acting like they were a brigade. The psychological impact on these guys who don't have the eyes and the ears that we have, the value of our intelligence versus their complete lack of intelligence, is incredible. For them to think there is a brigade out there and it's ten guys is a huge statement of what can be done.

But that's all based on our ability to understand, if nothing else, where we can and cannot move to next. Your intelligence may not tell you, "Well, this person or this group of guys is in this particular area," but we know they're likely to be in this area, and we know we can go from here to here and not have any contact. So we had the freedom to maneuver and strike them at different points, sometimes in minutes, to make them think there was a much larger force out there. And then when they went out to try to find that force, (a) it played into our

hand, because now they're moving; they solved our targeting problem, and (b) they would go to where they thought they were getting
this conventional attack from, nothing would be there, and it just blew
them away: "How were they able to do this?" It's depressing for the
other side; there was nothing they could do. And it's all based on air
supremacy.

Another perspective on both missions in western Iraq comes from one
of the SOF TACPs preparing to conduct those missions. T.Sgt. Ed Shulman had played a key role in helping the CAOC adapt its operations to
the unique SOF-CAS operational concept that had emerged in Afghanistan. In Iraq he found himself in a similar role, though at a lower eche-
lon, helping to fine-tune how that SOF-CAS team handled the Scud hunt
and refining the so-called Rat Patrol tactics used for pinning down much
larger forces. As Shulman illustrates, a lot of time, planning, and exercis-
ing went into polishing both modes of operations. He starts by describing
his participation in refining the Scud hunt procedures.

> We started in October—I actually didn't go to the first one—but then
> throughout December and January we went out to Nellis where we . . .
> exercised the entire Scud hunt package all the way from the British
> AWACS, down to the fighters and the bombers, and all the way down
> to the guys on the ground, executing the exact kill box deconfliction,
> the communications channels, the difference between a missile raised
> and a missile being transported, and support equipment, and the dif-
> ferent pro words [code words] associated with those things, and we
> basically went out and drilled the entire scenario. . . . The A-10 and F-16
> units that were flying in support of us—specifically in support of us—
> were at those training conferences, so we were actually, for the first
> time ever, face-to-face with the squadron commanders and the pilots
> that were actually going to be supporting us.
>
>   When an A-10 checked in with me I knew the guy's voice on the
> other [end]; we had developed that level of integration and that level
> of understanding of how we were going to operate. . . . I would go to
> [the A-10] squadron, talk to them, we would go out and do a scenario,
> and afterward go back and AAR [after action review] with them. . . .
> They would come over and check on our equipment. . . . They were just
> as concerned about how we were going to operate and how we could
> work with them as we were about how they would work with us. We all
> developed a real good relationship.

Shulman also helped develop the Rat Patrol tactics that were so effective against larger Iraqi forces. According to Shulman, these tactics were

not just an outgrowth of SOF-CAS operations in Afghanistan, though that experience had been an important catalyst. They were also heavily influenced by British experience in the first Scud hunt.

> We looked at a lot of the AARs [after action reports] from the first war [with Iraq], specifically the Brits, and I don't know if you've ever read *Saber Squadron*, but that was the story of the Brit regiment that was operating in the western desert doing counter Scud ops. [We] actually based a lot of our doctrine on *Saber Squadron*. . . . [Development and training involved] going out in the desert for two or three weeks at a time, learning how to operate out of the vehicles, learning the capabilities of the vehicles, learning the ranges and all—just how to make everything work out of the back of a truck, which is something that we were not really used to.
>
> We started working a lot on the type assets we were going to have, what type scenarios were we going to deal with. . . . We were trying to get our timelines down so we never wound up in a situation where the aircraft showed up and was waiting on us. We wanted to get everything down within the team where as soon as we identified a target everybody knew what to do. . . . We started building those crew drills so that as soon as it happened we could do it. . . . Then we did a thirty-day exercise where we went out and did our full desert training profile from the team level, and then [the teams] came together into a company.

As with those forces getting ready to invade Iraq from the south, the forces operating in western Iraq went in theater early, and as Shulman illustrates, they prepared extensively for their mission.

> We went to an exercise in Jordan in September 2002. We went there for the exercise, but obviously there was this lingering feeling that the war was coming. . . . In December we redeployed back to the States and stayed through Christmas. In the beginning of January deployed back to the same base we were operating out of in Jordan to get ready to go to the real war. Back in December we left all our equipment where it was under the pretense that if—we were still in that "if" phase—if the war kicked off we would just fall right back in on our vehicles, brush the dust off, clean the weapons, and we're ready to go. When we went back in January we knew it was for the war, but our biggest thing was we didn't know when the war was going to happen. . . . We were all leaning forward, we started doing the same refresher training, last minute getting issued some new medical stuff we had never seen before . . . but as soon as that stuff started rolling in we all went, "Okay, this wouldn't be here if we weren't going." [About five days before the

planned invasion] we drove to this holding area and did exactly that for three days—held for three days . . . and did our last little bit of planning. . . . We went across the night of the seventeenth.

The dual-mission nature of the western Iraq campaign as outlined by Bochain—finding Scuds and tying up Iraqi forces—caused some friction at first. Obviously preventing Scud launches took priority over harassing Iraqi army units, but in practical terms, how were guys out at "the tip of the spear" supposed to keep the two from conflicting with one another? As Shulman explains, this led to an episode that brought the potential conflict into sharp relief.

The first contact came when we started ringing the town of Ar Rutbah. . . . We hadn't been across the border long; I would say, it was between our second and our third day. We had been there long enough to where we [had] hit our primary objectives and didn't find anything, and that's when we started focusing a little bit on Ar Rutbah. . . . ODA 5-25 had two guys, their warrant officer and their communication sergeant, on a hill overlooking Ar Rutbah. . . . At some point they got compromised, and a bunch of vehicles came out of the city to start chasing those guys down, at which point they were totally on their own—two guys on top of the hill; they were basically screwed. . . . So when they started requesting air because they were about to get overrun, they called in a "Sprint." If you got on the radio and made a "Sprint" call it meant you were in an imminent overrun situation and they sent the fleet to those guys. A-10s started showing up and [the communication guy] understood CAS, he was real good at it. Immediately he jumped right on the radio . . . was controlling these A-10s and having them come in and strafe these vehicles that were driving at him. It was totally Hollywood—vehicles driving through the open desert, getting strafed by A-10s, catching fire, bursting into flames . . . and that was the end of that engagement.

Now the problem was . . . we pulled a lot of aircraft away from the Scud hunt, and at the time the Scud hunt was still a big deal. So all the aircraft that came to support us in the CAS environment were supposed to be Scud hunting. The command started catching some flack about, "Hey we just lost two hours worth of Scud hunt time." . . . After that happened the command started putting the screws down on the way the guys operate.

This episode occurred early in the Scud hunt, when everyone was sure Hussein had Scuds hidden somewhere in Iraq, so military leaders stressed the Scud mission over pinning down Iraqi forces. This came at a price, for hesitancy allows opportunity to slip away, as Shulman illustrates with another episode that followed soon after.

> So then they started saying, "Don't do that again, don't pick a fight. . . ." [Later] we had a team in place watching H-3 [an old Iraqi air base] as the rest of us were converging on the airfield, and they watched a thirty-vehicle convoy leave H-3 and they couldn't get permission to hit it. They started asking for aircraft to hit it, and these were trucks and vehicles towing artillery, towing all kinds of other stuff, and [the team was] trying to get aircraft, and it was at the FOB [forward operating base] that they were being denied. The FOB was saying, "Don't fire until fired upon. Don't initiate contact." There was this whole convoy leaving. It became, "Well, do you actually see people with weapons?" and it's like, "Yeah, we see vehicles towing weapons." And they just weren't allowed to engage them, so they wound up letting all those guys go.

As the initial phase of the Scud hunt turned up no Scuds, the "don't fire until fired upon" policy started to ease up, and the SOF teams were freed up to engage more aggressively, as Shulman illustrates with his team's operation to clear Ar Rutbah.

> If you can picture, a Wild West town is what this place reminds you of. . . . For the most part this town had about a five- to ten-kilometer ring of completely flat desert around it. So there was no way to get to the town without being seen. Likewise there was no way to leave the town without being seen. So as we had some teams go up and start probing, they were receiving some fire from the corners of the town.
>
> We had pretty well isolated the town at that point, set up some roadblocks, but we still hadn't actually made our way into the town. Through some of the intelligence sources we had with us, [we] started getting word about the centers of gravity within the town—the Fedayeen cells, the Baath Party headquarters etc.—so from that intelligence we were able to start templating [threat locations]. On the western edge of the city there was a huge prison compound. They were pulling locals into this prison compound and arming them and using it as a base of operations to mount their defenses against us.
>
> Something to keep in mind about Ar Rutbah is that it's one of the few towns that really had no involvement with the [Hussein] regime. Saddam did not go out to Ar Rutbah; there were some security concerns because it's very tribal out there. They never fell into the mold with the rest of Iraq. So it's also an equally shitty town because they didn't get any of the money that the rest of the places did. Nobody within the Baath Party or the regime wanted to go there, so they kind

of took care of themselves, and they were basically uninterested in the war. But there were Baath Party and Fedayeen cells that had taken up hiding in the town, and those were the ones that were the problem.

They were all hanging out in this prison. So we pulled up the prison on Falcon View and I did some plotting and sent a bunch of [CAS] requests up [to headquarters]. We had a B-1 check in and . . . they dropped a variety of delayed weapons into this prison and basically destroyed the entire thing. . . . [The bombs] threw stone all the way out into the highway, which is probably two hundred meters away. . . . And that kind of broke the back of the forces that were left.

Once we did that we got the whole company into a huge wedge and pulled up on the eastern side of the city with our psyops [psychological operations] team. We had the psyops guys get on the radio and tell the people in Ar Rutbah that we weren't there for them, that we weren't there to occupy, all the normal stuff. It's like, "Hey, tell us where the Fedayeen are, tell us where the Baath Party is. We'll take care of it." So we had a couple people come out of the town and tell us, "Hey, this is where these people are." Once we could confirm that's where the people are and [we] started taking some fire from that building . . . we dropped bombs on the building and that was pretty much the last of the strongholds in Ar Rutbah.

When we actually drove into Ar Rutbah we had an elaborate air show that I had worked out and I say air show [because] that's what it was: I had a B-1 fly over the city at like ten thousand feet moving at the speed of heat, and then we had F-16s fly over a little bit lower, and then we had A-10s buzzing the rooftops. The whole time we were moving into the city the A-10s were calling traffic to us, calling out vehicles moving around, any kind of suspicious activity. They were just making a lot of noise and being intimidating over the city for about three hours while we breached the police station and the Baath Party headquarters, and basically took over the city. But again, it wasn't a "blood and guts" street fight at that point. The people of the city were happy to have us there, they were open arms. I've got pictures of little kids jumping all over us, and adults walking up to the truck shaking our hands . . . so we didn't have any problems. By the time we moved into the city the threat was eliminated.

Everything else from that point on was low intensity stuff. . . . We caught a lot of guys coming out of Baghdad that were trying to get back to Syria . . . guys that were paid in Syria to come to Iraq to be suicide fighters that once the bombs started dropping had a change of heart, as one would expect. They were just trying to get home, so those guys were all driving through Ar Rutbah trying to get back into Syria. We rolled up [captured] . . . different HVTs [high value targets;

key figures in the old regime] here and there, but no large CAS conflicts or anything like that. . . . We stayed in Ar Rutbah until we exfilled
the first of May. We left Ar Rutbah, went back down to H-3, and then
basically reversed our infill. . . . I got to H-3 on May first and I was back
in my living room on May sixth.

In another part of western Iraq—the central part—was T.Sgt. Sean
O'Neill. Hailing from the "Live Free or Die" state of New Hampshire,
O'Neill was a thirteen-year veteran who had started as a vehicle operator-
dispatcher but after only a few years cross-trained into the TACP career
field and was ultimately selected for the SOF TACP program. Assigned
to the 17th ASOS and stationed at Fort Benning, O'Neill supported the
Rangers stationed there. He had been on two rotations in Afghanistan,
most notably as part of the combat jump into Camp Rhino outside Kandahar, but here in Iraq he and his team were tasked more with searching out Iraqi forces and reconnoitering airfields than looking for Scuds,
which as he explains was enough to get them into some serious action.

We got home [from Afghanistan] in December and had some time off
and started hearing some behind-the-water-cooler whispers here and
there [about Iraq]. Next thing you know we were doing a little exercise in February, and then we left right at the beginning of March. . . .
We deployed direct to the initial staging base [at an undisclosed loca-
tion]. . . . We did some rehearsals with the task force and then we drove
across [the border] on the night of the war starting.

We were going to recon for an airfield seizure; go in a couple of
days ahead of time and overwatch [the airfield] to confirm the intel
that is reported as far as what's there, and then myself being there to
talk to any preassault [airstrikes] that come across before the actual
seizure. . . . [After arriving at the staging base, though,] the call came,
"Stay where you're at," and then the next day it was, "Okay, now we
need you to go do this," which was never something we had planned
on doing.

We got on airplanes and flew to H-1 [an old Iraqi airfield] and used
it as our forward staging area. We got another mission; we were supposed to head east toward the place called K-3 [another old Iraqi air-
field] and recon it. . . . We [and another team] were supposed to start
there and leapfrog south. There were several objective areas on the
way; we were supposed to work one, and they were supposed to work
[the next one] south of us, and then we were supposed to hop down
south of them. . . . If we found some targets out there we were supposed to get some CAS and just start doing what we could. We got

about halfway there and they called the second team back and they told us to keep going.

We got to the vicinity of [K-3] a little bit before daybreak . . . and when it started getting light a little bit we started looking around. We had kind of parked on a little bit of low ground; it was pretty flat all around where we were, so we parked in as low ground as we could find, which wasn't much, and then just walked up a little bit to the higher stuff and we started watching movements. We started looking around and thought, "Hey, we might have some targets out here; we need to get some closer looks." But it's tough. We had two vehicles and six men, and it's tough to move those vehicles; it's tough to move as an individual around in there without being spotted. . . . So we stayed still and tried to look from as far off as we could [but] we were still pretty far away, so we moved a little bit closer to the airfield during the daylight. . . . When the sun went down we sent a two-man team out ahead of us on foot and they walked for an hour and a half to see what they could find. They found some wadis, so we went and parked our vehicle down in a wadi and then waited for daylight.

Then when [the sun] came up . . . we started seeing what we were pretty sure was military equipment around this area. The intel we were given said there were tanks, BMPs, and antiaircraft guns. There was just a bunch of stuff in this vicinity . . . so we were being careful approaching it. The team leader said, "Come on, I want to go up here and get a closer look." . . . So I grabbed all my stuff and we started walking. We started seeing a bunch of stuff and I started writing some [coordinates] down in my notes. . . .

We got behind [the airfield] and we could tell we were right next to a hard ball [paved] road, I think it was Highway 12. We got up next to it and it was all like embankments that had been bulldozed. They were revetments for parking a bunch of stuff it looked like. Either that or they had just bermed up the road real high—I wouldn't know why— but it was about twenty-five, thirty feet higher than the road. . . . We just kind of hunkered down behind that and we're peeking around and . . . we can see BMPs right in front of us. They were parked in revetments . . . we're like, "Hmm, wonder if there's people in those."

So I started calling for CAS and I got some airplanes to come a little bit later. Then the team leader is like, "Hey, I'm going up on this revetment here and see what I can see," and he and the assistant team leader went up there. Those two came back down and they were like, "Hey we got to get up in here. We can see the BMPs and there's tanks on the other side of this and antiaircraft stuff." For the rest of the day I called CAS and we bombed the BMPs and tanks. We worked [until] dark and then the team leader and I headed back toward our MSS [mission support site].

The next morning we got up and we walked from the other direction toward the airfield, and from there we got to a position where we could see a lot more stuff on the other side of the airfield. We got more aircraft and we started bombing that stuff. Then when we got back to [the MSS site] the guys were kind of going around frantically and we're like, "What's up?" And they were like, "They just called us, [a Ranger company at a nearby dam is] pinned down." . . . They rolled up there in the nighttime and there was no resistance whatsoever and they thought, "Oh, this is easy." The next morning they got up and they started getting shot at by a bunch of people. . . . They were fighting pretty hard and then they started getting mortars and artillery launched at them too. So it was pretty intense for them. . . .

They were estimating that [the artillery] was coming from somewhere in the vicinity of our location. . . . We went up a little bit farther to see what we could find and we thought we could spot some artillery pieces; and it looked like the grids matched up. So I got an aircraft that had some JDAMS—I'm pretty sure it was a B-1—and I gave them all five locations. They confirmed they could spot four of them good, and they dropped bombs on all four of those locations, and after that we didn't hear anything. The guys at the dam said that they didn't have any more shots come in, so I'm pretty sure we hit the artillery that was shooting at them.

We went back to the MSS, and the next day we went back [to K-3] and we got to hit a lot more stuff again. . . . There was triple-A all over the place out there. . . . The one highlight was when [one bomb] hit some sort of ammo supply location or something. [It] had to be maybe the second to the last thing that I cleared the [aircraft] on and it just lit up, you know, you could see secondaries, I could hear them where I was at, and I was a good thousand meters away from it and it was just pop, pop, pop, pop, pop, pop, pop. It was getting dark, so we were starting to go back to the MSS; [the ammo supply] was still going. It had been going for at least an hour when we started walking back, and when we got to the MSS we got up on the high ground and you could still see it glowing in the background—it was like two and a half hours later and it was still going off.

And then the last night we were there another platoon came down to do a raid on the airfield. And so I did a lot of airfield prep work—dropped bombs on the airfield itself, not just the equipment that was parked around it. . . . I was told to hit the airfield but not to hit the runway. . . . Once they came up and linked up with us, their

ETAC took over. . . . We put a blocking position at the intersection once they went up to do the raid on the airfield. . . . [Once they had cleared the airfield] the Ranger commander said, "We're moving out; we don't need you at the blocking position anymore."

O'Neill and his team were kept busy with various other missions through the closing days of war, but they too were sent home shortly after the regime collapsed. "We . . . went back to the dam and they said, 'Okay, we want you to go recon this one last site,' and we noticed that it was about halfway between the dam and H-1 airfield, which was the staging base, and we're like, 'Oh yeah, you're bringing us home, huh?' We went and [reconned the site] and it was just a farming site. . . . And then that was it. The next day we turned in all our equipment and packed our bags, jumped on a flight, went back to ISB [initial staging base]. I think we stayed there for one more night, maybe two, and [then] we went home."

12. The Drive from the North

From the first serious thoughts of taking out Saddam Hussein, the United States had big plans for its long-standing ally Turkey. Turkey not only shared a common northern border with Iraq but had also been the staging base for Operation Northern Watch, the UN-sanctioned effort to protect northern Iraq's Kurdish population. So invading Iraq from two directions was a natural option. While such a move would divide Coalition forces and dramatically increase logistical and political challenges, it would create far greater problems for Hussein.

The biggest advantage, though, was that the Coalition had a significant natural ally in northern Iraq: the Kurds, who had been waging a long battle for autonomy. America had strong ties with the Kurds dating back to their 1991 uprising in the wake of Iraq's defeat in Desert Storm. The Kurds had taken that opportunity to resume their old fight, and when Hussein suppressed the uprising with great brutality, America led the international reaction that resulted in a UN-protected semiautonomous enclave in northern Iraq. But protecting Kurds from Saddam was one thing; promoting their goal of independence was another. Turkey's Kurdish population had been waging a similar war for independence, and Turkey worried that toppling Hussein might embolden Iraqi Kurds, which in turn might exacerbate Turkey's Kurdish problem. But even without the Kurdish issue, the prospect of invading Iraq was deeply opposed by Turkey's Muslim population. The two issues combined to create an insurmountable problem.

The question of Turkish support played out in the worst possible manner for Coalition planning. If Turkey had made a quick decision for or against, planners could have set to work early responding to that variable, but instead Turkey vacillated for months. There were enough positive signals coming from Istanbul for planners to work up a northern invasion plan, designate forces, and put those forces in motion. All the while, though, the issue hung in doubt, and at almost the last minute Turkey refused permission for Coalition forces to cross their border. What was the Coalition to do? The United States had men and materiel on board ships in the Mediterranean ready to go ashore. There were even troops on aircraft that were turned back at the Turkish border and had to land elsewhere. The units on board ships had no choice but to make the long trip around Africa to the Persian Gulf, and there was no doubt they would never make the trip in time to be part of the original invasion plans—so they were, in a sense, out of the fight. But the northern option still had one more card to play—the SOF ace.

Unable to send a large conventional force into northern Iraq, the United States decided on a much smaller and riskier approach. Instead of the major conventional force of about sixty-two thousand the new plan called for only a few thousand. The largest group would be the 173rd Airborne Brigade, which conducted a combat parachute drop into Bashur Airfield near Harir in Kurdish territory. Their mission was to relieve Turkish concerns about the possibility of unchecked Kurdish ambitions. The real pressure on Hussein, though, would come from small Special Forces teams. Tenth Special Forces Group had been working with the Kurds since their 1991 uprising; now those numbers would be dramatically increased as more SOF teams were sent to link up with the Kurdish rebel forces. Together, SOF and Kurdish forces opened a "second front" by invading Iraq from the north. If this sounds familiar, it should—this was the same scenario used in Afghanistan, and it worked much the same way, achieving much the same results. Along with the SOF teams were SOF TACPs who performed the same functions that had proved so effective in Afghanistan. In fact, the same air-ground dynamic emerged: the Kurdish rebel forces were sizable enough that Iraqi forces could not disperse, and with Coalition air power being called in by SOF TACPs, these relatively small and poorly armed Kurds continually took on and destroyed or drove back larger and better-equipped enemy forces.

With one of these SOF teams was M.Sgt. John Knipe, who had seen service only a few months earlier in western Afghanistan. Knipe's experiences provide an interesting insight into several aspects of the northern campaign; for example, how Turkey's refusal affected Coalition plans and what it meant for some of the SOF teams sent into northern Iraq.

February fifteenth we left Fort Lewis, me and two other SOF TACPs from 1st Special Forces Group, and we did about two weeks of training with our team that we were going to infiltrate into Iraq with. . . . The planning we did prior to going in was excellent. We had a lot of maps, we

looked at the terrain, and we looked at what we needed to do quite a bit before we went in, so when we got on the ground we knew exactly where we were going. . . . [Then] we went to a forward staging area from the United States and went into isolation for a couple of weeks. We did some more training there, and then from there we [started trying to infiltrate] Iraq. The plan was to fly through Turkey to get into Iraq, but the Turks decided they weren't going to play, so that delayed us getting to where we needed to go probably by a few weeks. We kept spinning up to try to get in through Turkey and the aircraft would be turned around at the border . . . and we'd land again and this went on for a while.

In the grand scheme of things, the most significant consequence of Turkey's decision was undoubtedly the dramatic scaling back of Coalition plans, but for Knipe and several hundred others, the most significant consequence was arguably the route they now had to take to reinforce the SOF teams already on the scene with the Kurds. Loaded aboard six MC-130s, each with fifty troops, they were taking a decidedly different route from what had been planned. Knipe describes their infiltration on the night of 22 March.

We had to come in through a southwestern route, which meant we had to overfly Iraqi airspace for three hours to get to where we needed to go in northern Iraq, which exposed us to quite a bit of enemy fire. I was on plane number one, which lost engine number three, there was a bullet hole in the pilot's windshield, there were holes in the aircraft fuselage—it was like a roller-coaster ride the entire way. You could just see green tracers everywhere out the window for three hours. It was dangerous enough that [planners] had actually done a risk assessment that [predicted] some of those aircraft were going to get shot down that evening. And they were willing to accept that risk because they needed to have boots on the ground. One of the aircraft was not able to land in Iraq and actually had to do an emergency landing into Turkey.

Amazingly, there were no casualties from this air insertion. Besides the delay, the only thing that had changed for these SOF teams was the harrowing trip they had to take to get there.

Early in the Afghanistan campaign, coordinating and allocating air support for SOF operations had been a problem, but lessons had been learned and SOF TACPs hammered out procedures for coordinating air support in the north. This was all the more critical because with Turkish air bases out of the picture, all aircraft would have to come from bases far to the south. A SOF TACP with 5th Special Forces Group at Fort Bragg, North Carolina, who volunteered to augment 10th Group, describes this effort. A staff sergeant, Kevin asked that his full name not be used.

> The TACPs ended up getting together to create the air picture—how was it going to work . . . who's going to allocate the air. It turned out that the 10th Group guys that had been operating in that area already [had the capability] so we gave control to them. All of our requests for air would go to them and they would send it on to the [theater-level] ASOC, and whatever air would come into theater it would check in with [them]; they could distribute the air to whoever needed it first or whoever needed it the most. Due to . . . the Turkey issue [any un-planned CAS request] was almost a standard two-hour wait . . . so we planned it out in advance to have aircraft overhead no matter what. And it turned out that worked to our benefit and we had all kinds of different aircraft—F-14s, F-18s, F-16s, B-52s—everything was coming out to our area, and especially once we started getting into contact with armored vehicles, air was just nonstop.

In late March, Kevin's team was sent to an area along the Green Line—the line separating the semiautonomous Kurdish territory from the rest of Iraq—to prepare for the assault.

> [We started] moving out from the headquarters to probably within five kilometers of where we were actually going to be assaulting this key terrain. . . . Between the two sets of teams I think was fifteen to twenty kilometers. We were out there for I believe a day and a half to two days prior, so we were watching and plotting all the enemy posi-tions. . . . [The SOF command] wanted us to get a little closer so we can get more accurate positions with our laser range finders for using JDAMs. . . . Myself and another TACP went forward to about twelve hundred meters away from the closest machine-gun pits, and we were able to get more precise locations on a lot of the stuff—tents, sleep-ing areas, ammunition supply points, mortar tubes—basically all their fighting positions along the hill. Then we ended up pulling back, and once we got the word that the other teams were starting [that] night, we were told to bomb them [that] night as well.
>
> Once the assault started, the eastern team came into contact first, and they actually received tanks and BMPs coming onto their position and they had immediate CAS. . . . Once they had their area under con-trol our area became heavy with artillery, mortars, heavy machine-gun fire, and basically we rolled all the aircraft over to our location and we pretty much JDAMed the whole ridgeline.
>
> I don't know how long [the attack lasted]—it seemed like forever,

but it may have only been an hour; it took a long time in my eyes. We had a lot of aircraft coming in once our forces started to move. We were mounted in gun trucks, and once we started moving forward and receiving fire we obviously started firing back, calling for air. We were receiving mortars at the time. We were just outside of their reach, so then they started using heavy artillery. We started receiving a lot of heavy fire, so we started to pull back because they were very accurate and they were following us the whole way—you know, buildings exploding right next to us—and we were trying to get outside of that range. But . . . they followed us everywhere we went. We ended up going behind this other small ridgeline . . . and I was still trying to pinpoint [the enemy's artillery], 'cause [it] would move. They would fire a couple of shots and then they would move because they knew that we knew where they were and we were going to drop a bomb. As soon as they moved the bomb would hit. So it was quite taxing for me—jumping out and having to carry all this stuff, run up the hill, get eyes on, try to plot it real quick, give it to the aircraft. But as [we] were doing that they found where we were and they started hitting us again. . . .

We went back in, started doing more direct fire with all the gun truck munitions, .50-cal, 40-mm, 240, whatever else we had on there, while I'm dropping JDAMs with navy aircraft, F-14s, F-18s. The final blow was a B-52 carrying a lot of Mk-117s—the 750 pounders [dumb bombs]—and I believe sixteen CBU-87s. . . . We sent the other TACP that was with me forward 'cause we were going to be conducting possibly another [assault] in a different location. . . . His team ended up moving forward with the Kurdish military, so I let him take control of [the B-52] since he would be the most forward TACP. And it was nonstop bombardment with the B-52 until the last ordnance was falling off and exploding. That's when the Kurds took the hill—soon as the B-52 was done dropping. The Iraqi forces left a few guys to slow [the Kurds] down while everybody [else] ran away . . . and while the Kurds were taking the hill [the rear guard] ended up dropping their stuff and taking off.

Once combat operations began, many of the details, problems, tactics, and results were reminiscent of the SOF-CAS operational concept that had worked so well in Afghanistan. But Hussein had left a total of ten divisions to guard northern Iraq. Considering what was pitted against them, this was a sizable force with armor and artillery, and it was organized around a well-developed, in-depth defense plan that the Iraqis had had a long time to refine. Still, a key part of that plan dispersed those forces in penny packets among the many villages across the region, and this became the fatal flaw. Knipe describes what he and his team faced.

We immediately met with our Kurdish guerillas and started driving south down toward what was called the Green Line . . . and started gathering intelligence to start eliminating the Iraqi forces in their sector. . . . Pretty much all the way from the Green Line [south] to Kirkuk was like a no-man's-land and there was no agriculture or industry going on there. . . . [The villages] were pretty much all manned by Iraqi soldiers or families of Iraqi soldiers. . . . It looked like many of the civilians had evacuated quite a few weeks before we even arrived. . . .

[The villages were] from three to five kilometers apart. We had to fight another town, another village, another fighting position about every three to five kilometers. . . . It was continuous, it never ended. You'd get to a spot and you'd be secure, but you're in range of the next village, so they're shooting at you with something. Artillery was a constant reminder that they hadn't surrendered yet; no matter where we went we were getting shelled. All these positions we had taken [had been] occupied by the Iraqis, so they had them all registered on their target lists, which made it very easy for them to register their guns on us. . . . We fought a good twenty to twenty-five kilometers from the Green Line into Kirkuk [like that].

[Enemy forces] went from squad- to maybe company-size element. It was very difficult to tell how many because these positions had been dug in for years and years since the end of the first Iraq war. So these were hardened, well dug in, well-camouflaged, well-established positions that the Iraqis had been using to defend against the Kurds. The Iraqis had their basic complement; we were against tanks and BMPs and antiaircraft guns—their basic stuff. . . . Probably only one or two [tanks per village]. . . . I know that I physically saw and blew up at least ten to fifteen tanks. But there was quite a bit more that the aircraft could see with their [sensors] on the ridge line that I couldn't see that I [destroyed with CAS]. . . .

As happened with the Taliban in Afghanistan, having a friendly ground force in the area, even if only a guerrilla force like the Kurds, fixed the Iraqi forces, and by engaging them the Iraqis were forced to reveal their positions and strength. This made them vulnerable to airstrikes called in by the SOF teams working with the rebels. And as Knipe illustrates, the airstrikes, in turn, took most of the fight out of the enemy, thereby giving the guerrillas a decided advantage.

Our concept of the operation was to move up as close as we could, the Iraqis would engage us, we would fall back a little bit, I would call in an airstrike, we would destroy those forces as much as possible, send in our Kurdish guerrillas to clean up the town. We would then occupy that town or that fighting position and continue to do that in a leap-frog all the way into Kirkuk. . . . It was usually 6 [SOF] guys at the most forward OP at any given time, and the other 6 or 7 guys would be back at the mission support site resting or getting equipment together to replace the guys up on the front. We always had 12 Kurdish guerillas that were part of our personal security detachment, they were called Cobras, and they were with us 24/7; they never left our side—ever. Other than that we had anywhere from 100 to 150 Kurdish guerillas at our disposal all the time around us, camped with us; not in the same building with us, but they had followed us like traveling gypsies. It was our ready reserve. I would not go into the town after I dropped bombs in there. We would send our Kurds down there. It's their country after all. Most of them were returning to the homes they were evicted from in the first Gulf War.

Obviously we'd use enough [CAS so] they would stop shooting at us, for one. And then after that, depending on what that airstrike might dig up, something else. I was striking this one building where these guys were firing; after I dropped on that building, I saw a squad of guys run to another building. Well now I notice there's a BMP sitting in there that I didn't see before. It was like a domino effect. They'd start giving away other positions and I'd just keep working the air on these guys until there was nobody left. . . . The Kurdish guerillas would then go in and tell us if it was now safe to go in and occupy that village or that position.

How central air power was to this style of combat can be seen in a conversation between a SOF TACP and some 10th Special Forces troops. Conan Higgins, then a technical sergeant with the Washington Air National Guard, had jumped into Bashur Airfield with the 173rd and was scouting southward with his battalion commander when they ran into a SOF team. A member of the team was describing an air force guy whom Higgins recognized—"I asked if it was Johnny Knipe and they looked at me like yeah do you know him? [And they said] that his team was calling it 'The John Show.' They would get into a fight and he would just call in death and destruction and they would sit back and keep him alive."

One factor that helped this running engagement succeed was the aggressive way the Kurd-SOF teams pressed their enemy with attack after attack, in village after village, day after day. If the Iraqis had had time to consider what was happening, they might have decided that massing their forces and going on the offensive themselves would have been the better option. Of course, this would have presented even more lucrative opportunities for air attack, but it might have proved too much for the

small team to handle. Given the aggressive nature of the Kurd-SOF offensive, though, the Iraqis quite likely believed they faced a much bigger force than they actually did. This is what Knipe suspected, and it had
been the case in western Iraq. "I don't think they realized what they were
up against," Knipe explains. "They were trying to do an organized retreat
or falling back to Kirkuk, but trying to do it in layers. They weren't using
their whole force—their ring of security—at once, but they weren't trying to launch an offensive because they had no idea what size forces they
were against. . . . I'd have F-18s racked and stacked . . . waiting to pounce
on these people. They'd fire one round and they would get their nose
bloodied so bad they probably thought they were fighting a really large
force, when in actuality they were fighting six guys."

While Knipe depicts a slow, steady, almost methodical campaign,
it was hardly a simple matter of "bomb awhile, march forward, bomb
awhile, march forward." There were some tense moments that show not
only the incredible bravery of the SOF teams in their exposed positions
but also the audacity it takes to make this type of operation succeed. One
such battle took place not in a village but for control of what they thought
was a communications center between two towns. Knipe describes how,
after taking the first town, they started moving forward to the next, only
to find Iraqi forces firing at them from this compound.

> We didn't know it was an active communications center, but we en-
> countered heavy resistance from there. It was along the road kind
> of between [our current position and] the next village. . . . They were
> shooting the hell out of us from there, so we knew they were hiding
> something or there was something important there, because they
> weren't leaving. . . . There were probably about three large buildings
> there, and I had dropped a two-thousand-pound JDAM on the largest
> one. . . . We can only assume that dropping that JDAM and our Kurds
> moving in and shooting up that area a little bit [convinced them to
> leave]. . . . We were up there occupying it, and they weren't very happy
> that we were up rooting around. . . . It ended up being an old division
> headquarters and we found the entire defense map of Kirkuk under-
> neath the floor of that building.
>
> So now they wanted to destroy [the compound]; they knew they
> had left hastily and [now they] were trying to destroy what was left. . . .
> [They attacked] with whatever they had there, a couple tanks and a
> couple infantry squads, which was pretty significant. But we couldn't
> really see the tanks very well because of the terrain. . . . There were
> bullets flying all over the place, there was artillery coming in on us,
> you could hear the initial poof of the artillery and you know you have

about twenty seconds before it lands. I had to put my satellite antenna [out] in the open [because] it was the only place I could get it to hit the satellite. So I would have to continually run to my radio, make a couple calls, hear the artillery coming in or the small arms would be too much, and I would just throw the handset down and run back and take cover; artillery would go off, I'd run back to my radio and continue my transmission. I mean, I was literally in the middle of my nine-line or a talk-on with the pilot and I'd say, "Hey, I got about ten seconds and artillery's dropping on me, I gotta go." . . . That went on for about forty-five minutes.

That was a real dicey situation. The artillery's getting within fifty meters, and then twenty meters, and they do have us registered at that time, and they're continually putting fire right on the spot where we are at. . . . While all this is going on, the Kurds are getting in trucks leaving, and that's when I grabbed one of the interpreters, I pulled my pistol out, and said, "Listen, you can tell the Kurd commander that the next bunch of his troops that leave, I'm going to shoot them. . . . It's just showing the Iraqis that their attack is successful, 'Oh, they're leaving,' and then they'll send more troops and overrun us." That went on for quite a few hours. As a matter of fact, I think Jim Sciutto, an ABC News correspondent, was there with us at the time as well. They seemed pretty freaked out. . . . I was trying to find out where the fire's coming from and trying to get the aircraft's eyes on them to kill them. We eventually dropped [bombs] and killed those two tanks and knocked some artillery out, and also the Kurds fired about ten billion rounds of ammunition in every direction possible taking care of [the infantry] squads.

[The Iraqis] leapfrogged backward . . . and then eventually the firing dissipated. They melted away into the woodwork and we didn't see anybody. We didn't pursue obviously . . . we didn't have a force to pursue. . . . We just jumped in our pickup trucks and fell back to our last position because we knew that was out of range of any of their direct fire weapons and we could stop, assess injuries, assess ammunition. We could talk about what happened and how to deal with it next time.

Perhaps the most intense fight of Knipe's campaign came at the end, during a battle outside Kirkuk on 10 April, as Iraqi control in Baghdad and elsewhere was collapsing. The Kurdish community considered Kirkuk part of their ancestral territory—a Kurdish city. But for some years Hussein had waged a campaign to make it an Iraqi city by moving large numbers of ethnic Iraqis there. If ever the Kurds started marching south it was certain they would desperately want to capture Kirkuk, and just as certain Hussein would fight to keep it. Added to that is the terrain advantage enjoyed by the Iraqi forces. A ridgeline dominates the area just north of the city, which the Iraqi army had prepared well in advance with defensive positions. As the Kurds and SOF teams moved forward, surviving Iraqi army remnants fell back into a denser and more consolidated force, taking up positions in those prepared defenses on the ridgeline. As Knipe relates, they were somewhat surprised when they first encountered these defenses.

> Well, it was business as usual until we got to the ridgeline [and] that place that I call [the Last Castle]. It was a giant concrete castle-type fortress. . . . I had bombed—literally decimated—this place over the last few days. We finally went up and occupied it and we basically bit off more than we could chew that day.
>
> We got [to the castle], occupied it, . . . we're only about a kilometer away from the ridgeline, and right over the top of the ridgeline is the city of Kirkuk. We got into a big-time shooting match with these Iraqi forces and that's when some tanks and APCs, lots of dismounts came out from everywhere, and DSHKs just opened up on us. One of my team guys was shooting Javelins [shoulder-launched antitank missiles] knocking out the technicals, and I'm just dropping air in as many places as I can. At the time there were so many targets I couldn't process them as fast as I needed to. . . . I'm getting task saturated and this goes on and [the team guy says], "Hey, we're out of Javelins . . . we got to get out of here. If they're going to advance on us we don't have anything to stop them." So I had a B-52, and he dropped twelve Mk-82s. That kind of gave us [some cover] to get the hell out of there. . . .

Another perspective on the battle comes from Conan Higgins. Old friends, he and Knipe had linked up the day before, and though he provided critical help in this most desperate moment, as he explains, it wasn't enough,

> It was a firefight! They were pouring it on us and we had nothing that could reach them at the ridge. . . . We're just calling in CAS and I'm stacking [targets] up for John and he's pulling [them] out of my hands. I'm looking over the [ledge] calling [target] corrections. We just started systematically working from our left to our right and just pounding it and pounding it. But then the artillery . . . started getting too accurate. We had one about twenty-five meters from us and the only thing that saved us was that we had a [lot] of building between us. The decision was made, "All right, look, we need to break contact, we need to regroup, we need to figure out what we're going to do." You know, one

A team is not going to defeat an entire ridge of Iraqis. So we did the mad dash back across the open area. Stuff's just sailing right passed us—it was amazing, man it was amazing.

The strategic situation changed rapidly despite the check to U.S. efforts, and it changed without further American involvement. Knipe explains. "So we retreated and some of our Kurds stayed. . . . We only go back about two kilometers to our last location and we're sitting around, I'm eating an MRE, and then one of the Kurd commanders came back and said, 'We have got a foothold in the ridgeline!' I'm thinking, 'Well now, that's a bonus.' We all pile in the truck and we're driving down to see what he was talking about. Well, what he failed to tell us was they had punched through the ridgeline and Kurdish forces were now into Kirkuk. So that was it—all of a sudden Kirkuk is wide open." The sudden capture of Kirkuk signaled the collapse of Iraqi military power in northern Iraq as elsewhere in the country. For Knipe, the capture of Kirkuk spelled the end of the war for him as well. "There was no more organized Iraqi resistance after that. . . . It ended for me pretty much a week after the fall of Kirkuk. Most of the SOF TACPs got pulled out because there . . . was no more need of CAS, so we exfilled at that point." He did offer a couple observations about this campaign, though, and they reflect two distinct impressions of fighting the Iraqis; one is their tenacity: "Every day could have been the battle of Kirkuk really." The other point illustrates the disadvantage the Iraqis were up against, "You can only be tenacious so long as a B-52 is not dropping its entire load of bombs on you." These observations speak volumes about how and why this campaign was so successful against such overwhelming odds.

Conclusion

Wars may be fought with weapons, but they are won by men.

GEORGE S. PATTON

When John Knipe headed home, it wasn't for long. In fact, for most members of the TACP community, as for everyone else in the modern U.S. military—whether active duty, Guard, or reserve—today's reality is frequent deployments to either Afghanistan or Iraq. When commanders determined that Iraq's military had collapsed, their overriding concern was to get TACPs out of the country as quickly as possible to make room for other forces better suited for stabilizing and rebuilding a democratic Iraq. Unfortunately, the assessment that there would be no more organized resistance proved premature. Some within the TACP community thought it a mistake to rush them out of country—in fact, some wanted to stay longer. Most were glad to go home. Ever since Afghanistan proved the worth of CAS controllers they have been very busy people—what the military in its love for euphemisms calls "high demand, low density" assets—and this is particularly true of SOF TACPs. A chapter on post-Saddam Iraqi operations would look very much like the chapter on post-Taliban Afghanistan.

TACPs live in the nexus of the air-ground dynamic and they are essential to effectively exploiting it. A thinking enemy will wait till the last possible moment to consolidate his forces in the face of an advancing ground force covered by effective air power. This means any attempt to use air power when the enemy does consolidate must be done in close proximity to friendly ground forces, thus it will require the greatest skill in controlling CAS. Moreover, if friendly ground forces pull back to minimize fratricide, a thinking enemy will try to disperse and immobilize to lessen the effectiveness of air power. This again makes the enemy ripe for destruction by friendly ground forces, but as ground forces move in TACPs must remain ready, for the enemy is likely to consolidate again. This back-and-forth tension between enemy and friendly forces—consolidate and disperse, attack with air, attack with ground forces—is inherent in the air-ground dynamic. And U.S. training, organization, and doctrine should be postured to anticipate and exploit it as fully as possible.

The most important point to take from this study is the absolute necessity for CAS controllers to be experts at their craft. The most nefarious consequences of General Hagenbeck's claims of "air power's failures" in the wake of Anaconda came from his claim that the air force didn't provide him with enough TACPs. This led to a drive within the army to develop its own CAS controllers. On top of that, other groups have been jumping on the CAS control bandwagon and want to claim CAS controlling as part of their "skill set." Once the world saw in Afghanistan how effective CAS could be, controlling CAS became "sexy" and everybody wanted to get in on the action. On top of that, attention translates into money in the world of budgets, so a lot of money is being thrown at CAS controlling. Both of these trends point to a common misconception: that controlling CAS is easy. To the untrained eye it doesn't seem to take much to call "cleared hot" into a microphone. Nothing could be more wrong. Hopefully this study has highlighted how often modern combat calls on the ingenuity and skill of CAS controllers; these abilities are not easily acquired, and not every person can develop them. It takes years to develop skill and ingenuity, and they are both highly perishable if not continually honed. Keep in mind, also, that while controlling CAS may be relatively easy on the range or in a plain vanilla battle where everything goes as planned, the stress of bullets hitting nearby increases the need for long experience to break through the swirl of emotions. Even a little battlefield friction intensifies the need for split-second decisions and for instincts developed by years of experience.

This point must be emphasized: *It doesn't matter what service a CAS controller belongs to.* This study, for example, has highlighted the brilliant CAS work done in Iraq by three marines. Moreover, there are groups, particularly among Special Forces, that have controlled CAS to some extent for years. But controlling CAS is not something that someone can do as a sideline or part-time job. Moreover military services should not strive for their own CAS controllers simply to get in on what's hot or so commanders can employ CAS according to their own wishes without interference from CAS experts. This is fallacious thinking and is doubly dangerous. First, friendly troops are going to get killed by inexperienced CAS controllers. Granted, even the most experienced TACP can make mistakes, but it doesn't take much imagination to see that the accident curve will climb steeply as experience drops. Second, opening the floodgates to the CAS controller field will end up needlessly throwing away the advantages expert CAS controllers bring to the fight. Fully exploiting the air-ground dynamic will be hard and will require the best. A veteran of Pentagon doctrine battles once observed, "Joint warfare is not Little League warfare—not everyone gets to play in every game." Nor does everyone get to play every position. Simply slapping on a coat of CAS paint to placate service jealousies will end up creating worthless CAS controllers just as nations that try to solve fiscal problems by printing more money end up with worthless money. When deciding who should control CAS in your fight, your first priority ought to be someone who works CAS day in, day out, year in, year out. Anything less should be reserved for bona fide emergencies.

One final point, and this too must be stressed: *CAS did not defeat the Taliban or Saddam Hussein all by itself.* It is a sad fact that past efforts to highlight air power's contribution and capabilities descended into claims that air power was able to win wars single-handedly or was *the* decisive element on today's battlefield. Likewise, efforts to advance air power's capabilities have been stymied by critics who turned a deaf ear simply because "air power had failed to deliver on past promises." CAS worked dramatically well in Afghanistan and Iraq because air and ground forces consistently kept the enemy on the twin horns of the air-ground dilemma, but both halves of that equation are essential to make it work. Ground forces are necessary to exploit air power's success by completing the enemy's destruction and occupying the territory, but they also set the conditions for air power's success. Similarly, well-handled CAS can establish conditions for ground force success either through destroying enemy capability or by prompting him to disperse and immobilize. And CAS works best when it is exploiting conditions created by ground forces—that is, when ground forces compel the enemy to mass and maneuver.

The real secret to exploiting this air-ground dilemma, though, is the well-trained, highly skilled, dedicated people who work CAS, like the air force's ROMADs and ALOs. This book is the story of how they made it work in the past. I hope it will also serve as a guide to how they can keep it working in the future.

Appendix:
People Interviewed

The following individuals were interviewed on the record during the research for this book:

Achey, Stephen M., S.Sgt.
Bishop, Tim, Sr.A.
Blasinsky, Michael, S.Sgt.
Blocher, John W., Capt.
Bochain, Louis G., Lt. Col.
Bronakowski, Mark A., Lt. Col.
Brown, Daniel K., Gunnery Sgt., USMC
Carpenter, Russell B., S.M.Sgt.
Crosby, Travis D., S.Sgt.
Deas, William R. "Butch," Gunnery Sgt., USMC
DeLay, Dennis, M.Sgt. (Ret.)
Donnelly, Peter A., Maj.
English, Nathan, S.Sgt.
Fairchild, James E., Lt. Col.
Frazier, Jim (father of S.Sgt. Jake Frazier)
Glasscock, Charles G., Capt.
Green, Michael, T.Sgt.
Heidal, Charles E., M.Sgt.
Higgins, Conan, T.Sgt.
Hokkanen, Joel M., M.Sgt. (Ret.)
Hren, Joseph S., S.Sgt.
Jewell, Mark A., Maj., USMC
Keehan, Michael, T.Sgt.

"Kevin," S.Sgt. [last name withheld by request]
Knipe, John W., M.Sgt.
Knipple, Peyton C., Sr.A.
"Larry," M.Sgt. [last name withheld by request]
Lloyd, Sean W., S.Sgt.
Longoria, Michael, Col.
Maguire, Lance, T.Sgt.
McCabe, John E. "Vic," T.Sgt.
McGee, Michael B., Jr., Lt. Col.
Minyon, Sean, T.Sgt.
Murray, Brian F., S.Sgt.
O'Neill, Sean, T.Sgt.
Pinson, Jon, S.Sgt.
Rigney, Jim, T.Sgt.
Risner, Byron H., Lt. Col.
Shropshire, Michael S., S.Sgt.
Shulman, Edward W., S.Sgt.
Simmons, Craig, Capt.
Spann, Chris, S.Sgt.
Stamey, Tim, M.Sgt.
Stockman, John M., S.Sgt.
Sullivan, Hal, M.Sgt.
Tomat, Stephen, S.Sgt.
Wilchenski, Brian E., T.Sgt.

Glossary

AAGS. Army air-ground system.

A-FAC. Airborne forward air controller; also known as FAC/A or air FAC.

AFARN. Air force air request net; the radio channel used for calling in CAS requests.

AFSOC. Air Force Special Operations Command.

AI. Air interdiction; air strikes against forces or fixed targets far away from friendly forces.

ALO. Air liaison officer.

ANGLICO. Air and naval gunfire liaison company.

AOC. Air operations center; also known as CAOC.

Apache. AH-64 attack helicopter.

APC. Armored personnel carrier.

ARCENT. Army Central Command.

ASOC. Air support operations center.

ASOG. Air support operations group.

ASOS. Air support operations squadron.

ATO. Air tasking order; the master schedule of all air activity for any given day.

AWACS. Airborne warning and control system.

BALO. Battalion air liaison officer.

BCD. Battlefield coordination detachment.

BDA. Battle damage assessment; also known as bomb damage assessment.

Bingo. Fuel level at which you need to head home so you won't run out of gas.

BMP. A Soviet-era APC.

Bradley fighting vehicle M-2/M-3. Commonly referred to as the Bradley or the Brad. America's primary armored personnel carrier. First fielded in 1981, the M-3 is a cavalry variant designed for scouting.

BRDM. A Soviet-era APC.

BUFF. Nickname for B-52.

CAOC. Combined air operations center; also known as AOC.

CAS. Close air support.

CBU. Cluster bomb unit; antipersonnel cluster bomb, used against armor, personnel, and equipment.

CENTAF. Central Command, Air Force.

CENTCOM. Central Command, higher headquarters running the war in Afghanistan and Iraq.

Cleared hot. Radio call giving an aircraft approval to release ordnance.

Click. Slang for 1 kilometer.

CO. Commanding officer.

Coax. A 7.62-mm machine gun mounted "coaxially," that is, on the same axis as the main gun on M-1 tanks and Bradley fighting vehicles.

Danger close. Code word meaning the enemy is so close to friendly positions that fragments from bombs or artillery dropped on the enemy might also hit friendly forces.

DSHK (pronounced "DISH-ka"). Soviet-era heavy machine gun, similar to an American .50 caliber.

E-BALO. Enlisted battalion air liaison officer.

EPW. Enemy prisoner of war.

ETAC. Enlisted tactical air controller.

Exfil. Exfiltration; leaving a position and returning to friendly territory; also used as a verb, "to exfiltrate."

FAC/A. Forward air controller/airborne; also known as A-FAC or air FAC.

FARP. Forward arming and refueling point.

FSCL. Fire support coordination line.

FSO. Fire support officer.

GAU-5. Tactical variant of an M-16; similar to an M-4.

GBU-10. Two-thousand-pound LGB.

GBU-12. Five-hundred-pound LGB.

GPS. Global positioning system.

HEAT round. High-explosive antitank munition fired by the M-1's main gun.

HLZ. Hot (as in hostile) landing zone; a landing zone being defended by the enemy.

ID. Infantry division.

IED. Improvised explosive device; a homemade bomb.

Infil. Infiltration; going into a position, often by covert means; also used as a verb, "to infiltrate."

IR. Infrared.

JDAM. Joint direct attack munition.

JSTARS. Joint surveillance target attack radar system; sometimes called Joint STARS.

KICAS CONOPS. Killbox interdiction/close air support concept of operations (pronounced "kick-ass con-ops").

Kill box. A free-fire area (within the bounds of the rules of engagement, of course).

LD. Line of departure; a starting point; also used as a verb, "to cross a line of departure."

LGB. Laser-guided bomb.

LOCs. Lines of communication; supply routes.

Log trains. Logistical support.

LZ. Landing zone; where a helicopter lands to drop off personnel or supplies.

M-1 Abrams. U.S. main battle tank, first fielded in 1985.

M-4. Carbine variant of the M-16.

M-16. U.S. standard rifle firing 5.56-mm ammunition. It has been in use since the Vietnam era.

M-113. A Vietnam-era APC; it is not as well armored as a Bradley; often called a "track."

M-240. A 7.62-mm machine gun; replaced the old M-60 .30-caliber.

mIRC. A shareware internet relay chat client.

Mk (usually pronounced "mark"). Term that begins practically every weapon nomenclature, as in Mk-82. Why "Mark"? I haven't a clue.

Mk-19. A 40-mm grenade "machine gun,"

MLRS. Multiple launch rocket system.

NCO. Noncommissioned officer; a sergeant.

NCOIC. Noncommissioned officer in charge; top NCO noncommand supervisory position.

Nine-line. Pilot's briefing; the standard format used by a controller to pass key information to a pilot in a CAS mission.

NOD. Night optical device; also known as NVGs.

NTC. National Training Center.

NVG. Night vision goggles; also known as NODs.

ODA. Operational detachment-A, the tactically oriented half of a Special Forces team. (Operational detachment-B [ODB] is the half of a Special Forces team that performs most support functions; it also performs all the usual SOF tasks too.)

OGA. Other government agencies.

1C4. An entry level ROMAD who learns the ropes by assisting an ETAC or an ALO.

OP. Observation post.

PID. Positive identification; coalition members had to positively identify a target as hostile before engaging; also used as a verb, "to positively identify."

PJ. Pararescue jumpers. SOF personnel who rescue trapped or downed forces.

Predator. Name given the most commonly used UAV.

PZ. Pickup zone; where a helicopter lands to pick up personnel or supplies.

QRF. Quick reaction force.

ROE. Rules of engagement; the guidelines on when soldiers and airmen can fire.

ROMAD. Radio operator, maintainer, and driver; generic name for an enlisted TACP.

RPG. Rocket propelled grenade (similar to an old World War II–style bazooka).

Ruck. Military slang for a backpack.

S-60. Soviet-era single-barreled 57-mm antiaircraft artillery.

SALT. Supporting arms liaison team.

SAM. Surface-to-air missile.

SATCOM. Satellite communications; a radio or channel that uses satellite.

SAW. Squad automatic weapon; M-249 light machine gun, 5.56-mm, belt or magazine feed.

SCAR. Strike coordination and reconnaissance.

SF. Special Forces.

Shack. Military slang for a direct hit.

Shwack. Military slang for striking a target hard or a lot.

SIPRNET (pronounced "sipper net"). Secret Internet protocol router network; a secure computer network for passing classified information to military computers.

SOF (pronounced "soph"). Special Operations Forces.

SOFLAM. Special operations forces laser acquisition marker; a laser designator.

SOF TACP. Special Operations Forces tactical air control party; a TACP attached to SOF.

SOLE. Special operations liaison element; a SOF team working in a headquarters or command center to coordinate SOF operations with conventional forces.

TAC. Tactical air controller, or tactical assault center.

TACP. Tactical air control party.

TACS/AAGS. Tactical air control system/army air-ground system.

TACSAT. Tactical satellite; radio that uses satellite channels or a channel used by such radios.

TF. Task force.

TOC. Tactical operations center.

Track. Usually refers to an M-113 APC; also sometimes used as a generic term for any APC.

Triple-A. Antiaircraft artillery.

UAV. Unmanned aerial vehicle.

WCMD (pronounced "WICK-mid"). Wind corrected munition dispenser.

Winchester. Out of ammunition; also used as a verb, "to run out of ammunition."

XO. Executive officer.

ZSU (pronounced letter by letter or as "Zeus") 23-4. An armored tracked Soviet-era four-barrel antiaircraft system firing 23-mm shells.

ZSU 57-2. An armored tracked Soviet-era two-barrel antiaircraft system firing 57-mm shells.

Index

Note: Italicized page numbers refer to photograph captions

ISBN-13: 978-1-58544-624-7
ISBN-10: 1-58544-624-6